D1765616

Fixing the System

A History of Populism, Ancient and Modern

Adrian Kuzminski

continuum

NEW YORK • LONDON

2008

The Continuum International Publishing Group Inc
80 Maiden Lane, New York, NY 10038

The Continuum International Publishing Group Ltd
The Tower Building, 11 York Road, London SE1 7NX

www.continuumbooks.com

Copyright © 2008 by Adrian Kuzminski

Printed in the United States of America

9780826429605

Library of Congress Cataloging-in-Publication Data

Kuzminski, Adrian, 1944-

Fixing the system : a brief history of populism, ancient and modern / Adrian
Kuzminski.
     p. cm.
  Includes bibliographical references and index.
  ISBN-13: 978-0-8264-2959-9 (hardcover : alk. paper)
  ISBN-10: 0-8264-2959-9 (hardcover : alk. paper)
  ISBN-13: 978-0-8264-2960-5 (pbk. : alk. paper)
  ISBN-10: 0-8264-2960-2 (pbk. : alk. paper) 1. Populism--History. I. Title.

JC423.K95 2008
320.5--dc22
                        2007045342

To my wife,

T'nette,

who made this book possible

Contents

Preface

This book had its origins in my discovery of Thomas Jefferson's vision of a confederal democracy based on local assemblies or town meetings, which he called "ward republics." In a series of letters written mostly after he left office, he developed the idea that local communities ought to be self-governing direct democracies, and that they ought to be confederated together in a bottom-up system of accountable representative government. Despairing of the ongoing corruption of politics in the United States by big money and special interests, I was intrigued by the practical possibilities of Jefferson's neglected blueprint for accountable democratic decision making. Taking another cue from Jefferson, I came to realize that political democracy requires economic democracy—that is, a citizenry in which private property ownership is widespread and concentrations of wealth are minimal. This combination of democracy for all with property for all was the hallmark of nineteenth-century American populism, but I soon discovered that this populist outlook had important precedents extending far back into history, precedents that have been largely overlooked and never, as far as I could determine, integrated into a larger narrative.

At the same time as I pursued my research into the literature and history of populism, I had the opportunity to gain some practical political experience working in local advocacy groups—as a local public official, as a candidate for local office, and in party politics in both the Green and Democratic Parties (including a stint on the national platform committee of the Green Party). My often frustrating political experience, combined with my research, brought me to the conclusion that the populist program of decentralizing political and economic power—though marginalized in recent times—continues to hold the greatest promise for ensuring not only political and economic justice, but a sustainable social and natural world.

The current narrow box of mainstream left-wing/right-wing debate only perpetuates the presumption of elitist political and economic power, and prevents any serious consideration of increasingly needed alternatives. Populism is the genuine "third way" of politics, I concluded, transcending both the "big government" policies of the Left and the "big business" policies of the Right. By decentralizing political and economic power, populism aims to replace top-down with bottom-up politics. This book is an attempt to present populism in its historical context, to retrieve it from the oblivion into which it has been thrust by its opponents, and to demonstrate the promise it holds for the future. At a time when our political process no longer represents ordinary citizens, when disparities of wealth and poverty are enormous and increasing, when irresponsible hubris goes increasingly unchecked among government and corporate leaders, when criminal wars of aggression undermine our international integrity, and when the environmental costs of economic growth threaten the planet itself, it is more important than ever to find alternative and more promising ways of thinking about our political and economic problems. I focus on the history of populism in the West only because of the limitations of my own scholarship and experience. I leave it to others to write the history of populism in Asia, Africa, Latin America, and elsewhere.

How far do populists go? By "property for all" populists mean the widespread personal ownership of private capital sufficient to establish the relative economic independence of citizens vis-à-vis one another. Where none are rich enough to dominate others economically or poor enough to be so dominated, populists argue, the public interest rather than private interest is likely to be served. In an earlier agrarian era, populists called for the distribution of land (then the principal form of capital) among citizens, while in modern commercial economies they propose to distribute credit (now the principal form of capital) directly to citizens through various systems of public credit. The most comprehensive system of public credit—developed by the nineteenth-century American populist Edward Kellogg—proposed to replace our privatized financial system with a decentralized but state-regulated monetary system based on direct low-interest loans to citizens.

By "democracy for all" populists mean full and direct participation in empowered local citizen assemblies—such as those found in ancient city-states, and in the town meetings of colonial and early federal America—suitably confederated together into broader accountable representative bodies, as Jefferson outlined. In calling for a wide distribution and decentralization of both wealth and politics, populism offers a radical but plausible reform of the political and economic system found today in the United States and most other developed countries, where credit and property remain highly concentrated in private hands, and where representatives chosen in impersonal mass elections frustrate democracy by serving private interests rather than the public good. Populism seeks to complete a half-begun American revolution by establishing the full measure possible of individual political and economic liberty. In our time of crisis, this pragmatic program for fundamental social reform deserves serious consideration.

Acknowledgments

I am grateful to Hartwick College, where I have been resident scholar in philosophy since 1997, for giving me the academic setting necessary to undertake research for this book. I would like to thank the following persons, who aided or encouraged this project in varying ways, sometimes unbeknownst to themselves: Stanley Konecky, Sylvia Tesh, George McGuire, Tony Gronowicz, Howie Hawkins, Michael B. Millard, Stefan Kuzminski, Jan Kuzminski (who gave me my title), my wife T'nette Kuzminski, and lastly, David Barker, my editor at Continuum.

Chapter One

The Insight of Phaleas

The word *democracy* literally means the rule of the people, from the ancient Greek *kratio*, to rule, and *demos*, the people. This popular self-governance is achieved in its fullest sense, I shall argue, by more or less equal citizens meeting in local, face-to-face, decision-making assemblies in which they are free to participate equally, fully, and directly. The word *democracy* is widely misused in our time, most commonly to indicate any kind of political system claiming popular sovereignty on the basis of elections or plebiscites, even though such periodic mass voting reduces citizen participation to a minimum while giving elected officials wide latitude for action with minimal accountability to their constituents. I use the word *democracy* in its original, stronger, and fuller sense of direct rule by the people; that is, the right of unimpeded participation—minimally, historically by heads of households, and maximally, by all adult community members—in self-government through empowered face-to-face assemblies of the kind found, among other places, in most kinship clans and tribes worldwide, in numerous ancient and medieval city-states, and in various modern assemblies such as New England town meetings. Direct democracy was arguably the first form of human polity, the natural embodiment of social justice, a once universal condition manifest in kinship societies around the world. It is essential to democratic societies, I shall argue, that their members do not differ significantly in personal wealth and power, not enough for some to control others. But democracy has been uprooted almost everywhere by thousands of years of war, conquest, and appropriation, with wealth and power conspicuously concentrated in relatively few hands. Though democracy in the postkinship state societies we call civilizations has been a rare exception, it remains an ever-present possibility, provided that the inequalities in wealth characteristic of war-based state societies can be significantly narrowed. This work hopes to contribute to that possibility.

Direct democracy is possible only on the local level, where citizens can meet and act personally in face-to-face assemblies. It can be extended over a broader area only if local assemblies are somehow confederated through wider representative bodies, whose members also meet face-to-face, and if these wider bodies are in turn made accountable to their constituent assemblies by ensuring that their members are elected by those assemblies and recallable by them. Assemblies for still larger areas, such as regions and nations, can similarly be constituted with regard to the regions and nations they represent. Thus, for example, if the United States were a democracy in this sense, we can imagine that county councils would represent local assemblies, state legislatures would represent county councils, and a national congress would represent state legislatures. This combination of local democracy and accountable representation, a democracy of individuals at the grassroots and of communities and regions beyond the grassroots, is the hallmark of confederal democracy. Although some kinship societies evolved into strong confederal democracies, such as the Native American Iroquois,[1] there have been relatively few confederal democractic state societies. Among these can perhaps be included the Aetolian and Achaean leagues in ancient Greece, and the Lydian and Etruscan leagues, among others.[2] The United States under the Articles of Confederation and the Swiss Confederation are, at least in part, more recent examples.[3] Confederal democracy would be the realization of democracy on a large scale; it would constitute not only its actual institutionalization locally but also its integration across a variety of communities and regions.[4] It would replace that oxymoron "mass democracy"—the system under which we live—with an integrated series of democracies of individuals, communities, and regions. The relative absence of confederal democracies in the historical record reflects the relative absence of democracy itself. Why this should be so, and how it might be remedied, are among the questions before us.

It is the principal thesis of this work that democracy so understood can be achieved and sustained only if its citizens are economically independent of one another to the degree necessary to allow them to come together more or less as political equals, not as masters and slaves, nobles and peasants, patrons and clients, employers and employees, bosses and workers, and so on. Economic independence means each citizen's personal or direct ownership of resources, sufficient to establish a degree of material self-sufficiency not absolutely but relatively vis-à-vis other citizens. It presupposes the right to private property *per se*, not just the right to an opportunity to struggle *for* private property. To insist upon economic independence is to claim the right to direct and full control of some fair share of the wealth of the community—that is, the resources or capital adequate for the realization of minimal personal economic self-sufficiency through one's own individual labor and investment, not just the right to claim economic benefits from property controlled by others, including the state. This work will consider how the direct right to property might be realized. My thesis is that a direct right to property is a necessary condition of genuine democracy, and that this presumption lies at the heart of the political movements we call "populist." The political economy of populism, which this work hopes to help revive, is based on the twin pillars of a right to private property by all and a right to democracy by all.

My thesis is not original. The term *populism* comes out of postbellum nineteenth-century American politics, but the insight it represents goes far back into ancient times. It was first articulated in the West, as far as I can determine, by an ancient Greek thinker, Phaleas of Chalcedon, who has come down to us only through a discussion in Aristotle's *Politics*. In Phaleas's view, as reported by Aristotle, for any democracy to be successful its citizens must have neither so much personal wealth and power as consistently to be able to dominate others, nor so little as to be dominated consistently by others. In Aristotle's words:

> For some persons think that the right regulation of property is the most important; for the question of property, they say, is universally the cause of party strife. Therefore the Chalcedonian Phaleas was the first who introduced this expedient; for he says that the citizens' estates ought to be equal, and he thought that this would not be difficult to secure at the outset for cities in process of formation, while in those already settled, although it would be a more irksome task, nevertheless a leveling would most easily be effected by the rich giving dowries but not receiving them and the poor receiving but not giving them.[5]

If Phaleas is right, free and full participation in democratic governance depends upon each citizen personally commanding resources sufficient to maintain his or her relative economic independence vis-à-vis other citizens. This command of personal resources can be established only by somehow ensuring the availability to all of some fair share of societies' resources, some part of the "common wealth." Phaleas is no socialist advocating common ownership; he speaks rather of "citizens' estates." This does not have to mean, as we shall see, taking resources away from anybody; it does mean equal access by each person by right to some equal portion of the wealth available to society as a whole. We shall explore, in what follows, some overlooked ways this might be done. If such a circulation of resources could be established it would have the effect, over time, of reducing the extremes of conspicuously rich and conspicuously poor, gradually melding them into a broad middle class of citizens. Justifiable differences of wealth would and should remain. If honestly earned wealth can only reflect honest differences among individuals and their endeavors, it seems such wealth should be retained by individuals and their families on a personal basis, but not necessarily institutionalized and perpetuated through corporate entities and special economic privileges. It is these latter, as we shall see, that allow for concentrations of wealth and power incompatible with democracy. A partial but steady diffusion of wealth throughout the citizenry, as Phaleas seems to have argued, is necessary to sustain the diffusion of political power in a democracy. This balance of democracy and property, to be struck in each individual, is the heart of Phaleas's insight, the core of his political economy, and the essence of populism.

In any society, there can and should be richer and poorer, given natural human differences in productive talents, skills, energies, motivations, and knowledge, all of which deserve their suitable rewards. But in a populist democracy there would be neither dramatically rich nor dramatically poor, neither those powerful enough to constitute a coherent and self-perpetuating ruling class nor those dependent enough to constitute a coherent and self-perpetuating client class. To avoid these all-too-familiar extremes, property, Phaleas tells us, must continuously be recirculated through an established, ongoing system of distribution. It must not be diverted and concentrated into the hands of authorities and bureaucracies, bypassing the people, but rather distributed individually and personally in equal shares to all. This distribution should allow those with productive talents to enjoy a generous return for their efforts, to become relatively richer, but not overwhelmingly so. It must be great enough to ensure that those who find themselves relatively poor can maintain a level of material self-sufficiency adequate to exercise independent and uncoerced judgment as free citizens. The point is not to strive for an impossible goal of absolute material equality, but to dampen the extremes of wealth and to broaden out the middle class. To this end, it is only necessary that citizens enjoy access to an equal share of such capital as is currently available to the community, a kind of ongoing minimal grubstake, or claim against the future resources of society, by personal right.

Part of the purpose of this work is to explore some unusual ways of circulating wealth devised by populist thinkers with the conscious intent to avoid the evils of direct taking or appropriation while fulfilling the promise of the populist equation of property and democracy. If Phaleas is right, true democracy—collective decision making by otherwise more or less free and equal private citizens meeting together in committees of the whole—can be successful only to the degree that citizens personally are materially self-sufficient enough to be economically independent of one another, or any other power. For only then can they hope to achieve a measure of objectivity and responsibility on social issues free of the biases inherent in being rich or poor—the fundamental source of political faction. Private property widely distributed is, in this view, an indispensable requirement of democracy, just as private property narrowly distributed has been democracy's worst enemy. A responsible democracy is impossible without the ability of each person to command as personal property his or her share of the resources necessary to develop freely the fruits of his or her own labor, and—paradoxical as it may sound at first—there can be no lasting security for personal property and the fruits of one's own labor without democracy. Indeed, it is their combination—the merger of public accountability with private production—that defines the democratic populist political economy envisioned by Phaleas.

By wealth or property I mean the right to command some equitable share of the resources of nature and society as a matter of effective personal (not merely token or symbolic or indirect) ownership. This is not merely the "right" to labor for others who control resources, where one is reduced to selling the property of one's own body or mind. It is rather the right of each individual to claim direct ownership of a fair share of the resources acknowledged by right as necessary to carry out one's own productive labor for one's own purposes. Ownership here means full personal control, including the freedom to wholly alienate (to sell or otherwise transfer) the distributed capital in question. This claim to private resources means that some resources must somehow continuously be circulated more or less uniformly to all, rather than disproportionately appropriated by a relative few. Such uniform circulation, modern populists have argued, can best be achieved through an alternative monetary system based on low-interest loans available to individual citizens with good collateral. Unlike other critics of the shortcomings of corporate capitalism, populists have zeroed in on the established debt-based financial system as the principal culprit driving unsustainable economic growth and unduly concentrating wealth; the serious alternatives to that system they have proposed are well worth considering in our troubled economic times. The fullest idea of such an alternative system was developed in the nineteenth century by the American protopopulist Edward Kellogg in *A New Monetary System* and other works. A government obligation to offer citizens low-interest loans was seen by Kellogg as the best means of equitably distributing future capital, and we shall examine his views in detail later in this work.

Socialists have sought to abolish private property and the market, while capitalists have sought to reify private property into an independent force. Phaleas and the populists point out a third way: the combination of full public, democratic rights with full private, resource rights, with democracy and property for all, not just for some at the expense of others. They offer a new path toward establishing a just social and economic order, one hitherto only marginally explored. This combination of property and democracy is no more or less than the balance of private pursuits with public responsibilities. It allows for the maximum freedom possible, with freedom understood as the mutual range of activity that you and I and our fellow citizens allow ourselves in our individual and collective pursuits of happiness. The false reduction of freedom to individual freedom (as found in corporate capitalist ideology) tends to anarchy, just as the false inflation of freedom to collective freedom (as found in socialist and fascist ideology) tends to tyranny. Freedom, it is here proposed, might better be served by the sustained balance of private individual resource rights with public collective democratic rights. A just society, in this view, can be established *only* when all citizens have full and direct access to both the political process and the resources necessary to maintain a level of relative personal economic security adequate to sustain an independent outlook on public issues.

The promise of a populist program speaks directly to our political and economic failures, and to the bankruptcy of our misrepresentative system of government: a plutocratic oligarchy perpetuated through manipulated mass elections or plebecites that insists upon calling itself a "democracy." Populism holds out the hope of dissolving, peacefully and over time, the domineering personal and corporate concentrations of wealth and political power that characterize our society, so as to free and advance, rather than hinder and exploit, the private energies of labor, talent, and ambition. The populist program, first envisioned by Phaleas, proposes to establish and sustain democracy by economically empowering ordinary citizens. In our day that means transforming them from dependent wage earners into property owners personally controlling significant resources, and thereby independent and responsible enough to be truly and successfully self-governing. It is an old vision once more worth taking seriously, a vision perhaps more relevant than ever in the twenty-first century.

***

We live, of course, in a very un-Phalean, unpopulist world. It is the world of corporate finance capitalism where political accountability is minimal, the operative forces not personal but controlling abstractions backed by force, the influence of oligarchic ruling elites indirect but decisive, and wealth highly concentrated in few hands, leaving most people as clients of one sort or another. The state is the ultimate corporation, set off against the people, the one by which all others are sanctioned. The private corporations sanctioned by the state have in many instances gone on to accumulate sufficient powers to influence, even dominate, the state itself.[6] Corporate entities are highly various, and include, for instance, the federal government, Microsoft, the States of the Union, the IRS, the Catholic Church, the Farm Bureau, General Electric, the Sierra Club, the Rotary Club, the Veterans of Foreign Wars, the Teamsters Union, Exxon, and the Rockefeller Foundation, among countless others, including family trusts, nonprofits, many small businesses, and so forth. The United States and most modern industrial countries are essentially corporate oligarchies. They are ruled by shifting corporate coalitions of governments, businesses, and related institutions, dominated by a peculiar system of private finance; taken together these institutions constitute the principal instruments for perpetuating vast discrepancies of wealth, blocking the possibility of a populist political economy.

These various corporate financial entities are controlled by relatively small numbers of individuals—including, variously, politicians, lobbyists, public officials, donors, directors, executives, board members, CEOs, and trustees, among others—most of whom are only indirectly accountable, if at all, to most of those affected by their decisions. The social and political power of any corporate institution is determined mainly by its relative size, its legal standing and regulatory force, its assets and financial influence, and its productive power—that is, by the various means at its disposal to appropriate and control resources to its own ends. Whether private enterprises or governmental bodies, corporations have become the premier means of concentrating enormous power and wealth in few hands. With minimal public accountability, these curious abstract entities, large or small, are in a special position to reward those who control them. The vast majority of people (citizens, consumers, stockholders, employees, the self-employed, and so on, as the case may be) control no such entities. They remain social and economic dependents, atomized and isolated for the most part, whose decisions in the marketplace or voting booth are all too often predetermined by the mass advertising of the corporate media, or the fear of losing one's job.

Leftish-liberal critics of the status quo in America traditionally have seen private corporations, or "big business," or Wall Street, as the main source of social injustice, while looking favorably upon government as a key instrument of social virtue. Rightish-conservative critics of the same status quo traditionally have seen "big government" as the main source of social injustice, while looking favorably upon business and the marketplace as key instruments of social virtue. Both accept corporate structure (one public, the other private) as fundamental. The ideological dovetailing is nearly perfect. The Left tells us that business is bad (exploitation, injustice, etc.) and government is good (social programs, environmental protection, etc.). The Right tells us that government is bad (regulations, high taxes, etc.) and business is good (profits, jobs, etc.). This is an oversimplification, to be sure, but it highlights a key fault line in American political discourse, a fault line that has long obscured a deeper, pathological, common structure. The radical left-wing tendency to endorse government and distrust private corporations, and the radical right-wing tendency to endorse private corporations and distrust government, are two sides of the same coin. It is not big business that is solely the problem; nor is it big government; it is both of them together, effectively unaccountable to the people, and controlled by small elites. The Left has yet to recognize that corporate government, even in its liberal representative versions, is a democratic sham accountable only to special interests, not to the public interest. The Right has yet to recognize that corporate competition, especially when "deregulated," is a license to steal, not a "hidden hand" leading to utopia. The left wing at its most vocal has thought business a crime and government the answer; the right wing at its most vocal has thought government a crime and business the answer. Each has been right about the other, and wrong about itself.

These pseudoalternatives demonstrate the *reductio ad absurdum* that has lain at the heart of American political discourse at least since the defeat of the populist movement at the end of the nineteenth century. For well over a century now, debate in the United States has failed to move beyond an illusory big government versus big business dichotomy. Each side fails to recognize the corporate nature common to both business and government. Corporate structure is essentially a semipermeable membrane insulating those in control but allowing them to exercise largely unaccountable power over others (members, voters, employees, clients, consumers, etc., as the case may be). Once the common antidemocratic corporate structure of both big government and big business is recognized, their common measure can be taken. In the corporate world, stockholders vote like citizens for the management of their corporations, and have about as much influence over management as voters do over governments, which is next to none. This has become painfully evident with the latest wave of corporate scandals, beginning with the collapse of the Enron Corporation in 2001. Private corporations, like the public corporation we call the government, are run from the top down—not from the bottom up.

Peacefully disestablishing unaccountable corporate power, public and private, including the fiction of corporate personhood, is a major precondition of fundamental political and economic reform, particularly in the United States, but in most other modern industrial countries as well. If the traditional left/right spectrum sustains a common illusion, how can we begin to think about political economy? From a populist perspective, resources have be shared more equitably, and politics carried out more democratically, with corporate privilege replaced by community accountability. In the process, politics would become repersonalized. Ending the misrepresentative system of pseudodemocratic government means refounding government on the basis of bottom-up, local democracy. Ending corporate tyranny means ending the legal fiction of corporations as persons in the law and repersonalizing property relations. Ending government tyranny means ending the American misrepresentative system of pseudodemocratic government in favor of an actual democracy. Ending the legal fiction of private and public corporations as "persons" means removing the mask of corporate being, with its power to deflect responsibility from living individuals to controlling legal abstractions. It means, as we shall see, devolving decision making back into partnerships of flesh-and-blood citizens.

Just as corporate government is the principal mechanism today concentrating political power, so the principal mechanism today concentrating wealth is the corporate finance system. That system is based upon a monopoly over capital established in our banking and monetary practices. The ability of commercial banks and other financial institutions, acting through the Federal Reserve System, to control interest rates and money supply allows them to control who gets credit and on what terms to their private profit. They are in a position to use this power to private advantage rather than public good. The public must often borrow, often at usurious rates of interest, to have any access to capital at all. This, more than anything else, frustrates the economic independence of citizens and makes them clients of one sort or another of corporate finance power. The power of creditors over debtors is an old issue, going back to the very beginnings of recorded history. The populist tradition, as we shall see in detail, came to focus on this issue and advanced, particularly in modern times, the novel idea of making credit available without interest to citizens with good collateral. The nature of the money system became central to populist concerns, and in the work of Edward Kellogg and others, we shall consider how such an alternative system might work.

***

These notions may appear utopian, yet anything less, I would argue, risks failing to address the fundamental problems facing our society. This work hopes to persuade the reader that populist democratic and economic reform of our most important institutions is not only desirable, but possible and even necessary. These issues, of course, are not new. They have been debated since the founding of the republic, and go back deep into antiquity, but they are perhaps now as pressing as they ever were. A brief historical sketch may be useful. The Civil War, with its demand for credit and resources, brought corporate power dramatically to the national stage in the United States, enabling it over time to restructure the economic and financial system to its advantage. Rural populists and urban radicals resisted the consolidation of corporate and financial power, but to little avail. By the 1890s, through a series of legislative and judicial acts, corporate power in the United States broke free of effective public accountability.[7] The new financial-corporate system, now in control of the government, managed to overcome the challenges posed by World War I, by the Depression of the 1930s, by World War II, by the Civil Rights and countercultural movements of the 1950s and '60s, by the oil shocks and economic upheavals of the 1970s, and by the Japanese challenge of the 1980s, to go no further. Although the New Deal in particular imposed a measure of accountability on corporate and financial activities—the minimum wage, the Securities and Exchange Commission, the Glass-Stegall Act, and various labor laws, among others—much of this control was rolled back, especially in the late twentieth century; and in any case the New Deal never challenged the core power of private finance. By the 1990s, after the collapse of the Soviet Union, the corporate financial system came to stand virtually unchallenged domestically and internationally. Under the slogan of "globalization" it sought worldwide preeminence. It took the attacks of September 11, 2001, and the subsequent war on terror, the Iraq war, corporate scandals, volatile markets, economic slump, global destabilization, peak oil, debt burdens, and other threats to American power, to remind everyone how vulnerable this system remains.[8]

It is not unreasonable, I submit, to describe early twenty-first-century America as a corporate-plutocratic society, driven above all by the profit motive, predicated on a presumption of endless "growth" driven by the obligation to service debt burdens, and justified by what is in fact an antidemocratic version of misrepresentative government. After the Vietnam defeat and the economic shocks of the 1970s and early '80s, relative prosperity returned in the Reagan era, fueled by large federal deficits. That prosperity continued in the 1990s in the wake of the successful Gulf War and the collapse of the Soviet Union. Under the powerful stimulus of government spending and corporate globalization, rooted in the exploitation of cheap labor and cheap resources around the world, corporate profits and stock prices soared. This new prosperity of the Clinton years was widespread among the upper and middle classes, but it failed to address a long series of chronic problems, including:

- racism
- increasing class division
- the pollution of air, water, and land
- an often ugly and degraded human landscape
- an inefficient and gridlocked transportation system
- illegal immigration
- dependence on overseas resources
- an exploitive global economy
- outsourcing of jobs
- the deterioration of public education and public institutions generally
- the loss of independent producers
- the corruption of elected officials by campaign finance contributions and other perks
- the worldwide deployment of the American military
- excessive power in the executive branch over the use of the military
- the decline of public services and safety
- the atomization of individuals and families
- the consolidation of corporate power
- a real decline in national income for the majority
- a heavy debt burden on taxpayers
- lack of access to capital by individuals and small businesses

- a heavily debt-financed economy
- high levels of debt generally
- cultural reduction and homogenization through consumerism and the media
- serious deterioration of local and global environments, and so on.

All these made up the seamy underside of corporate globalization and "prosperity" in the 1990s. Under the administration of George W. Bush, these problems only intensified, compounded by the war on terror, the suspension in principle of constitutional rights and civil liberties, even greater debts, intensified global warming, and the looming prospect of energy shortages related to peak oil.

If anyone doubts claims about the maldistribution of wealth and power in America, a few statistics may be useful. Often cited, they remain mind-boggling. The vast class of the nonrich in the United States encompasses the lower and middle classes, including most of the professional and literary-artistic sectors of the middle class. The nonrich, unlike the rich, have to work for a living. The nonrich are almost everybody, some 98.5 percent of the population. Ferdinand Lundberg's classic study of this subject, *The Rich and the Super-Rich*, was published in the 1960s. He produced exhaustive data to show that, at that time, "1.6 percent of the adult population own at least 32 percent of all assets, and nearly all the investment assets, and that 11 percent of households . . . own at least 56 percent of the assets and 60 percent of the net worth. It is even possible . . . that 1/2 of 1 percent own more than one-third of all productive assets as of 1965-67. It is evident that this leaves very little to be apportioned among 90 percent of the population."[9] It is the "investment assets" that count. Nearly all subsequent commentators agree that these disparities have worsened since the 1960s. As Kevin Phillips put it in his 1990 book *The Politics of the Rich and Poor*: "By the middle of Reagan's second term, official data had begun to show that America's broadly defined 'rich'—the top half of 1 percent of the U.S. population—had never been richer. Federal policy favored the accumulation of wealth and rewarded financial assets, and the concentration of income that began in the mid-1970s was accelerating. . . . No parallel upsurge of riches had been seen since the late nineteenth century, the era of the Vanderbilts, Morgans and Rockefellers."[10] Arthur Schlesinger Jr., writing in the op-ed page of the *Wall Street Journal* on June 7, 1995 stated: "Britain is notorious as a class-ridden society, but the top 1% of families in Britain own only about 18% of the nation's wealth. In America the top 1% own more than 40%." More recently, the gap between the rich and poor has been persistent, even intensifying, to the point where even conservative apologists have stopped trying to refute the claim.

Writing in 2002, Kevin Phillips in *Wealth and Democracy* observes that "thanks to earned income tax credits and a long overdue minimum wage increase, the second Clinton term produced a slightly less skewed income distribution than the previous GOP regimes. The gap between top and bottom, still widening from 1993 to 1996, was mitigated by gains for the two bottom fifths during the peak of the business cycle from 1997 to 2000. The widening crevice between the top 1 percent and the beleaguered middle, however, was untouched."[11] And so it has been for a long time. Writing in the 1850s, Edward Kellogg, whose work we shall later consider at length, states:

> In all probability, four thousand of the most wealthy citizens of the city of New York own a greater amount of real and personal property than the whole remainder of its inhabitants. Their wealth is vested in real estate in the city and country, in bank, railroad, State, and other stocks, loans of money, etc. Allow five persons to form a family, and the four thousand men and their families would form a population of twenty thousand, or two and a half per cent of eight hundred thousand, the present population of the city. Upon this estimate—and a little observation and reflection will show that it is not an extravagant one—two and a half per cent of the population are worth as much as the remaining ninety-seven and a half per cent.[12]

***

We now have a government in the United States run almost openly for the benefit of this small minority. The argument that this is so—for those who still doubt it—can be found largely if not entirely in the works of a series of self-styled "progressive" writers and critics of the last half of the twentieth century, including C. Wright Mills, Ferdinand Lundberg, Herbert Marcuse, Barry Commoner, Richard J. Barnett, Ronald E. Muller, David Noble, William Greider, Howard Zinn, Noam Chomsky, David C. Korton, Jeremy Rifkin, Richard Douthwaite, Kevin Phillips, Ralph Nader, Donald L. Bartlett, James B. Steele, Stanley Aronowitz, and many others.[13] These authors have relentlessly chronicled deregulation, the globalization of corporate power, the corruption of election financing, the maldistribution of wealth, the liberal-conservative pseudodebate, the decline of labor, tax evasion by the wealthy, corporate welfare, the advantages of offshore banking and production, foreign competition, the influence of finance and central banking, the power of the media, the corruption of education, the decline of Keyensian economics, and the general triumph of debtors over creditors in the new, ruthless global economy.

One of the more popular of these writers, William Greider, summarized his agenda for "reform" as follows:

> Restore national controls over global capital. Tax wealth more, labor less. Stimulate global growth by boosting consumer demand from the bottom up. Compel trading nations to accept more balanced trade relations and absorb more surplus production. Forgive the debtors, especially the hopeless cases among the very poorest nations. Reorganize monetary policy to confront the realities of a globalized money supply, both to achieve greater stability and open the way to greater growth. Defend labor rights in all markets, prohibit the ancient abuses renewed in the "dark Satanic mills." Withdraw from the old labor-capital battleground by universalizing access to capital ownership. Reformulate the idea of economic growth to escape the wasteful nature of consumption. And, in the meantime, defend work and wages and social protections against assaults by the marketplace.[14]

Greider's prescriptions—like those of most of his fellow progressive critics—point toward but do not describe what a decorporatized America might look like. His appeal to labor power is inherently democratic, and his call for "universalizing access to capital ownership" is fundamental. But he stops short of calling for the radical political changes necessary to implement and sustain these ideals, leaving his agenda hanging in midair and the status quo in place. He fails to develop in any detail just what his most important points—democratic accountability and universalizing access to capital ownership—might mean and how they could reasonably be implemented and work. This inability to specify the populist interconnection between democracy and resources permits their separation to persist. Resources without democracy produce the tyranny of wealth; democracy without resources produces the tyranny of the mob. Grieder senses this failure to probe deeper when he laments the lack of a basic theory that would show us how to domesticate the marketplace in the name of social and environmental justice:

"Perhaps, in this next age of capitalism," he writes, "an original thinker will arise somewhere in the world with a new theory that reconciles the market's imperatives with unfilled human needs, without having to destroy the marketplace to do so. This would be an intellectual achievement for the ages . . . it is not inconceivable that someone might someday solve this problem."[15]

In fact there have been a number of such thinkers, and even some practical applications; indeed, there is a long if somewhat disrupted tradition going back to Phaleas, a tradition largely overlooked by recent radical writers. Grieder's "intellectual achievement for the ages" has already been achieved, at least in principle, though obscured in our time. Prescriptions for the future, as so often, can be found in the past, in this case in a very old, nonsocialist, radical perspective that I seek to revive for serious consideration. I call it populist, though it's also been called Jeffersonian and "classical republican," and it goes back, as we shall see, through a long line of thinkers including the populists of the Farmers' Alliance and the Peoples' Party, Edward Kellogg and the greenbackers, Thomas Paine, Thomas Jefferson, Bishop Berkeley, James Harrington, and even farther back to the social struggles in Rome, to Aristotle and the practice of democracy in classical Greek city-states such as Athens, and to its early expression by Phaleas, and beyond that to its more or less spontaneous practice in the natural populist political economies of kinship societies. In America, it goes back to the radicals of the Revolutionary era, to Benjamin Franklin, Thomas Jefferson, John Logan, Tom Paine, Sam Adams, Daniel Shays, Ethan Allen, and others. There are links and important parallels with Native American traditions. This property, prodemocracy populist tradition was incorporated into Jefferson's vision of a democratic American republic, a vision held by Tom Paine, John Taylor of Carolina, Edward Kellogg, Charles Macune, Henry George, greenbackers, populists, and many others. For all of them, the central insight was the one-to-one correlation between property and democracy, the recognition that more or less political equals must also be more or less economic equals. This does not mean, again, equality of possessions, but rather access to capital by each and all sufficient to preclude any domineering concentration of possessions by a few. Actual, not potential, economic freedom (actual ownership, not just the "opportunity" to compete for ownership) is the precondition of genuine rather than faux democracy.

***

Some terminology and background may be useful. *Republican* comes from the Latin, *res publica*, the public thing, or the peoples' business, while *democratic* comes as noted earlier from the Greek, *demos*, the people themselves, and *krateo*, to rule. Their meanings are overlapping but distinct, and sometimes confusing. The public thing does not require direct democracy, or any democracy at all; it might be done by proxy, by representatives, by a conquerer, by some of the people, even just a few, or even none of them rather than all of them, or by a monarch or dictator. And indeed, *republic* in modern times has come to mean a state in which the sovereign power resides formally but passively in the general body of the people, the citizens, but is exercised in fact by governments set off from those citizens, and linked to them only by representatives, delegated with power, and chosen in mass elections but otherwise only theoretically responsible to the citizenry. This modern definition, which boils popular sovereignty down to the right to vote in periodic elections, in effect excludes any meaningful democracy. Only elected representatives actually exercise power in modern republics, in contrast to genuine democracies, such as found in many ancient city-states or in modern communities governed by town meetings, where citizens enjoy direct voting powers over legislation and other matters. The *demos*, on the other hand, is undeniably the people and no one else, gathered together face-to-face in open assemblies, ready to exercise power. The term *democracy* has been obscured by its modern confusion with "representative government," so that "democratic government" in the popular sense today is really republican, or representative, government; it is not democratic at all. Modern representative government is really a form of oligarchy, not of hereditary title but in our case of money (a plutocracy), which money, however, is often bequeathed through hereditary connection, so we have, like the ancients, like Sulla and Pompey and Caesar, our own dynasts (e.g., the Roosevelts, Rockefellers, Kennedys, Bushes, etc).

Before the eighteenth century, republicanism in the West was associated with small city-states, which could and sometimes did include direct democracy, as in various people's assemblies, or communes, as in the Swiss cantons, but was more often oligarchic, as in Venice. The term *republic* nonetheless included at least the possibility of democracy, of the exercise of direct power not only by some body of citizens, but all of them. Most classic city-state republics, from Athens and Rome to Venice and Florence and Geneva, variously combined democratic and representative elements. No legislation could pass in the Roman Republic, for instance, without a vote by the citizens meeting in assembly, a clear exercise of direct democracy quite foreign to our current system.[16] Some city-states, like Athens in the fifth and fourth centuries before the common era, were close to being pure democracies for their qualifying citizens, if not for women and resident aliens such as slaves, foreigners, and so on. Others, like Venice, evolved into restrictive oligarchies, with some citizens consistently ruling others. Still others vacillated between forms of popular sovereignty, as well as monarchy and tyranny.

Democracy in premodern city-states sometimes degenerated into tyranny, as seen in Thucydides' description of civil strife in the city of Corcyra at the start of the Peloponnesian War.[17] It is instructive, however, that this breakdown usually occurs not when citizens are economically free and wealth widely distributed, but when they are indebted and impoverished, without property, and dependent on the rich, either directly as clients or one sort of another, or indirectly through other obligations. These propertyless often urban but sometimes also rural poor (we see them in the *sans-culottes* of revolutionary Paris and in the Roman soldiers demanding land in the Late Republic under Marius, Sulla, Caesar, and other leaders) were often motivated by anger and resentment, and vulnerable to demagoguery. Too often they wished only to emulate rather than improve upon those perceived to be more successful than themselves, or else to punish them out of resentment. Unable or unwilling to contemplate a substantial redistribution of their wealth, the rich then and now have consistently played on this resentment, using it to oppose democracy, seeking to effect an identification of democracy with the mob that, by their appropriations of wealth, they created in the first place.

Economic class warfare has been a chronic feature of state society since the first civilizations. We see it in the struggle of indebted, dispossessed farmers and artisans against oligarchic rule in Athens, and later in Rome, and in many other ancient cities, in fact probably in most of them, and often from an early date.[18] These conflicts resurfaced with the recovery of commerce and the growth of cities toward the end of the Middle Ages in Europe. In early America, however, a continent with an abundance of resources open to European immigrants made it possible for them to realize some approximation of a populist society, most noticeably on the frontier and in places such as Vermont, Pennsylvania, parts of New England, and the hinterlands of most of the colonies. For a time in early America, class warfare was significantly diminished, though hardly eliminated. European settlers spread over a vast continent, with only weakened resistance from Native Americans reduced by disease. There was plentiful access to resources for the new settlers, and fewer dramatic disparities between the rich and poor among them than in Europe. They

could, and did, tend to organize themselves spontaneously along more
or less democratic lines, regularly holding town meetings and local assemblies, displaying the spontaneous passion for democracy chronicled
so clearly in Alexis de Tocqueville's *Democracy in America.* Colonial and
early federal America constituted in modern times an unprecedented
series of more or less populist states—most notably, perhaps, independent Vermont, as we shall see—where democratic participation and
personal economic freedom were very widely combined, and where there
were some poorer and some richer, but where most if not all had enough
personal property to avoid economic dependency.

The central image of the populist or Phalean vision, as I have suggested, is a society of independent producers, of individuals personally
owning productive private resources as sole proprietors or partners in
independent business ventures. These same independent producers
come together as equals in local people's assemblies, like New England
town meetings or committees of correspondence, to manage their common affairs. The key precondition for free deliberation is enough property per household, if not per individual, to allow for a modicum level of
independent subsistence, the rough equivalent of the old homestead on
the frontier. Drew McCoy succinctly summarizes what I am calling the
American populist vision in *The Elusive Republic*:

> American republicans valued property in land primarily be-
> cause it provided personal independence. The individual with
> direct access to the productive resources of nature need not rely
> on other men, or any man, for the basic means of existence. The
> Revolutionaries believed that every man had a natural right
> to this form of property, in the sense that he was entitled to
> autonomous control of the resources that were absolutely
> necessary for his subsistence. The personal independence
> that resulted from the ownership of land permitted a citizen to
> participate responsibly in the political process, for it allowed him
> to pursue spontaneously the common or public good, rather
> than the narrow interest of the men—or the government—on
> whom he depended for his support. Thus the Revolutionaries
> did not intend to provide men with property so that they might
> flee from public responsibility into a selfish privatism; property
> was rather the necessary basis for a committed republican
> citizenry.[19]

One other quotation might be useful here, this time a longish one from Alexis de Tocqueville's *Democracy in America*. Tocqueville famously worried over the egalitarian implications of what he saw as an inevitable movement toward democracy, a possible stifling of the human spirit in a society where all are more or less equal economically and politically. While I am more optimistic about the virtues of human diversity under such conditions, even Tocqueville, toward the end of his influential work, ends up offering a rather positive populist analysis of what society based on more or less political and economic egalitarianism might look like. He does not tell us how wealth can be circulated to guarantee such a society—a point to which we shall return—but he paints an accurate enough picture of what is desired:

Remove the secondary causes which have produced the great convulsions of the world, and you will almost always find the principle of inequality at the bottom. Either the poor have attempted to plunder the rich, or the rich to enslave the poor. If, then, a state of society can ever be founded in which every man shall have something to keep, and little to take from others, much will have been done for the peace of the world. I am aware that among a great democratic people there will always be some members of the community in great poverty, and others in great opulence; but the poor, instead of forming the immense majority of the nation, as is always the case in aristocratic communities, are comparatively few in number, and the laws do not bind them together by the ties of irremediable and hereditary penury. The wealthy, on their side, are scarce and powerless; they have no privileges which attract public observation; even their wealth, as it is no longer incorporated and bound up with the soil, is impalpable, and as it were invisible. As there is no longer a race of poor men, so there is no longer a race of rich men; the latter spring up daily from the multitude, and relapse into it again. Hence they do not form a distinct class, which may be easily marked out and plundered; and, moreover, as they are connected with the mass of their fellow citizens by a thousand secret ties, the people cannot assail them without inflicting an injury upon itself. Between these two extremes of democratic communities stand an innumerable multitude of men almost alike, who, without being exactly rich or poor, are possessed of sufficient property to desire the maintenance of order, yet not enough to excite envy. Such men are the natural enemies of violent commotions: their stillness keeps all beneath them and above them still, and secures the balance of the fabric of society. Not, indeed, that even these men are contented with what they have got, or that they feel a natural abhorrence for a revolution in which they might share the spoil without sharing the calamity; on the contrary, they desire, with unexampled ardor, to get rich, but the difficulty is to know from whom riches can be taken. The same state of society which constantly prompts desires, restrains these desires within necessary limits: it gives men more liberty of changing and less interest in change.[20]

***

In its presumption that the right to wealth—that is, private property—is a necessary condition of responsible democracy and social justice, the American populist tradition collides head on with the socialist tradition, which is deeply suspicious of private property and still informs much oppositional thought in America. European-inspired socialism, though not as influential as it once was, today remains for many educated people the only broadly held critical alternative to corporate capitalism. Socialism's response to the problem of the rich and poor has been to recommunalize property, making it more public, less private, and to plan the overall economy through centralized government agencies on every level. The idea was to fight the growth of large, private corporations by developing the countervailing power of the public corporation we call the government to the point where the latter would neutralize and ultimately absorb the former. In the process, however, the poor were all too often transformed from clients of private interests into clients of the state, which became the effective owner of resources in socialist countries, albeit in trust for its citizens, an arrangement which left most citizens as dependent as before, unable to act freely or responsibly. The result was a series of more or less bureaucratic, more or less tyrannical, socialist states, including the USSR and Communist China, where centralized power in the worse cases allowed for totalitarian-scale abuses and monumental crimes against humanity. But even milder, more limited, liberal socialist governments, like those of the Scandinavian countries or the Labor governments in Britain after World War II, tended to a bureaucratic, top-down approach in the name of supporting their client voters, with direct democracy largely overlooked, or not even recognized. Socialists normally favor government-run monopolies, little different in the end politically or environmentally from the private cartels of corporate monopolists, both being structured internally along similar pseudodemocratic representative lines, with real authority flowing top-down, with wealth tending to concentrate in a distinct ruling class. Socialist presumptions continue to confuse and bedevil radical politics in America, effectively marginalizing it. When the relative failure of classic Soviet-style bureaucratic command economies became apparent in the 1980s, some American socialists turned to a decentralized version of socialism, a view perhaps best articulated by Murray Bookchin in his vision of "social ecology." In a 1986 pamphlet, "Municipalization: Community Ownership of the Economy," Bookchin writes:

> Libertarian municipalism scores a significant advance . . . by calling for the municipalization of the economy—and its management by the community as part of a politics of public self-management. Where the syndicalist alternative re-privatizes the economy into "self-managed" collectives and opens the way to their degeneration into traditional forms of private property—whether "collectively" owned or not—libertarian municipalism politicizes the economy and dissolves it into the civic domain. Neither factory or land appear as separate interests within the communal collective. Nor can workers, farmers, technicians, engineers, professional, and the like perpetuate their vocational identities as separate interests that exist apart from the citizen body in face-to-face assemblies. "Property" is integrated into the commune as a material constituent of its libertarian institutional framework, indeed as a part of the larger whole that is controlled by the citizen body in assembly as citizens—not as vocationally oriented interest groups.[21]

In Bookchin's vision of municipalist socialism, taken up by Greens, neohippies, and others, property is just as collectivized and "politicized" as in the old Soviet-style command system, only the focus is now local, on the immediate community and its governing assembly. Individuals, however, still remain powerless as individuals. They receive no direct and unqualified private shares of public resources; they are reduced rather to dependence upon the local assembly, now empowered to run local enterprises. Most citizens would end up working for their local municipality, of which they would also be, in theory, the collective owners. Citizens meeting in local assembly are not likely to be able practically to manage a local economy. This work would quickly be given over to representatives, committees, experts, professionals, consultants, managers, and so on. These municipal corporate monopolies, if ever established, would very naturally concentrate power in few hands, and in the absence of real competition might seriously lag in production and efficiency. Comprehensive management can engender a hierarchy of authority as much at the local level as anywhere else, and citizens would have few private resources with which to protect themselves against it. Consider the private economic enterprises in your community, and try to imagine them being municipalized. The likely result would be bureaucratic state socialism in miniature, but no less collectivist and potentially totalitarian for that. With no provision for acquiring significant personal property, and with most property communalized, individuals would have no bulwark against local tyranny, no check on demagogery, no independent security against the all-powerful local assembly and its leadership. Local demogogues need be no less pernicious, after all, than national ones. We would likely see under such conditions the fierce local factionalism of ancient city-states reappear.

Modern populists, by contrast with socialists, insist upon the private and personal, rather than the public and collective, ownership of resources. And populists, by contrast with capitalists, insist upon a right by each person to wealth, to actual property ownership, not simply upon a right of opportunity to compete for property with no obligation to the losers. Populist ownership is individual and personal, not corporate. Populists reject the capitalist privileging of capital over labor, just as they reject the socialist privileging of labor over capital. They seek rather to balance labor with capital. Capital and labor are recognized not as ends in themselves, but as necessary complementary means to human fulfillment, and therefore as equivalent rights for all persons. Populists place a universal right to one's own capital next to a universal right to one's own labor. While socialists have advocated that the fruits of production go primarily to labor, and capitalists that they go primarily to capital, populists advocate that labor and capital share these fruits equally insofar as capital and labor are both equally necessary to production, and best combined in each person. Society owes to each of its members some minimal claim on its resources, again, not so great as to exploit unduly the labor of others as to deprive them of their just desserts, nor so little as to deny the necessities of life. Only when this claim is recognized and honored can genuine democracy be achieved and maintained. The populist world pivots on this balance. Only by respecting both of these, by economically empowering all citizens, can genuine democracy be enabled, as Phaleas saw. The balance is one between private and public, between personal independence and freedom from coercion on the one hand, and the opportunities and responsibilities to participate in common self-government on the other.

***

In recent decades the socialist critique of corporate capitalism has been supplemented to an increasing degree by what might be called an ecocritique, advanced under the overlapping labels of environmentalism, ecology, sustainability, peak oil, and relocalization. E. F. Schumacher's *Small is Beautiful*; Barry Commoner's *The Poverty of Power*; Jane Jacobs's early works, beginning with *The Death and Life of Great American Cities*; the essays of Wendell Berry, beginning with *The Unsettling of America*; and *The Limits to Growth* by Donella Meadows et al., along with other works that appeared in the 1960s and '70s, launched the new eco-critique.[22] Its distinguishing feature is a shift in focus from the exploitation of labor to the exploitation of nature. The eco-critics are suspicious of the centralization of political and economic power in the name of "growth," whether under corporate capitalism or state socialism. For them, large-scale, industrial economics is an unsustainable linear process, taking raw materials in amounts far exceeding any provision for their replacement and turning them into consumer products and infrastructure that, after a period of use, become so much unusable waste and harmful pollution—of which carbon dioxide emissions fueling global warming are perhaps the best example. The challenge is to reestablish a sustainable political economy, replacing linear with circular processes (closing the ecological loops, as it were), and for most eco-critics this has meant some kind of decentralization of political and economic power.

A succeeding generation of eco-critics has pushed these issues even further. William R. Catton Jr.'s *Overshoot*, published in 1980, may still be the most comprehensive of the major eco-critics' works.[23] Richard Douthwaite in *The Growth Illusion* and Herman E. Daly in *Beyond Growth* systematically catalog the environmental toll extracted by conventional economic "growth," while the overall factors conditioning "growth" are updated in the latest edition of *Limits to Growth* (2004).[24] In recent years eco-critics have come to focus on the prospect of declining oil reserves in particular. The modern industrial world is based primarily on oil and other cheaply extracted fossil fuels, such as coal and natural gas; as they run out or get more difficult to extract, there is nothing to replace them—so far—as a comparable source of energy. Richard Heinberg in *Powerdown* argues that no combination of alternative energy sources can come near to supplying current energy demands based largely on oil, and James Howard Kunstler in *The Long Emergency* dramatizes the consequences of arriving at "peak oil" supply, after which a drastic reduction in global standards of living seems inevitable, barring some *deus ex machina*. In worst-case scenarios, they suggest, the energy shortfall might be as much as 90 percent.

None of these writers identifies himself particularly as a populist. Yet the relentless analyses of unsustainable economic and political concentrations of power—especially by the more recent peak-oil-influenced writers—return us to the basic ingredients of the populist perspective. Even if they are half right, their predictions remain dire; if the present and projected populations of the earth cannot expect access to anything like the resources still available today to maintain current standards of living, there will be a social global catastrophe. These writers offer a more or less doomsday senario, warning of a drastic reduction in energy resources and consequently a drastic and perhaps horrific decline in population, sometime in the coming decades, perhaps sooner rather than later. The only recourse consistently offered in this literature is relocalization—that is, the radical downsizing of political and economic activity back to the grassroots—an inherently populist impulse. It means diversifying and decentralizing production and exchange in large degree back into local communities, replacing global and national networks with regional and local ones, and that implies local control, where the prospects for widespread local ownership and democratic decision making—key populist principles—would naturally be heightened.

Most eco-critics have little to offer beyond the somewhat abstract concept of relocalization, however, often leaving the specifics vague.[25] How can relocalization avoid anarchy? How can widespread personal ownership be established without resentment and class warfare? How can democratic local communities be integrated into regional, national, and perhaps global networks that serve rather than exploit those communities? And just what is local? I suggest that the populist tradition—based on the insight of Phaleas combining local democracy with widespread individual citizen ownership of wealth—has some answers to these questions. Indeed I would argue that populism is the logical alternative (if there is enough time) to any anticipated collaspe of the large-scale "growth" economies promoted by both corporate capitalism and state socialism. The populist tradition has a long history of confronting these issues, and it has developed, as we shall see, important strategies and precedents for implementing political and economic democracy, strategies that have been neglected in the industrial age of "growth," but that now deserve fuller consideration.

The political economy of populism, after all, seeks not only to establish local autonomy but also to provide for institutions integrating local communities on broader scales to their mutual benefit, rather than to their detriment. The populist aim is not to confine all power or all production to the local level, but to ensure that political and economic power flows upward while remaining subject to local control, so that decisions taken on a broader level reflect local desires and are accountable to local communities. The populist aim is not to redistribute property arbitrarily from some to others, but to provide access to resources for all, which will facilitate such a redistribution, over time, without class warfare. Before the industrial age, when the earth's bounty seemed adequate for all, populists sought to secure democracy by providing land to individuals; more recently, with economic power shifted from control of land to control of credit, populists have looked to fundamental reforms of the credit and monetary system to put capital into the hands of individuals in a general and equitable way. We shall explore these long-neglected but now ever more relevant possibilities in the chapters that follow.

Chapter Two

Kinship Precedents

In this chapter, I turn to the historical record of populism, beginning with kinship societies. If populists are right about the connection between wealth and democracy, their separation is the great enemy of liberty. And the separation of wealth and democracy is a hallmark of the transition from kinship societies—everywhere the earliest known form of human association—into nonkinship or state societies, beginning with the appearance of complex city-states in the Middle East and elsewhere at the end of the Neolithic Era. Kinship might be regarded as the natural form of populism, where small face-to-face human communities allow their members more or less equal access to resources and decision making. The consequent upsetting of this spontaneous populism by the rise of state societies—where kinship is subordinated in a larger social system including non-kin strangers—brings with it an exercise of power and authority outside the bounds of the community, and inevitably, it seems, at its expense. In the state societies that have dominated the five thousand years we have of recorded history, wealth has tended to be highly concentrated and democracy largely evaded or suppressed. True democratic assemblies in the history of civilization, with important exceptions, have been rare. On the other hand, in nonstate or kinship societies, which everywhere preceded and long paralleled state societies, wealth and democracy are deeply intertwined. Whatever their many differences and shortcomings, kinship societies have normally managed their affairs through direct democratic decision-making practices, and they presume whatever resources they have to be available to all. Their democratic pratice usually involves the adults of the community meeting together, if not all at once then in separate but equal clan or gender groupings, in what amounts to a committee or committees of the whole. One way to develop a sense of the possibilities of direct democracy is to look seriously at the nonstate societies of our ancestors who were able to practice it.

Kinship peoples live intensely in small groups either as mobile hunters and gatherers, or in villages or small towns as more or less sedentary agriculturalists. There is little anonymity within such groups, no place to hide in the camp or village. But there is also little violent coercion of individuals, and considerable opportunity for isolation and escape in the wilderness beyond the village. Everyone in the community usually can be heard on any issue, and important decisions are ordinarily vetted through open discussion, usually in councils of families, clans, or tribes—more or less committees of the whole—usually issuing in some consensus. Authority figures are minimal, scattered about, variously limited; their reputations are based on specific knowledge and experience (a keen hunter, a powerful medicine woman, a wise elder, etc.). The members of the clan are partners in a common enterprise, enjoying a certain mutual respect and a proportionally fair share of access to resources. Such face-to-face democratic kinship societies—from deep in the Paleolithic to the Neolithic villages of prehistory to the last disappearing rain forest peoples of today—we now know to be primitive only in their small numbers and low levels of technology. While such societies are limited and confining in important ways, they are more subtle than modern societies in a number of other interesting ways, particularly in the interpersonal relations that underpin their direct democracy. A kinship tribe—unlike a modern society—is built through a sacred union of clans or descent groups that regulate marriage and most social activities. Kinship societies have no distinct structure we would call a state or government set over against the members of the community. State societies, by contrast, are organized hierarchically along class lines, usually among non-kin, or strangers, with state power conspicuously separated from civil society. Power in state society is not dispersed among the people but concentrated in a separate corporation called the state, which generally rules a particular territory and its inhabitants in the interest of an elite.

This power to alienate people from the community, to dehumanize them, is based most plausibly, it seems, on conquest by force, through war, of one community by another. The conquering community—free to plunder and otherwise appropriate men and women and other spoils from the conquered community—short-circuits the clan exchange ritual of reciprocity and gifting by brute force and taking. When the conquerors bring home their captives (or settle down to live among them), the natural populist balance of kinship society is upset in favor of a stratified state society (rulers and ruled) organized top down on the basis of force (the warriors of the chief, the knights of the lord, the soldiers of the king, the police of the government, etc.), with a hierarchy of classes (slaves, peasants, yeoman, wage earners, merchants, gentry, creditors, debtors, professionals, aristocrats, tycoons, royalty, celebrities, etc.). State society is class society. It creates parallel but unequal communities that are largely strangers to one another, even when in close contact, a society in which various public and private spaces are shared only unevenly, if at all, by individuals from different classes, who normally do not share commonly recognized ancestors. The more or less equal world of clan members is replaced by a world of masters and slaves, lords and peasants, families and servants, bosses and workers, rich and poor. The rulers, recognizing only one another as full members of the community, create an elitist, exclusionary class marked off by its own spaces and etiquette, whether at the ducal court or at the country club. The ruled—depending on the character of the regime—find themselves in one or another dependent class, more or less vulnerable, more or less excluded from debate and decision making, more or less subject to extortions and tyrannies. The movement from kinship to state societies has been a piecemeal, complex, and sometimes sudden but often gradual process, unfolding over thousands of years. The revolution establishing state society was no single event, but a series of many events over millennia; by the same token, most state societies, even the most modern ones, retain important kinship elements, particularly the family.

Why have kinship societies succumbed so consistently and apparently inevitably to state societies? It is not my purpose to propose a historical explanation of the transition from kinship to state societies. I merely wish to point out some features of this transition. Groups of humans who do not recognize the same clans, the same common ancestors, need not recognize one another nor any mutual obligation. Different ancestors mean something like a different species, an essential otherness, a foreign thing. This failure to recognize and integrate strangers makes it possible to justify warfare, slavery, exploitation, denial of partnership, and other forms of interclan dehumanization. State society has been the expression, not the solution, of these problems. In their earliest forms, in the first cities in the Middle East, state societies institutionalized violence and invented new superhuman sky-gods to justify it. Violence is at the heart of the matter. Perhaps the very success of kinship society, its profound cohesiveness, made strangers so incomprehensible as to be feared and denied—not even recognized as human beings, or perhaps only as something counterhuman, superhuman, or subhuman. Under the impact of state society, kinship was first transformed into tribalism as a generic identity, and gradually into ever more abstract identities, whether sacred or profane, ranging from traditional religious, ethnic, and cultic communities to secular ideological beliefs defining societies such as racism, nationalism, fascism, communism, and libertarianism. The intensity of the kin community's energy was, over time, captured and co-opted into these displaced beliefs, which then battled one another for survival. Along with state society came religion and ideology that transformed kinship values and practices, hitherto natural and continuous with nature, into detached standards of right and wrong, generally intolerant of contradiction, and beyond appeal.

The granting of full rights of citizenship in modern times to slaves, peasants, colonials, women, nonheterosexuals, and others has reintroduced to some degree the old kinship idea of common inalienable rights within the community. But the continued separation of political from property rights has ensured that citizenship in the modern state has remained a limited, mostly symbolic, corporate membership, nearly a sleight of hand; the separation of property rights from political rights makes impossible, it seems, an integrated kinship community. State society consists mainly in the rule of law, and its political activity, at least in modern times, mainly in the right to vote. The modern state provides no right of direct participation in government; nor is the right to equal protection before the law always available. Voting is in many ways an alienation of one's right to political participation; it is the surrender of politics to another, to the representative. Equal protection before the law even in modern state societies is often available only to those who can afford it. The right to vote remains at best a passive and blunt instrument that can occasionally moderate the worse excesses of government ("throw the bums out"), but for the most part it is successfully manipulated by the powers that be. In addition, modern citizenship as we know it allows certain nonpersons—that is, corporations—important political rights and exemptions reserved for real persons in kinship societies, exacerbating the split in state society between property rights and political rights, between institutions and persons.

As good a summary as any of the distinction between kinship and state societies is found in the work of the pioneer nineteenth-century anthropologist Lewis Henry Morgan in his classic study *Ancient Society*: "All forms of government are reducible to two general plans," he tells us. "The first, in the order of time, is founded upon persons and upon relations purely personal, and may be distinguished as a society (*societas*). The gens [the clan] is the unit of this organization. . . .The second is founded upon territory and upon property, and may be distinguished as a state (*civitas*). The township or ward, circumscribed by metes and bounds, with the property it contains, is the basis or unit of the later."[1] The clan, the outstanding feature of kinship society, relates its members to those of other clans in the community in complex, highly defined ways (including patrilineal or matrilineal descent, marriage rules, property use, customs of hospitality and visitation, gift-giving, etc.). State society, by contrast, is a organization of strangers based on a territorial ruling authority, within which families and kin are singular but subordinate and often disjointed elements. What matters in state society is the law as laid down and enforced by state authority. Kinship ties continue to be important in state society, manifest most conspicuously in royal and aristocratic families, but they are only a part of society, and no longer all of it.

State society has not always existed, and it need not continue forever. State societies since at least the fourth millennium BCE have been able to exploit nature and one another with increasing skill and impunity, it seems, consuming resources in pursuit of a competitive acquisitiveness that has become increasingly lopsided and destructive worldwide. That this competitiveness has often been beneficial (for example, as a spur to technological innovation), and that state societies have sometimes been generous in their allotment of material benefits (at least to some of their members), is plain enough. But that should not blind us to the high price state societies have extracted repeatedly in conflict and violence, poverty, social injustice, and environmental degradation. Even the most enlightened of state societies have been unduly exploitative of persons (class conflict and war) and nature (global warming, peak oil, sprawl, species extinction, overpopulation, etc.). State society has not done well in domesticating human aggression, and indeed appears to have exacerbated it. The kinship world is worth reexamining in light of its greater relative success with human aggression and social justice.

***

But first, let us consider the state societies in which we live, which have been long in the making. These are mostly national political entities with precise territorial definitions, like the United States, France, China, Nigeria, or Brazil, and their many subdivisions. I happen to live on land I own, a fifty-acre fee-simple parcel, in the 5th electoral district (or precinct) of the Town of Otsego, Otsego County, New York State, United States of America, the boundaries of which are carefully laid out along the survey lines of groups of deeded real estate parcels of record, exactly as Morgan pointed out with regard to state societies. Anyone could look it up at the county courthouse. In state societies, in addition to territory, we find minimally a state apparatus (with executive, legislative, and judicial functions, and their extensions, including bureaucracies, police forces, armies, etc.) organized as an independent entity or corporation distinct from the people, with powers within and over that territory and over personal activities within that territory. Some behaviors, like murder, rape, theft, and so forth are generally prohibited by law, while others, like production, trade, education, and so on are generally permitted, but usually and variously regulated, and often taxed. These regulations are generally set by ruling elites. The inhabitants of state societies are commonly split, it cannot be overemphasized, into classes, or levels, or hierarchies, mainly along lines of relative wealth and relative poverty. State society is so penetrating and widespread that it is usually taken for granted. But in fact state society had distinct beginnings, and it may have a distinct end.

The traditional alternative to state society is not anarchy (which is its negation) but kinship society, a society in which hardly anyone is a stranger to anyone else, not merely because numbers are small, but because most everyone is related to everyone else and most have lived together continuously. Kinship societies are local and mostly self-ruling, like the families that compose them, with members related through blood and marriage; indeed, they are organized almost wholly as extended families, or clans. Originally all human societies were more or less small self-sufficient kinship bands composed of individuals known to one another and descended from common ancestors, often totemically represented. Kinship societies (unlike state societies) have no separate state or corporate authority over and against themselves, no Leviathan, in Hobbes's sense. They have, as Jefferson noted with regard to Native Americans, no government as we know it, but function instead as spontaneous democracies. That Hobbes could imagine only anarchy as an alternative to state society (the famous "war of all against all" in which "life is nasty, brutish, and short") is a testimony as to how profoundly (and mistakenly) we moderns take the inevitability of state society, and how easily we dismiss important kinship precedents.

Up until the twentieth century, kinship societies were generally portrayed by scholars as a prior step in human culture, narrow and primitive, while state societies (or "civilizations") were presumed to constitute the higher synthesis destined to overtake them. Academic fashion subsequently largely reversed those evaluations. Kinship societies in the twentieth century were often touted as integrated into the natural world in a way civilizations have lost, and their traditions were often sought out as alternative inspirations. State societies by contrast were often described as separated and isolated from the natural world, which had become externalized and alienated as an object to be dominated. Spirit and matter, self and other, consciousness and its objects, the inner space and the outer world—which appear as opposing dualisms in the psychology of state societies—are said to be harmonized in the kinship world so as to be compatible with one another, so that the presense of any one of them automatically implies the other. Matter is understood as having spirit, as something animate, and spirit is understood to manifest itself through matter; the other (any other) is acknowledged to have a self of its own, and every self to have some particular manifestation, its own thinghood or body; and so on. Nature—the sky and the trees and the earth, with its waters and stones, and all creation—is alive, animate, and conscious, and human beings in kinship cultures live within this seamless web. The web is cut and dualism appears when the self behind the other is denied. That leaves the other a kind of objectified artifact, devoid of spirituality, a material object, an inanimate thing. In state society these dualisms predominate; the networks of reciprocity are broken, and the natural world becomes desanctified and objectified, ready for consumption on our terms, not its.[2]

This loss of identity with nature is sometimes offered as an explanation for the rise of state societies, with their exploitation of people and nature. Whether a cause or effect, the break in consciousness seems to correspond to the transition. In kinship society, nature (sky, earth, lands, waters, plants, animals, etc.) is not an absolute and opaque other, but a reciprocal self, something with which one can communicate. The hunter becomes the game he or she stalks and kills out of respect and with restraint, and with at least symbolic compensation. We see it in the sacrifice of most traditional societies, in the libations of wine the Greeks and Romans—still driven by some important kinship values—poured on the ground.[3] There is much truth in this postmodern characterization of state society, and much that was innocent and naive, if not arrogant and patronizing, in earlier accounts of the "rise of civilization." I will take a middle view between these extremes, however, one that respects the virtues of kinship societies without romanticizing them, and which accepts as well the fundamental if unfulfilled imperative of civilization, which is to construct a just society including strangers as well as kin. And we cannot forget that, distinct as kinship and state societies are, aspects of kinship society have remained embedded in the state societies that have overwhelmed them. There has not yet been a pure state society, though some might suggest that the mass, anonymous, atomized, consumer society of modern America, with its communities and families fragmenting and disappearing, comes closest.

***

The earliest non-kinship or state societies of which we have evidence arose nearly six thousand years ago in parts of Western Asia, particularly in what used to be called the fertile crecent, in the fourth millennium BCE, if not earlier. They created the first urban centers anywhere in the world, the first common homes, at least in part, of different peoples, with one usually dominant over the others, with a distinguishable state apparatus. These centers were larger in population and scale than earlier kinship-exclusive villages or towns, and they first appeared in the major river valleys of what is now the Middle East, and then almost at the same time in Egypt, India, and China. Among the best known of the very earliest state societies are the Sumerian cities of the Tigris-Euphrates Valley, places like Ur and Lagash and Uruk. Similar centers independently appeared somewhat later in interior North America—including the mound sites at Cahokia in Illinois and elsewhere, and the temple complex cities in Central and South America. The beginnings of state societies are evident with the Mayans, Aztecs, and Incas, among others, where some tribes conquered others and built permanent cities with class structures, such as Tenochtitlan.

What differentiated these new urban centers in both the old and new worlds from older kinship villages and towns is that the people living together in them were often strangers to one another, of different kin, often speaking different languages, with no common recognizable ancestors. Most noticeably, these peoples were politically and economically unequal. The cities of Sumer, for instance, seem to have had from early on peoples speaking Semitic as well as Sumerian languages, with sometimes one group dominating, sometimes another.[4] Early city-states across the world almost everywhere seem to have been hierarchically organized into dominant and submissive groups, and subject to centralized control; their territory was carefully zoned, with private spaces (palaces and sanctuaries) and special semiopen non-kinship areas like army camps and temple-marketplace complexes that attracted traders, travelers, and other outsiders. Kinship mores were necessarily adapted, and often radically transformed, to function in cities as codified rules or laws among strangers, but their force became less psychological and more physical and explicit, ultimately manifesting itself in a state monopoly on lawful violence, with the state generally in the hands of a conquering kin group whose mores became law, with other kin groups or fragments thereof in various ways dependent upon their rulers; slavery, unknown to kin societies, represents perhaps the extreme of kinship dissolution. The broad pageant of state society has included, over time, besides early city-states, theocratic monarchies, aristocratic republics, religious universal states, polyglot empires, commercial oligarchies, federated leagues, feudal principalities, nation states, fascist states, communist states, and (in our own case) corporate plutocracies under one or another form of what might be called misrepresentative government. None of these variants of state society has managed to overcome the contrasts of rich and poor, patron and client, dominant and subservient, seemingly endemic to such societies (and viturally unknown to kinship societies); nor has any state society (with a few partial exceptions, like classical Athens and some other ancient city-states, and early Vermont and some other frontier communities) allowed for the kind of self- or direct democracy that seems to come naturally in kinship societies—namely, political participation by the adults in the community in an assembly functioning, at least in some important respects, as a committee of the whole. The earliest civilizations from the start demonstrated antidemocratic, centralized state power and impressive inequities of wealth, though important kinship features persisted.[5] Impersonality and hierarchy, it seems, are characteristic of state—as opposed to kinship—societies, whenever and wherever they appear. Our modern, for-profit, corporate society (public and private, government and business) is, from this perspective, but the latest form of state society.

State societies are usually characterized by historians as sharing a familiar ensemble of social features: literacy, agriculture, taxes, classes, patriarchy, police, armies, monumental architecture, money, markets, and so on. While some of these features—classes and patriarchy—do seem endemic to state society, others—like literacy and agriculture—are arguably prestate innovations absorbed by state societies. The complexity of some kinship societies in the neolithic and paleolithic—from Catal Huyuk, to the Vinca culture in Europe, to early East Asian cultures—has been documented by a number of scholars, including Alexander Marshack, Marija Gimbutas, and Denise Schmandt-Besserat. As Richard Rudgley makes clear in *The Lost Civilizations of the Stone Age*, these scholars and others have persuasively argued for complex notational systems, or "artificial memory systems," in many ancient kinship societies worldwide, perhaps even a kind of writing, along with surprisingly complex technologies related to astronomy, pottery, mining, cooking, medicine and surgery, crafts such as textiles and rugs, architecture, as well as "high" arts, as in the famous cave paintings at Lascaux and elsewhere.[6] Some scholars extend the term *civilization* back to include these earlier societies, but the effect is to blur the distinction between kinship and state societies. I use the term *civilization* in its more traditional sense, as coextensive with state society, that is, with post kinship societies that incorporate strangers into an inegalitarian, top-down, class-based polity sustained by war and appropriation. Kinship societies are fragmented and their elements reblended in the crucible of state society, with profound effects on conquerers and conquered alike. Today only a few more or less intact kinship societies persist on the verge of extinction in remote corners of the world. Yet some of the substance of the kinship world lives on in our personal families, and among our closest friends and acquaintances, where human interactions are governed mainly by the more emotional kinship logic of direct personal relations, and less by abstract rules of law or dogmas of faith. The law (religious or civil) steps in, as in divorce court or a religious tribunal, only when the family ends, or breaks down. Only when we cross over the line in social contexts from acquaintance to non acquaintance, to encounters with strangers (the public, the man or woman in the street) do we find ourselves firmly in state society.

State societies appear to be the inevitable successors of kinship societies almost everywhere. The growth of population and the increasing complexity of human interactions seem to point to the need for something like state society to organize human affairs beyond the village kinship level, although some kinship societies, such as the Iroquois Indians of North America, managed to develop complex confederations of clans and villages covering a large territory.[7] And it is only in state societies, it appears, that wealth and sophistication and many of the good things in life seem possible at all, even if state societies have often been tyrannical and unjust. How many of us would be able to go back and live and hope to survive like our Stone Age kinship-oriented ancestors, even if we desired to? Most residents of modern industrial countries live in a creature-comfort, consumer paradise that seems like science fiction come true to anyone still in a subsistence kinship economy. Technologies developed in state societies have literally transformed the face of the earth, for better and worse. The distance from a rural, still largely kinship village in a West African country like Ghana, for instance, where this writer lived for a time, with no electricity and few basic amenities (no clean water, no sewage treatment, virtually no health care, etc.), to any middle-class American suburb is very nearly a direct measure in material terms both of the benefits of human civilization and its costs.

State societies, modern as well as ancient, have produced great wealth, not because they enjoy special intrinsic merit as social systems (much evidence suggests otherwise), but because of their historical ability to repeatedly jump-start their economies by sudden forceful accumulations of resources from the outside.[8] Even relative overpopulation will lead to a competition for scarce resource, promping violent interactions. The defining step, it seems, in establishing a state society is the violent subjugation and enslavement of one group by another, mainly as a result of war, whether the raids of ancient tribes or the intrusions of modern imperial powers. Warfare powerfully promotes the mixing of different kinship groups—initially conquerors and conquered—that is the mark of state society. This mixing is not on equal terms, of course, but on terms of dominance and subjugation. Stendhal's famous aphorism—that at the source of every family fortune lies a crime—seems to apply as well to every state society. The forceful breakup of kinship ties and the triumph of violence is a two-edged sword. Wealth is accumulated more quickly as a result, but only for some and at the price of impoverishing and humiliating others. No doubt the human imagination may be somewhat liberated in the process, but at the cost (it would seem) of a persistent social pathology marked by a loss of moral bearings.

The story of the fateful transition from kinship to state society turns on the frequently repeated discovery by male-dominated hunting parties, scouring for resources that they could subdue, of alien humans, where *alien* means anyone not descended from one's own ancestors. They also discovered that they could control resources (hunting and gathering grounds, land for settled farming, etc.) by force. Once such conquests became routine, male war chiefs (gang leaders) found themselves in a position to come home and dominate their own societies as well. Eventually, the standing military or police necessary to control conquered subjects came to be used at home, while the booty and slaves from outside gave the chiefs new resources for personal rather than common needs. The incentives to institutionalize their new powers must have been overwhelming. Gradually, over many generations, it seems that the war chiefs subverted the roughly balanced male-female relations of kinship culture into the male-dominated patriarchies characteristic of state society for most of its long history, a process evident with the earliest historical records in Sumer, Egypt, China, the Olmec and Mayan cities, and elsewhere. The kinship emphasis on reciprocity was replaced by concentrated accumulations of property under state (ruling class) control, often justified by new sky-god religions. Once they were routinely mobilized for war, these incipient state societies became predators ready to overrun their neighbors, even in "self-defense."

A predatory state society, with a windfall of resources and labor appropriated through conquest, can dramatically raise its standard of living (at least for some and sometimes, albeit disproportionally, for all of its members) without having to work fully to earn it (beyond the labor of conquest and the burden of administering and enforcing exploitation). The real work is done by soldiers and slaves and forced labor (including wage labor). By separating themselves and their booty from the communal kinship system of shared property rights, the war chiefs create a new kind of property: state, class, or private property, defined through ownership backed by force rather than use and custom, and under the control of an elite—a pattern that has endured in one form or another right down to the present. By contrast, almost everywhere we can learn about them we find that kinship societies maintain a high degree of material reciprocity in which distribution predominates over accumulation. Local chiefs and "big men" are often the poorest people in kinship villages because of the redistributative demands placed upon them. By busting up kinship bonds, chiefs and war leaders were able to reverse this situation. They were able for the first time to accrue resources for themselves and their dependents at the expense of others.

It was kinship (not state) societies that arguably made the greatest incremental leaps in human ingenuity and productivity: inventing fire, domesticating animals, and developing agriculture, the wheel, pottery, textiles, architecture, metallurgy, writing, art, calculation, astronomy, and religion. Had kinship societies somehow avoided transformation into state societies, had they somehow preserved their internal integrity, it seems reasonable to suppose that technologies born of human ingenuity would have continued to evolve. In spite of their creative destructiveness, their ability to change and adapt quickly when necessary, especially in military matters, we should be wary of presuming state societies enjoy some kind of monopoly over human ingenuity. Indeed, key features of state society such as slavery and coerced labor have often discouraged technological innovation. To command the labor of others, to use them as if they were robots, is to discourage the production of true robots that might free humans of undesirable labor. If regional and global integration had occurred under kinship rather than state societies, it would probably have richly shaped and compounded the development of technology, and led it in new and more humane directions. But kinship societies had a fatal flaw. They could not deal with non-kin, with outsiders.

   A small kinship society isolated in a bounteous nature can freely
appropriate and transform its given resources—in a balmy tropical paradise, say, where the fruit of the land can be plucked by hand. Problems
arise when my claim to resources is contested by another, when I find
myself in competition with others for the things I need to live and prosper,
and particularly when I find myself in competition with those who are
strangers to me, to whom I need have no obligation. Most kinship societies with their primitive, labor-intensive technologies could make but
limited use of natural resources. Insofar as fertile lands were available to
absorb excess populations, competition for resources was muted, perhaps nonexistent.[9] Without competition raising the "mine" or "yours"
question, resources were more or less held in common by the group, but
available to its various members for their personal uses. However, as
human ingenuity and invention and technology contributed to increased
productivity—that is, to less labor per unit of resources transformed—
populations increased. At some point, we can imagine different kinship
societies (strangers to one another) coming into contact and beginning
to impose upon one another, becoming competitive for resources, a
development that raises for the first time the question of property. One
might almost say that the beginning of the closing of the open frontier
of resources worldwide began in the first state societies of the Nile, Tigris-
Euphrates, and Indus river valleys over five thousand years ago, and
ended only with the closing of the American Western frontier in 1890 by
the United States Census Bureau. Along the way, many factors inter-
vened. The domestication of the horse in the later Neolithic and early
Bronze Age, for instance, allowed nomadic tribes to range widely and
freely over vast areas, appropriating the resources of more sedentary
agriculturalists, extracting tribute if not converting them into property.
   The encounter with aliens over resources leads to the notion of private property. If I must contend with a stranger to use some resource, I
am forced to recognize the possibility that I can be denied that resource,
no matter what my needs. The resource itself becomes objectified and
externalized. The presumption that it has an inner self, or spirit, is obscured by the struggle for control, in which it becomes a pawn. If I prevail,
my triumph is not only over my competitor, but over the resource, which
I now can and must dominate, if I am to survive. I must be prepared to
defend any use of it I can establish. I can no longer presume that it is
available to me if I want it, or collectively to my people. I become deaf to
its spiritual voice, to any mutuality or codependence with the resource.
Instead, my (our) use of it must be established and maintained by force,
if necessary. Force (physical violence) is the court of last resort because

aliens—strangers—are not bound by the network of mutual obligations shared among kinfolk. They cannot be controlled by social sanctions such as embarassment or ostracism. The ancestors of strangers are not my ancestors; with them there are no binding obligations, no constraints of love, guilt, responsibility. Appearances notwithstanding, strangers need not be considered human. They are not accountable to me (nor I to them), whereas I and my kinfolk remain mutually accountable. Whatever I can take by force from a stranger is mine to keep (and vice versa). Competition between strangers brings illicit risks and opportunities—in conspicuous violation of the mores of kinship society—precisely because competition outside the kinship circle is no longer balanced by cooperation. I must share with my kinfolk, not fight with them. It is almost the reverse with strangers. I do not need them, and I must be prepared to fight with them, if necessary; cooperation and exchange are secondary. Fighting with strangers introduces immoral behavior, which, when sustained, inevitably infects domestic life.

What kinship societies offer their members that state societies cannot is psychological security, and a reliable system of social and material justice, where everyone has more or less the same voice. With common access to resources, there is little difference among kinfolk in material wealth; with direct democracy, there is little opportunity for internal tyranny. Archaeological and ethnographic investigations by Gimbutas, Maallert, Fairservis, Braidwood, Evans-Pritchard, Morgan, and others over many decades have shown that early kinship cultures enjoyed a relatively uniform distribution of housing and artifacts, complemented perhaps by small ceremonial structures utilized in common.[10] There was personal property (including residential space), but not what we would call either private or public property. Personal property in kinship societies depends on personal use, not on the abstract ownership that characterizes both private and public property in state societies (public property merely being property "owned" by the state). Many authorities (see Gimbutas, Lerner, Baring and Cashford, Graves) highlight the relative importance of women in kinship societies, where men could not yet dominate by force alone.[11] The individual had little alternative but to submit to the mores of the group in the same way as everyone else, in return for which one received the group's support and protection. Malefactors were shamed into submission, or ostracized, rarely physically punished or killed. Seldom, if ever, were individuals able to remake society in their image—at least not before the rise of "civilization." It would have been unimaginable.

There is no reason, however, to romanticize kinship society. Far from constituting some kind of paradise, such societies were frustrating in many ways. Life in the kinship band or village was highly circumscribed. One lived from birth to death with a relatively small number of people, no doubt sometimes too close for comfort. The exhilarating freedom (and anxiety) of anonymity among strangers was unknown. Life was often (if not always) difficult, dependent on following the game or on the capricious nature of subsistence farming. The range of activities and interests open to individuals was relatively narrow, if sometimes intense. Comforts were few and far between; there was little protection against accident and disease. The delights of luxury were largely unknown. All evidence suggests that life expectancy in the Neolithic Era was considerably less than in later state societies, and perhaps less also than in earlier paleolithic societies (some paleolithic hunters and gathers, including some Neanderthals, may have lived better and longer than early agriculturalists, who were more subject to animal-borne diseases).

I am suggesting that the key element distinguishing kinship from state societies is violence between kin groups that are strangers to one another. How did this happen? A speculation offered by William Irwin Thompson in *The Time Falling Bodies Take to Light* presents a plausible account. Thompson suggests that the very inventiveness of kinship societies in producing new wealth is what made them vulnerable to one another:

> Hunters and gathers have little property, and what they have they can carry, but sedentary collectors begin to have stores of grain, grinding stones, and clay bins that they cannot easily leave. They begin to have wealth, and the hunter with his spear and bow and arrow discovers a new use for his tool and his trade. If his manhood is insignificant in producing food in the chase, it can become significant in protecting women and wealth. It must have been frustrating for the Neolithic hunter to come home and lay his deer before all to admire, to realize his catch would last a few days, women's a whole year. No doubt the hunter would demean the porridge of cereals and seeds as "women's food" and make loud noises about a thick steak of venison, but the furious activity around him continued in spite of all his celebrations of the noble chase. And that, too, triggered a positive feedback system of accelerating change. The more insignificant male activities were, and the more women's activities produced wealth, the more some men were attracted to

steal and other men attracted to defend the new acquisitions. The men discovered a new way to get together and warfare was born.[12]

Thompson might have added that additional wealth encourges greater population, leading once more to scarcity and competition. The windfall of a raid or military victory became a new kind of wealth, however, no longer presumed to belong to the community, but rather to those who fought (and risked their lives and bonded together) to gain it. Only such a powerful claim could offset the rights of the community. By risking their lives, the warriors stepped outside the bounds of their kin group. They acted like gods, not men. Like the gods, they could act immorally, and like them, they could pretend to immortality. Hence the deification or semideification of many early rulers, most famously the Egyptian pharaoh, but also some Sumerian kings, and many others, including the semidivine Caesars and the Emperors of China, who were "sons of heaven." As long as the resources won by warriors were relatively insignificant, they merely gained prestige at home, not exemption from kinship mores. But if the fruits of their conquests were important enough—vast hunting grounds, large flocks, rich agricultural lands, precious metals, subject cities, masses of slaves, control of trade routes—and reaped often enough, they could impose a whole new economy on their own kinfolk, one in which the warriors personally controlled ("owned") the relevant resources, including the labor required to exploit those resources. The warrior band thus may have evolved into a ruling elite, an aristocracy, controlling property, supported by clients and slaves: a new kind of society with decision making in the hands of fighting males, but closed off to everyone else.

State society, in this view, was born out of the accumulation and distribution among themselves by male hunter-warriors of resources taken from others, including female slaves captured from foreign tribes. Such chattel women would have undermined the status of the warrior's own mothers, sisters, and daughters, not least by allowing the hunter-warriors to create new, non-kinship families. Eventually, even the "legitimate" women in the community were reduced, perhaps more politely, to the status of property. The leading men, having betrayed their mothers, sisters, and daughters, justified themselves as supermen by claiming ultimate descent from male warrior gods—like Zeus, or Maui, or Chac, or Ra, or Marduk—whose worship they promoted at the expense of the Great Mother and other female deities. A conspicuous feature of early state society was this new pantheon of gods reflecting the new reality in which warrior males plundered, looted, and raped their way through their endless, immortal lives. Beginning first in Mesopotamia, India, and Egypt in the fourth millennium BCE, and subsequently independently duplicated in Europe, East Asia, and the New World, we see a wholesale change of society and culture, the rise of state societies, and the subordination and eventual virtual eclipse of kinship societies.

State society, if this analysis is correct, is rooted in the triumph and institutionalization of force over democracy and property over persons. We find this process fully engaged in the earliest literature we can read, dating to the Sumerian city-states of the third millennium BCE. The semidivine hero-king Gilgamesh publicly competes with the stranger Enkidu, his future bosom buddy, in a no-holds-barred brawl, where the prowess of force is established. The encounter between strangers is a dance of violence. In the ancient words: "They grappled with each other, snorting like bulls. They shattered the doorpost, that the wall shook." Or consider the lament of those victimized among his own kinfolk: "Gilgamesh went abroad in the world, but he met with none who could withstand his arms till he returned to Uruk. But the men of Uruk muttered in their houses, 'Gilgamesh sounds the tocsin for his amusement, his arrogance has no bounds by day or night. No son is left with his father, for Gilgamesh takes them all; yet the king should be a shepherd to his people. His lust leaves no virgin to her lover, neither the warrior's daughter not the wife of the noble; yet this is the shepherd of the city, wise, comely, and resolute.'"[13] Cooperation and democracy hardly disappeared overnight in these new, early state societies, but no longer could they team up to neutralize this new kind of aggression. The natural populist balance of the kinship world was overthrown. The men discovered "a new way to get together," as Thompson puts it. Popular assemblies and councils of elders slowly but steadily give way to the "big men"— kings and warriors, and their advisors and dependents—who as a group controlled the new forms of property.

Harriet Crawford sums up the state of knowledge about this process in ancient Sumer in her *Sumer and the Sumerians*:

> [W]e do not know how the earliest secular rulers emerged. It has been suggested that they may originally have been temporary war leaders, drawn from the best warriors, whose posts became institutionalized. Possibly they were, in some cases, charismatic men with special powers of some sort, or merely the seniors of a group of elders or the heads of the most

prosperous extended family in a locality. . . . What we do know is that . . . the office of ruler had become largely hereditary, passing from father to eldest son. The inscriptions from Lagash, for instance, show a continuous descent for at least six generations. Sometimes the ruler would record that he had been specifically chosen for the job by the city's god, but this was frequently a device used by usurpers to justify their seizure of power. Sargon of Agade claimed to have been specially selected by the goddess Ishtar, though his origins were obscure and later tradition said he was illegitimate.

The growth of royal state society was slow but steady. Crawford continues: "[W]hen Gilgamesh wanted to go to war, he was unable to do so until he had obtained the approval of the people. There seems to have been two assemblies in Uruk at the time of Gilgamesh and, having failed to obtain the approval of the council of elders, he then went to the council of young men, who enthusiastically endorsed his proposal."[14] What is pertinent here is the ability of big men like Gilgamesh to prevail, if not always, then often enough. In the best of circumstances—later in city-states like Athens—the ruling males remained a large group, including most heads of households, who participated in more or less egalitarian, democratic assemblies. More often, however, oligarchies of the more powerful men controlled the state. And in many cases, in tyrannies and monarchies, a single despotic figure—nearly always a male, a monarch or tyrant, but sometimes a woman, a queen—would concentrate all power in his or her hands. But even where male householders constituted a democracy among themselves, competition and force continued to be validated in many ways, generating a new definition of property as private or otherwise exclusive, no longer shared by the community as a whole.

This earliest form of private property was likely, and somewhat paradoxically, what we today would call state or public property. It was the private property of the king, or the god he more or less incarnated or represented; this property was increasingly separated from direct claims by the kin community and controlled instead by the king or temple priests, their authority backed by the last resort of force. Harriet Crawford sums it up: "The advent of the deified rulers of Ur III brought church and state together into one integrated system, administrated from one centre and controlling all the Sumerian plain."[15] Similarly, property commanded personally or "owned" by the warriors of the god/priest/

ruler (their share of the loot—land, slaves, cattle, etc.) likely also took on this new private form, exempt from generalized claims by the larger community. Unused property no longer reverted to claims by others in the community; it remained under the control of its "owners." What we now call "public" property emerged gradually but steadily as a resource separated and controlled by the state, open under limited conditions to citizens (who were largely redefined as the warriors of the ruler-priests, and as members of the ruling tribe most broadly). These new restricted forms of property included not only the temple spaces of the ruling gods, but the palaces of the kings, the fields where the armed men assembled, associated military areas, and other common spaces now under under central administration (marketplaces, granaries, etc.). What we call private property likely came about through dispersions by the king of land and resources to his principal retainers, who in turn enjoyed exclusive and arbitrary rights over that property. Kinship societies, which by contrast take resources for granted as collectively theirs, are not conscious in this sense of property. Resources for them are in effect collective private property, but unconsciously so and mostly taken for granted. Only when resources are challenged by strangers through war do they become objectified into property. The new notion of property is then incorporated domestically, detached from kin-group claims and "privatized" by the new elites, through exchange or appropriation backed by force, not morality.

The fact that even the ruler's dependents have limited access to parts or aspects of his or her property is the germ of what we call public (or government) property. What we consider today public or state property is derivative of what is essentially a private form of ownership based on conquest and violence invented thousands of years ago. The property of the state or government can be just as exclusive of general use as any private property, just as much "off-limits to unauthorized personnel." The proliferation of these new forms of property slowly reduced what was left of kinship property—"the commons"—to relative insignificance, to the point where today the commons has almost entirely disappeared. Kinship resources were not controlled by some at the expense of others, but were open to all in the community, which remained the ultimate authority but allowed individual use with certain exclusive rights. Resources were freely available assets, or capital, in the shape of land and natural resources, regulated by the community, but distributed and controlled individually. In state societies, however, property is literally divided up and sectioned off, with the largest and the best parts going to the most powerful: a process that has continued down to the present, with mere vestiges of kinship usages still found here and there. Free-range cattle in the South and West of the United States in the nineteenth century, for instance, still utilized a "commons" of open land; even today the open seas, the Anatarctic continent, and the moon and the planets and outerspace each remain a kind of commons, yet to be divided up and enclosed.

***

Far from perpetuating the original free distribution of property characteristic of prehistoric societies, state societies separate property from public accountability by the use of force in the service of a dominating group. This pattern has continued under nearly all forms of state society, from priests and kings down to prime ministers, politicians, and CEOs. The result has been class society, a division between the rich and the poor, the strong and the weak, found in no authentic kinship society. This is not to say that kinship societies practiced public ownership or socialism of some sort, while state societies specialized in developing private property. Rather, kinship societies practiced a kind of conditioned personalized ownership, neither public nor private. From that perspective, a socialist bureaucracy of apparatchiks controlling resources in the name of the people, but without any effective accountability, differs little with regard to the function of property from an oligarchy of private interests in a capitalist state controlling the same resources. Both arbitrarily define and restrict access to resources, making them into scarce and exclusive commodities, available to some and not others, with ownership backed up by the coercive power of the state.

Private property in kinship society is conditional upon use and subject to the overall mores of the community, more or less as determined by the community assembly but strongly conditioned by tradition. Kinship mores reflect the small-scale localism characteristic of most kinship societies. They are usually highly restrictive: narrow and inhibiting, perhaps, although intense and supportive. In state societies, property is normally exempt from such social considerations. The danger in state society is rather the irresponsible free-for-all, with the community often at the mercy of power struggles over property untempered by social and moral considerations. Modern economic development, for instance, is not a function of community decision making; rather it is imposed upon communities by powerful and largely unaccountable interests. One might speculate that the "inward" psychological violence of kinship society is replaced by the "outward" physical violence of state society. The impersonal brute force at the bottom of state society finds its counterpoint in the constant threat of anarchy. Far from vacillating in this way between authoritarianism and anarchy, kinship society promotes stability by linking property with socially sanctioned use, though it does so at a cost of limiting human freedom most of us moderns may be reluctant to pay.

How did it work? In his work on the Iroquois, *The Ordeal of the Longhouse*, Daniel K. Ritcher writes:

> Iroquois economic principles . . . "rested on need and use rather than mere possession. Food, clothing, tools, houses, land, and other forms of property belonged to those individuals and kin groups who needed and made active use of them". Conversely, excess of abandoned property was largely free for the taking, and in times of shortages all shared in the meager fare. Early seventeenth-century Dutch and French colonists rich in excess material possessions learned a lesson in Iroquois economics when they accused natives of "always seeking some advantage by thieving" and found them taking up residence in abandoned barns and houses. As the Indians saw it, unused items should be free for anyone who needed them, and hospitality required owners to yield them to those without.[16]

Notice that ownership in this kinship society is by individuals as well as kin groups, any of whom can "own" houses and land and other resources, but only as long as they use them and can justify that use to the community. Property in state society, in contrast to Iroquois ways, is conditional not upon use but upon legal ownership: the more or less unlimited possession or control of real estate and other goods, claims to which are reenforced by the power of the state. Although modern ownership of property and assets usually entails taxes and a degree of state regulation, it is otherwise mostly independent of community obligation. Conspicuously absent is any limit on the amount of property any individual or corporation can own, or control, nothing like the use limitation of the Iroquois. Modern ownership separates property from community accountability, from the reciprocity characteristic of kinship society.

The point of kinship accountability is not to take resources away from individuals, but to ensure a minimum of distribution of available resources to all individuals, enough to provide each of them with relative economic independence vis-à-vis the others. Since all members of kinship society have equal access to unused resources, none who are able are forced into dependence on others for their material well-being. Kinship society, by insisting that individuals (or families or clans) can own (hold as personal possessions) only what they can actually use, make any reserve of resources available to all. A limit is recognized on individual possession, beyond which items are automatically recirculated back to others lacking them—a principle of maximum wealth, as it were. A modern society cannot literally return to the "use" criteria of kinship folk, but it can take steps to reestablish the right of every citizen to a fair claim to be able to use the resources of the commonwealth. In our own time, such claims involve "a taking" or appropriation by the government from some to be distributed to others. This approach, however, as we see from the failed experiments of socialist state societies, has only shifted and not relieved the dependency of the many on the few. In subsequent chapters we shall explore in detail possible ways of making claims to resources available on a fair basis without resorting to taking. The kinship idea of direct personal use may not be appropriate to a poststate society as a standard of ownership, but equivalents can be found, particularly in the distribution of modern credit.

In nondemocratic state society, legislation is carried out not by the community as a whole (by persons meeting in a governing assembly or committee of the whole, or in its subcommittees), but by separate, removed corporate bodies (by royal courts, national legislatures, political parties, boards of directors, CEOs, etc.). At best, these bodies and individuals are indirectly and loosely accountable to the community, or some part of it, and even those that are indirectly and loosely accountable (for example, those whose members are elected representatives) have a responsibility to constituents that is more symbolic than real. What has been lost in all forms of state society, from the earlier times to today, is the populist combination of the kinship idea of democracy—that everyone in the community has, or can have, a direct role in decision making—with the kinship society idea of open access to wealth, that is, resources. State society creates material dependency and hierarchy. It benefits mainly large resource owners and their more immediate clients, leaving most people relatively powerless, even if sometimes comfortable. It is not a myth that modern state society exudes stress and anxiety in a manner unknown to kinship societies, often remarkable for their relaxed ease of life—a fact noted by explorers from Columbus to Captain Cook, and by many anthropologists.

This condition of state society dependency old-time leftists used to call exploitation and alienation. They correctly saw it as part of a historic process involving the loss of self-sustaining resources by ever larger groups in the long and often violent history of state society. The losers in that social struggle became dependent for survival on the winners. The more fortunate losers were able to work for a living under more or less favorable conditions as dependents or clients of the winners. Those less fortunate were variously exterminated, deported, enslaved, ghettoized, unemployed, and so on. This movement from self-controlled or independent product labor to dependent wage labor—as revealed, for instance, by the enclosure movement in the British Isles, or the more recent destruction of family farms in the United States—is very nearly complete in the modern consumer society of today. The overwhelming majority of people now work for some individual or corporate body (large or small) over which they have little if any influence. Hence their vulnerability.

Everyone in modern corporate plutocracy is "free" mainly to accumulate—to own—as much property as he or she can, for which a minimum of personal freedom is necessary. The trick, however, is that the most effective means of accumulation involve one or another form of exploitation, not only of the environment, but of the labor necessary to production. Here we see the deadly legacy of the violent birth of state society in war. Basic human rights—freedoms of person, speech, assembly, property, and so forth—are tolerated in state society not for their own sake (even if they are so valued by some of their strongest advocates), but because even those uncomfortable with them see that they are necessary for the most basic right in corporate state society: the freedom to accumulate and concentrate property without having to meet most social and environmental responsibilities. Without some human rights, and the access to information they make possible, profitable business could not be conducted. This is first of all what is meant by a "free and open" society. In this system of virtually unconditional license to property, however, a very few will nearly always succeed in accumulating vastly disproportionate shares of the total. In time, such accumulations are organized into corporate structures that take on a life of their own as independent centers of power and influence, with their "owners" as their principal beneficiaries. Most fortunes start with individuals and continue through families. In premodern state societies, family control remained the rule. The most complex premodern states, like ancient Rome, were dominated by family plutocracies embedded in a web of ancient customs and mores involving clients and other dependents, a mix of kin and stranger groups; they were not, like the United States and other modern countries, ruled by depersonalized private corporate entities. But whatever form state societies have taken, "freedom" within such societies has included the right to forceful domination, the right to exclude others from what used to be common resources. It is no surprise, that from Gilgamesh to today, criminal behavior has often paraded as a right of self-expression—the social and cultural effects of which are all too evident. This confusion of freedom with individualism, even with narcissism, is one of the hallmarks of modern, "open" state society. Both liberals and conservatives defend the autonomy of the individual as the supreme value. Liberals promote individualism by relying on wealth-transferring government programs to ensure equal opportunity to acquire marketable skills and a modicum of personal economic security. Conservatives promote individualism by relying on wealth-producing market forces to provide opportunities for personal gain and security through private enterprise. Liberals have traditionally sought to temper the excesses of individualism by a sense of social justice and public responsibility. Conservatives have traditionally sought to temper those same excesses by appeal to religious and cultural norms. Yet each of these temporizing appeals appears to have limited success, at best. The liberal public ethic of social justice appears too broad and abstract to be effective, and the conservative private ethic of culture and religion seems too narrow and divisive. The "permissiveness" decried by conservatives and the "greed" decried by liberals are really two sides of the same individualistic coin. Liberalism and conservativism both have failed to temper individualism. A society of atomized individuals, each bent on his or her own private interests with no intrinsic regard for the needs of others, is at once undisciplined and egocentric; this "culture of narcissism," as historian Christopher Lasch called it, has become the American common denominator. It is the very antithesis of a democracy; indeed, it is state society verging, in many ways, on anarchy.

    The individual who respects and enjoys mutual freedom or liberty with others does so only by virtue of participating in a direct democracy. Unlike representative government, where the voter deliberately surrenders his or her political rights to some representative, the citizen in a real or direct democracy can exercise every right to participate in government, and through that he or she has the opportunity to exercise civic virtue. I cannot hope fully to discover who I am as an individual without the give-and-take of personal encounters, including encounters in the political arena. I can do this freely and fully, however, as Phaleas noted, only to the extent to which I come to the democratic assembly already minimally self-sufficient in material terms. Otherwise I will be more or less inhibited, intimidated, and ignorant. In my efforts at personal production, even if they prove unsuccessful, I will have learned enough to qualify for

participation in the assembly. And it is only in the assembly that can I
can mix the fruits of my private ventures with the experience of others
in a common public endeavor. There is a therapeutic element here. An
assembly provides a rare opportunity for a community to plumb the
depths of its character, and to explore the possibilities of mutual deliberation and self-transformation. This is a largely lost but important way
to find out not only who we are, but who we can be—an experience that
produced a number of promising exceptions among state societies,
including the genius of the ancient Greek democracies, the energy of the
Early Roman Republic, the vibrant free city-states of early Europe and
Asia, and the wisdom of some of the American founding fathers.

***

Thomas Jefferson's recognition of the importance of both the public
and the private, of their mutual indispensability, was linked to an appreciation of kinship societies, where he likely saw in operation what I have
called the populist principle still in its original context. Living near the
early American frontier in direct contact with the Native Americans of
his day, and as a student of Native Indian culture, Jefferson was in a
position to appreciate the contrast of kinship and state society. He notes
in a letter to John Adams, on June 11, 1812, that from "the very early
part of my life, I was very familiar, and acquired impressions of attach-
ment and commiseration for them [the Indians] which have never been
obliterated."[17] And in his *Notes on the State of Virginia*, Jefferson offers
an observation of the Indians'

> circumstance of having never submitted themselves to any laws,
> any coercive power, any shadow of government. Their only
> controuls are their manners, and that moral sense of right and
> wrong, which, like the sense of tasting and feeling, in every man
> makes a part of his nature. An offence against these is punished
> by contempt, by exclusion from society, or, where the case is
> serious, as that of murder, by the individuals whom it concerns.
> Imperfect as their species of coercion may seem, crimes are very
> rare among them: insomuch that were it made a question,
> whether no law, as among the savage Americans, or too much
> law, as among the civilized Europeans, submits man to the
> greatest evil, one who has been both conditions of existence
> would pronounce it to be the last: and that the sheep are happier
> of themselves, than under care of the wolves. It will be said, that

great societies cannot exist without government. The Savages therefore break them into small ones.[18]

A full life, it seems, requires both private and public pursuits. The wholly public life, as Jefferson realized, was as incomplete as the wholly private life so lauded today. Both are nightmares. The populist balance of democracy and property, still practiced among the Native Americans of his day, is a balance of public and private, outer and inner. Richard K. Matthews, author of that remarkable book *The Radical Politics of Thomas Jefferson*, puts it this way:

> The pursuit of happiness, in its dual interdependent [public and private] facets, can provide a fully human life; but the pursuit of either at the neglect or expense of the other will lead to personal perversion in the individual and to social decay in the corporate body. Because his grand vision of a society of ward-republics [local assemblies] has yet to be implemented, the sole avenue for Americans to pursue happiness has been restricted to the private realm, which, even in Jefferson's day, was increasingly becoming synonymous with the market.[19]

Another populist, Thomas Paine, also came to have some firsthand knowledge and appreciation of Native Americans and recognized the kinship precedents of populist values. He attended a conference in 1777 in Pennsylvania with representatives of the Iroquois tribes, where he was one of several negotiators for Pennsylvania and the Continental Congress on issues of relations with the Indians, an experience that much impressed him. In "Agrarian Justice" he writes: "To understand what the state of society ought to be, it is necessary to have some idea of the natural and primitive state of man; such as it at this day among the Indians of North America. There is not, in that state, any of those spectacles of human misery which poverty and want present to our eyes, in all the towns and streets of Europe. Poverty, therefore, is a thing created by that which is called civilized life. It exists not in the natural state."[20]

Jefferson, Paine, and others, including Benjamin Franklin, saw that American Indian kinship communalism was predicated on decentralization, on authority being vested in small democratic groups or councils, which may have helped inspire Jefferson, along with other sources, to conceive his notion of ward republics (to be examined in more detail in chapter 4 and in the appendix). Jefferson and Paine accepted the kinship

principle that property is not a wholly unrestricted individual right for
some but a socially accountable means of developing human potential
for all, whether individually or cooperatively. They saw the virtues of
private, individually held property, of its liberating potential for all, provided each individual could personally acquire a sufficient measure of it.
Paine had little material ambition, and tended to give away any money
he made, even as he endorsed personal capitalism. He was a creature of
commercial society; he sailed with a privateer for profit in the wars
against France before he came to America, and he tried his hand, un-
successfully, as a small business partner while still in England. Jefferson's
development of his own land—Monticello and the area around it—
testifies to his belief in the redemptive personal virtues of private property. Ownership for Jefferson and Paine was tied to use, however, and
through use to preservation and sustainability, to future uses by others,
to stewardship and responsibility. Force in defense of mere possession
ceased at least in principle to be acceptable to them as a final justification
of ownership. Ownership had to be legitimized by the community not
on the basis of conquest, but as a necessary means to individual fulfillment, to "the pursuit of happiness."

In his oft-quoted letter of September 6, 1789 to James Madison,
Jefferson wrote: "I set out this ground, which I suppose to be self-evident:
'that the earth belongs in usufruct to the living': that the dead have neither
powers nor rights over it."[21] *Usufruct* means the right of temporary use
only, in contrast to the right of absolute, unconditioned, perpetual use,
what we normally call "ownership." Usufruct captures the populist definition of property. It implies accountability, the populist mechanism
for which is democracy. The power and rights of the dead include all
forms of indebtedness fostered by any generation upon its descendents.
Jefferson denies any right to consume the resources of nature without
insuring their renewal for subsequent generations. Jefferson, of course,
included slaves among his property (Paine was opposed to slavery).
Nothing could be less in the spirit of kinship society than slavery, a contradiction Jefferson was well aware of, and which he was never able to
resolve. His personal failure, though, is no indictment of his populist
insights; indeed, it rather serves to confirm them.

In the populist vision of Phaleas, reflected by Jefferson and Paine,
our relationship to property ought to be reciprocal, as it is in kinship
societies, not one way, or exploitive, as it is in modern state societies. I
ought to have not just the right to compete for property, but an actual
right to property (resources, capital) as a means to my happiness; such
property, however, I am responsible to maintain and pass on. This does

not mean communal ownership, as modern socialists have advocated and practiced it, which precludes important individual uses of property and ensures dependency, but it does mean private ownership with public responsibility to the larger community. This is no vague dream, as we shall see, but a practical proposition involving direct distribution of resources to private individuals under the aegis of genuinely democratic government. It means providing access for all individuals to the minimum of personal property necessary for engaging in the pursuit of happiness. As we shall see in succeeding chapters, for populists this meant distributing land in the preindustrial era, while in the modern commercial era it means distributing credit.

A populist political economy is natural to kinship societies. Access to resources and to political decision making is open to all in the community, not just to some. One of the principal features of populist political economy lies in its personal scale and expression. Democracy and property are meaningless if not oppressive notions when they become abstracted into impersonal processes or entities that stand over and against individuals. If elected representatives can claim to represent an abstraction called the "government," as opposed to their individual constituents, and if property becomes a force in its own right, embodied in a "corporation," an independently existing legal entity, set apart from and against flesh and blood persons and manipulated from within by owners and their agents, and unchecked by community accountability, then we should not be surprised to find injustice and inequality. Few such independently existing entities are to be found in kinship societies, apart from the kinship elements themselves (clans, etc.). And even they are not abstractions, but collections of particulars, ancestors living and remembered, as well as those of flesh and blood to come, when and if they come. The challenge for modern populists is to preserve the personalized democratic political economy of kinship society in a modern context.

**

State society, even in its modern corporate form, even with its rhetoric of human rights, has not overcome the original sin of its birth in the violent rupture of kinship relations. Since the eighteenth century in the West, the modern revolutions have established that any native adult of the community enjoying citizenship is free, not to make any populist claim on resources, but only to contend for wealth and power. Secular modernity, with its roots in the rationalism of the eighteenth-century European Enlightenment, has reestablished "the people," though only in an abstract and alienating sense, as the ultimate source of political authority, while giving individuals an equally abstract set of civil rights. It has confused humanity with naturalistic materialism and the struggle for existence. These non-kinship standards of social justice (now modernized) see in nature necessary competition rather than cooperation, thereby justifying the intensifying economic inequalities and disenfranchisements that modernity has continued to generate, especially with the growth of corporate power, public and private.

Only a few major modern political theorists have linked popular sovereignty to popular access to resources. Even what has been perhaps the most radical modern critique of corporate capitalism—the nonviolent movements of Gandhi, Martin Luther King Jr., Nelson Mandela, and their followers—has largely missed the populist point; for the most part this movement has failed to link personal access to resources with personal access to politics, a failing common as well to liberal and left-wing critics of corporate capitalism. Modernity has by and large rejected nonviolence and appeals to conscience; moral appeals have been increasingly discounted in recent decades. Instead we have seen the triumph of the principle of conquest, sublimated in the glorification of competition, and overtly affirmed in militarism and the recognition of the right of the stronger through continuing recourse to war. The modern media—television, film, popular music—have notoriously glorified violence. Far from moving toward an integrated society, modernity has been relentlessly atomizing. First it destroyed the larger structures of kinship, then the extended family; now even the nuclear family is disintegrating.

The law of the jungle, formally limited to warriors, far from being repealed has now been thrown open to the many, if not all, albeit in the more regulated and domesticated form of the competitive market economy regulated or manipulated by the state. The good intentions underlying modern slogans like "liberty" and "national sovereignty" suffer from a disjunction between rights and responsibilities once united in kinship sensibilities. To be "free" is a laudable goal, and one that has been indispensable to overthrowing the tyrannies of earlier versions of state society. But as Dostoyevsky, Nietzsche, and the existentialists made clear, freedom in itself knows no bounds, no limits, no moral values. Who is not to say that anything goes? We have seen in modern times an incremental leap in freedom for many in the wake of the emancipation movements for slaves, women, and others (for example, colonials, nonheterosexuals, racial and ethnic minorities, etc.). But without an accompanying sense of social responsibility and reciprocity, "freedom" in state society has also been a license to steal, kill, and take revenge. The vice president of the United States, Dick Cheney, has declared the American way of life to be "nonnegotiable," and the United States has not hesitated to launch wars of aggression to protect its "national security." The freedom of the warrior to transgress social mores, to steal, rape, and kill, was confined in earlier versions of state society to the aristocratic classes, while strong kinship values and mores lived on in the submerged communities subject to aristocratic rule, and among aristocrats themselves. Today, however, modern freedom has come to mean that even the lower orders of society demand the kind of amoral freedoms formally restricted to their rulers.

The stability of state societies has depended on the middle classes, on those poised between riches and poverty. If the middle classes—the principal clients of the elites—get enough of the benefits of the good life available to the elites, state society will be relatively stable though socially unjust. This has been the case in the United States and most so-called developed countries in the world in modern times. But if the middle classes feel, like the impoverished classes, that they are being denied most of those benefits enjoyed by the powerful, state society will be destabilized, as it was in much of the industrialized world in the period between 1914 and 1945. State society has persisted as the dominant social form because it has managed by and large to recirculate to its dependents just enough of the resources it has appropriated to keep them happy. That it has done so selectively, from the top down, in many ways unfairly, on the basis of a continued exploitation of resources and labor, and with more or less conscious calculation and manipulation, has been recognized but generally tolerated by these dependents. The immediate gratification of conquest (foreign and domestic, colonies and enclosures) has usually proved more tempting than the slower and more virtuous road of sustainable development on a populist basis in which all individuals have a reasonable claim on the totality of resources.

Like many quick fixes, appropriation by conquest usually can be repeated when the going gets tough. State societies can perpetuate themselves like parasites as long as they can find vulnerable, productive lands, near or far, to enslave. The Iraq War launched in 2003 by the Bush administration is almost a textbook case of a great power seeking to secure at least indirect control over oil, perhaps the fundamental modern resource. Eventually, though, as limits are reached, particular state societies, if they are not attacked from outside, tend to ossify around their authority structures. Privileged patterns of appropriation tend to stifle innovation and inhibit flexibility; such state societies become top-heavy, arrogant, and vulnerable. This may account for the widespread decline of most state societies after an initial period of exaggerated growth, a process that fascinated universal historians like Vico and Toynbee and Spengler in an earlier day, and Paul Kennedy and Samuel P. Huntington more recently. Reinvigoration frequently has come from yet another round of warfare, which provides the creative destruction necessary to further innovation, and so the cycle goes on.

Chapter Three

European Populism

The recognition of the link between property and democracy can be traced back, as I have suggested, to prehistoric times. In literate societies, at least in the West, perhaps the earliest conscious recognition of this link can be attributed to Phaleas of Chalcedon. In the European tradition, ancient and modern, we find notable instances of populism expressed not only in theory, but to some degree in practice. I project back the word *populism*, of course, and I hope with sufficient justification. Its root is the Latin *populus*, the people, and populism is the political economy of the people; it is their claim to private property as a correlate to their claim to public power. Let us begin our account of European populism by examining more closely what Aristotle has to say about Phaleas, and how Phaleas may have influenced him. We begin with a closer look at the important passage in Aristotle where Phaleas is discussed. To quote Aristotle again:

> For some persons think that the right regulation of property is the most important; for the question of property, they say, is universally the cause of party strife. Therefore the Chalcedonian Phaleas was the first who introduced this expedient; for he says that the citizens' estates ought to be equal, and he thought that this would not be difficult to secure at the outset for cities in process of founda-tion, while in those already settled, although it would be a more irksome task, nevertheless a levelling would most easily be effected by the rich giving dowries but not receiving them and the poor receiving but not giving them.[1]

The key phrase is translated as "the citizen's estates." The Greek reads *tas kteseis ton politon*, literally the property of the citizens. Property—*kteseis*—here has the strong sense of personal possession or private property, so the citizens are to have equal claims of some kind to the resources of the community, but on an individual rather than a collective basis. In spite of the importance given to property distribution among ancient lawgivers, most notably Solon, Aristotle is initially skeptical, indeed rather critical, of Phaleas's idea, particularly about the importance Phaleas gives to equality of property. "Now equality of property," Aristotle says, "among the citizens is certainly one of the factors that contribute to the avoidance of party faction; it is not however a particularly important one."[2] Most people, he goes on to say, will not be satisfied with an equal share of property, however defined, "for appetite is in its nature unlimited, and the majority of mankind live for the satisfaction of appetite."[3] Only an adequate system of education can hope to "level men's desires,"[4] Aristotle observes. Phaleas, he notes, might agree about the need for equality in education as well as property, though Aristotle makes it clear that equality of education, like equality of property, is an idea that needs further definition. Phaleas seems to have raised more questions than answers for Aristotle, and he appears to be dismissive of Phaleas's idea: "We cannot approve what Phaleas has said about equality of property," he states, "for he makes the citizens equal in respect of landed estate only, but wealth also consists in slaves and cattle and money, and there is an abundance of property in the shape of what is called furniture; we must therefore either seek to secure equality of some moderate regulation as regards all these things, or we must permit all forms of wealth."[5]

The issue, however, is more subtle, and we see that Aristotle's critique of Phaleas is not necessarily that Phaleas is wrong but something very different—namely, that Phaleas is not explicit enough about what is involved. Aristotle's main concern is with virtue as a condition of good politics. Given the power of desire and passion in most people, in his view, what he calls virtue normally will be found only among a few, and not necessarily the rulers. Most people are victims of their fears and desires, and fixated on security, or if they have some security, then on wealth, ambition, lust, or some other object of desire. Lack of virtue among the people leads to many inequalities, including inequalities of wealth. The strong (not necessarily the virtuous) overcome the weak; they conquer them, intimidate them, cheat them, and so forth. Aristotle uses the word *democracy* sometimes in a neutral, sometimes in a negative sense. If most citizens lack property as well as virtue, but gain political power in a democracy, then abuse of power (a tyranny of the majority) is likely, given their envy, anger, or resentment. The alternative to this becomes rule by the virtuous few, what Aristotle calls an aristocracy, literally the rule of the best, the *aristoi*, or else a monarchy, ruled by the single best. But he also makes plain that the few or the one may not necessarily be any more virtuous than the many; perhaps even less so. The rich, for example, are relatively few but not likely to be virtuous precisely because, being rich, they are prone, unlike the poor, to excess and a lack of the moderation and self-discipline essential to virtue. Aristocracy thus tends in his view to degenerate into oligarchy, and monarchy into tyranny. Clearly the democracies of the poor and the oligarchies of the rich—the major political alternatives—are not the best kinds of states.

Scholars seems to have taken all this as an excuse to dismiss Phaleas's ideas, but nowhere does Aristotle say they are mistaken, only incomplete. In fact, he finds himself revising his estimation of the importance of property to democracy. Indeed, Aristotle, in a rather startling reversal, in the end returns to the Phalean kernal, places it at the center of his argument, and develops it into a broad vision of the best kind of government, which is what his *Politics* is all about. The key role of property in defining rich and poor forces him into a reevaluation of his earlier dismissal of property's role as relatively unimportant.[6] It is useful to recall that Aristotle's approach at the onset of any inquiry is generally to assess critically the contributions of his predecessors to the problem at hand; only later does he offer his own views, which are generally presented without further reference to others. But just as we can often recognize the influence of views initially criticized in the substance of his subsequent arguments—for example, as we can see the influence of Plato's theory of forms in his *Metaphysics*—so it is possible to see the insight of Phaleas at the heart of his description of the best possible polity that he offers toward the end of *Politics*.

So it is only later, in book 4, chapter 9, that we get to the crux of the matter, as Aristotle moves from theory to practice: "But what is the best constitution and what is the best mode of life for most cities and most of mankind," he asks us, "if we do not judge by the standard of a virtue that is above the level of private citizens or of an education that needs natural gifts and means supplied by fortune, nor by the standard of the ideal constitution, but of a mode of life able to be shared by most men and a constitution possible for most states to attain?"[7] His answer combines Phaleas's emphasis on equal distributions of private property (however property might be defined) with his own emphasis on education to instill virtue. He doesn't give credit here to Phaleas, nor mention him at all, perhaps because he thought Phaleas's germ on an idea was not sufficiently developed, but what he writes at this point is essentially a vindication of the populist insight of Phaleas. Consider the following series of passages, where it is important to quote at length:

> For if it has rightly been said in *Ethics* that the happy life is the life that is lived without impediment in accordance with virtue, and that virtue is a middle course, it necessarily follows that the middle course of life is the best—such a middle course as it is possible for each class of men to attain. And these same criteria must also necessarily apply to the goodness and badness of a state, and of a constitution—for a constitution is a certain mode of life of a state. In all states therefore there exist three divisions of the state, the very rich, the very poor, and thirdly those who are between the two. Since then it is admitted that what is moderate or in the middle is best, it is manifest that the middle amount of all of the good things of fortune is the best amount to possess. For this degree of wealth is ready to obey reason, where for a person who is exceedingly beautiful or strong or nobly born or rich, or the opposite—exceedingly poor or weak or of very mean station, it is difficult to follow the bidding of reason.[8]

He cites other examples of the dangers of extremes in society, and continues as follows:

> Hence the latter class [the poor, the dependent] do not know how to govern but know how to submit to government of a servile kind, while the former class [the rich, the independent] do not know how to submit to any government, and only know how to govern in the manner of a master. The result is a state consisting of slaves and masters, not of free men, and of one class envious and another contemptuous of their fellows. This condition of affairs is very far removed from friendliness, and from political partnership—for friendliness is an element of partnership, since men are not willing to be partners with their enemies even on a journey. But surely the ideal of the state is to consist as much as possible of persons that are equal and alike, and this similarity is most found in the middle classes; therefore the middle-class state will necessarily be best constituted in respect of those elements of which we say that the state is by nature composed.[9]

Aristotle then concludes, in an explicitly populist vein:

> It is clear therefore also that the political community adminis-
> tered by the middle class is the best, and that it is possible for
> those states to be well governed that are of the kind in which the
> middle class is numerous, and preferably stronger than both
> the other two classes…. Hence it is of the greatest good fortune
> if the men that have political power possess a moderate and
> sufficient substance, since where some own a very great deal of
> property and others none there comes about either an extreme
> democracy or an unmixed oligarchy, or a tyranny may result
> from both of the two extremes….[10]
>
> That the middle form of constitution is the best is evident;
> for it alone is free from faction, since where the middle class is
> numerous, factions and party divisions among the citizens are
> least likely to occur. And the great states are more free from
> faction for the same reason, because the middle class is numer-
> ous, whereas in the small states it is easy to divide the whole
> people into two parties leaving nothing in between, and also
> almost everybody is needy or wealthy. Also democracies are
> more secure and more long-lived than oligarchies owing to the
> citizens of the middle class … since when the poor are in a ma-
> jority without the middle class, adversity sets in and they are
> soon ruined. And it must be deemed a significant fact that the
> best lawgivers are from among the middle citizens; for Solon
> was of that class, …and so was Lycurgus … and Charondas and
> almost the greatest number of lawgivers.[11]

Scholars have sometimes opined that no eloquent voice from antiquity
defending democracy has come down to us, yet Aristotle's *Politics* can
be read that way, given its populist recognition, derived as it would
appear from Phaleas, that property must be integrated into citizenship
in any just and democratic state. Aristotle makes it plain that democracy
in itself is not necessarily a good thing, and that it can be quite a bad thing.
The trouble arises when we have democracy *without* property, or the
rule of the poor, or the mob; it also arises when we have the rule of the
rich, the oligarchs. What is wanted is a society with citizens all of moderate means, with none either conspicuously rich or conspicuously poor,
as Tocqueville later pointed out; such a society will not only be a natural
but a successful democracy. Aristotle tends to use the term *politas*, or

polity, for this form of government, in the sense of its being the most natural and proper form of a body politic, the others being pathological or deformed states. But as the rule of the many, the *politas* would necessarily be a democracy. Not that Aristotle's democracy isn't framed by certain prejudices. *Politics* turns on a struggle between a deep recognition of what we would call human inequality, manifest in his notorious opening endorsements of slavery and the subordinate status of women as natural conditions, and the contrary democratic universalism expressed in his famous dictum that "man is a political animal," as well as his view that the end of the state is the realization of human potential and the good. Aristotle noticibly does not oppose slavery, but takes it for granted; nor does he object to the exclusion of women or barbarians from society—that is, the polis. Inequality may reign within the geographical space of the polis (where those who are not citizens live with those who are); but among citizens extremes are to be moderated, and the more or less egalitarian middle is to prevail. Whatever the definition of citizenship, the best society for citizens, the highest good, in Aristotle's view, seems to be a populist society.

There is no evidence that Phaleas, Aristotle, and other early democrats, such as Protagoras and Democritus, were concerned to recognize as citizens women, slaves, and others routinely excluded from the ancient assemblies, though some democratically inclined ancients, including the sophist Alcidamas and the playwrite Euripides, objected to slavery.[12] Indeed, Aristotle tells us that Phaleas held that "artisans are to be public slaves."[13] Ancient city-states at their core remained exclusionary and tribal, unions of families and clans, and of individuals only secondarily through them; hereditary descent was normally required for citizenship; they included, nonetheless, especially in later centuries, significant populations of noncitizens, of strangers. Athens, it seems, never conquered during the Dark Ages after the end of the Bronze Age, but perhaps retained, more than most Greek cities, important defining kinship traditions. There seems to have been no articulated ideal of humankind as a whole, however, no conscious presumption of fundamental equality among persons in the West before the Epicureans, Skeptics, and Stoics of the Hellenistic era, though we see the sensibility of a common humanity in a writer such as Herodotus.

Nevertheless, to enter the polis, to become a citizen, is to pursue the practice of virtue. Democracy is the best, most stable form of government for Aristotle, and the most promising for virtue in the long run, as long as the citizens have sufficient property to be more or less independent agents, not somebody's client, just as Phaleas said. *Politics* is written for those who would found cities, preferably democratic ones, and Aristotle's final advice to them in book 6, section 3, is to aim at distributing at least some of the community's wealth, to prevent the corruption of democracy: "the truly democratic statesman must study how the multitude may be saved from extreme poverty; for this is what causes democracy to be corrupt. Measures must therefore be contrived that may bring about lasting prosperity. And since this is advantageous also for the well-to-do, the proper course is to collect all the proceeds of the revenues into a fund and distribute this in lump sums to the needy, best of all, if one can, in sums large enough for acquiring a small estate, or, failing this, to serve as capital for trade or husbandry, and if this is not possible for all, at all events to distribute the money by tribes or some other division of the population."[14]

This is almost pure Phaleas. What Aristotle criticizes in book 2 of *Politics*, he now makes in book 4 the centerpiece of the best possible state that can be achieved. Where desire was earlier said to be infinite, and men incapable of controlling it, apparently even when given equal shares of property, now unequal property is acknowledged to be the principal cause of both the corruption of democracy and the abuses of oligarchy. And it turns out that the men best capable of controlling their desires, of being virtuous, are those in the middle, neither rich nor poor, for they both rule and are ruled, and act both as masters or slaves, and so are prepared for the give-and-take of genuine citizenship. It is these citizens of middling status, for Aristotle, who strike the balance that allows them to be rational and prudent, the hallmark of virtue.

Many of Aristotle's texts, I suggest, including *Politics*, can be read not as deductive treatises but as reports of evolving views, as exercises not in conclusions but in dialectics, in the processes of thought and discovery, of testing propositions against one another. If so, the contradiction between seemingly rejecting and then endorsing Phaleas's views may be apparent. Phaleas may have spoken only in practical terms about circulating wealth, but he clearly got Aristotle's attention. Aristotle's criticism is that Phaleas seems not to have shown *how* his regime could be a virtuous one. In doing exactly that, Aristotle can be read as appropriating and vindicating the insight of Phaleas. The cultivation of virtue by self-sufficient, middle-class citizens acting together democratically he presents as an ever-present ideal, as well as a practical goal, perhaps to be approximated in certain circumstances, such as the founding of a new city, but without any unrealistic expectation that it could be indefinitely sustained. It remains, however, the norm for which to strive.

***

Perhaps the most successful democracy for which we have considerable evidence, at least in Western history, and the one most widely cited, is the Athenian democracy of the fifth and fourth centuries BCE, where legislative, executive, and judicial authority were exercised wholly by the citizens meeting in public assemblies. It's worth noting that democracy was very widespread among largely still-tribal ancient Greek and other city-states, though almost all surviving evidence comes from Athens. Athens was hardly alone. Other Greek city-states that had at least periods of democratic government include: the Achaian cities, Acragas, the Arcadian Confederacy, Argos, Byzantium, Caulonia, Corcyra, Cos, Croton, Cyme, Cyrene, Elis, Ephesus, Epidamnus, Eretria, Erythrae, Gela, Heraclea Pontica, Heraea, Hestiaia, Himera, Iasos, Istrus, Leukas, Mantinea, Megara, Miletus, Mytilene, Paros, Rhodes, Samos, Selinus, Sicyon, Sybaris, Syracuse, Tarentum, Thasos, Thebes, and Thessaly.[15] The overwhelming evidence of ancient democratic practice nonetheless comes from Athens, and it is worth reviewing the Athenian record as part of the tradition of European populism.

We know that Athenian citizenship was far from inclusive, and no doubt neither were the others. Critics frequently remind us that the Athenians excluded slaves, foreigners, and women, among others, from political participation. Athens was essentially a democracy of male heads of households organized on a tribal model. But these limitations, important as they are, should not allow us to overlook the genuine degree of democracy—far in excess of our own—actually achieved by the Athenians who qualified as citizens. We should not confuse "who is a citizen" with "what is citizenship." As C. Douglas Lummis puts it in his *Radical Democracy*, "The Athenians did not invent slavery and patriarchy, neither did they abolish them; what they did was to discover public freedom."[16] Or rather, it may have been preserved there from kinship times in a particularly pure form, if Athens was indeed the only major Greek city not conquered by foreigners during the Dark Ages that followed the Bronze Age. We moderns, by contrast, come nowhere near realizing the kind of direct political power enjoyed by the large numbers who were able to participate in the Athenian assembly and its related institutions. It is astonishing, even a shock, to see how much of a complete democracy ancient Athens was for its citizens by contrast with our representative system, which is no democracy but rather an oligarchy legitimized by symbolic popular sovereignty established through plebicitory approval. There is some accountability in modern representative systems, but very little compared to something like the Athenian democracy. In Athens, the adult male resident population included a very wide social spectrum (from the richest landowners to the most humble, propertyless artisans and workmen), but more important for our purposes, it offered genuine, not symbolic and occasional, participation in government. It was a democratic society where property, if not distributed equally among citizens, remained available to many and probably most of them. As Victor Davis Hanson puts it: "Rural Greeks often resided on their farms, or at least in clusters of small homesteads, rather than commuting from nucleated centers to distant plots. This is an important distinction if one believes in a uniquely rural culture as the basis of the city-state. Agrarians probably owned average-sized plots, lived on them, and acquired a slave or two to help with the intensive regimen of homestead agriculture. Thus classical Greeks were not exploited peasants, but could be better characterized as a chauvinistic and proud middle class that defined much of the original military, political and economic thinking of the polis."[17] It was only later, after the Athenians acquired an empire, that extremes of wealth and poverty appeared, with the poor able to justify their political participation only by virtue of their military contributions, often as rowers in the city's fleets.

The Athenians were their own legislators, something we in modern Western countries have never allowed ourselves to be, save for town meetings and other mostly exceptional and small-scale circumstances. Mogens Herman Hansen, in *The Athenian Democracy in the Age of Demosthenes*, estimates the Athenian citizenry in the Periclean age at sixty thousand.[18] Another scholar, Josiah Ober, in *Mass and Elite in Democratic Athens*, estimates twenty to forty thousand citizens "through most of the fifth and fourth centuries."[19] Citizenship was hereditary, based on tribal records. Citizens who came of age were registered in their local precinct, or *deme*, and then served two years of military training and duty, after which they would assume their responsibilities as citizens. These citizens were a clear minority of the total population of ancient Attica in the fifth and fourth centuries BCE, an area of about one thousand square miles, almost exactly the size of Otsego County, New York, where I live. We think of the Athenian democracy as a city-state, but it is better understood on a county scale: a central town or city plus the surrounding countryside, where many citizens had small farms.

Citizens met in assembly in Athens, often on the hill across from the Acropolis called the Pnyx, almost on a weekly basis. The assembly was comprised of citizens from all Attica, though required of none. In later years, citizens were paid to participate. A quorum of six thousand (fantastic as it sounds) was required for most meetings in the fourth century BCE. These meetings were conducted largely as a committee-of-the-whole constituted by the citizens who were present. Though any citizen could speak as well as vote, most of the speakers (as we might expect) seem to have been drawn from a self-selected pool of politically active individuals (natural leaders, as it were). The agenda and much of the work of the assembly was done by a council of five hundred, a kind of executive committee, drawn by lot. Proposals could only be introduced by the council, which fixed the agenda for assembly meetings, and had to be accepted or rejected in the assembly session in which they were introduced, though any action taken in one sitting could be reconsidered in another.

Leadership—open to anyone at any time—was a matter of publicly persuading the Athenian assembly or council to take a certain course of action, or not. The ability to speak (open to all) rather than the ability to get elected (open to few) was the only prerequisite to leadership. The ordinary American citizen stands almost completely outside the political process, and merely has an opportunity, on rare occasions, to vote for one or another representative known usually only by reputation. And modern voting by citizens is not carried out as part of any deliberative assembly, but in separate voting precincts isolated from the rest of the political process. The very privacy of voting (alone in a curtained booth) is the very antithesis of the public give-and-take in the assembly. The Athenians were inside their own political process from beginning to end, on a continuing basis, being their own representatives. So little did the Athenians trust elected representatives that almost all government officials—generally functionaries of the assembly—were chosen by lot, frequently rotated, and had no special standing in the assembly. The chairman of the assembly himself presided for only one sitting. The only officials Athenians elected were military commanders—something virtually unimaginable in modern America—and some treasury officers, and the overseer of the water supply. Even then, they rarely if ever elected just one official, but usually a committee (there were normally ten generals elected, as a committee, with no designated leader). Large juries composed of hundreds of citizens were separately constituted to try cases and determine verdicts. Our jury system is the one modern institution with an Athenian flavor, in which important public matters are managed by a committee of citizens chosen largely at random, with some restrictions, by judges, lawyers, and so forth.[20]

The Athenian democratic system was instituted in its essentials in 508 BCE on the initiative of Cleisthenes. As Barry S. Strauss points out in "The Melting Pot, the Mosaic, and the Agora," Cleisthenes went so far as to have the Athenians renounce their tribal patronymics in favor of the names of their demes or places of residence.[21] Here we see imposed an articifial kinship system (something the Romans used as well, in a milder form). It would be as if I, a resident of the Township of Otsego in Otsego County, New York, were to give up my patronymic, "Kuzminski," in favor of "Otsego," becoming Adrian Otsego. Such a renaming must have been a powerful reintegration—almost unimaginable to us—of previously separated individuals into a single, highly democratized community. The system, brought to completion by Ephliates in the 460s, lasted, with two brief interruptions of oligarchic rule, until 322 BCE, when Antipater, a Macedonian general, put down a revolt of the Athenians after the death of Alexander the Great, and ended the democracy as an independent force on the larger historical stage.

Athens never again enjoyed the freedom of an independent state. She lost her ability to conduct her own foreign policy and became subject to taxation and other imperial requirements by Hellenistic and later Roman rulers. It is important to note, however, as Christian Habicht has shown in his *Athens from Alexander to Antony*, that the democracy continued, though only as a local form of self-government (still much cherished by the Athenians), on through Roman times. These later centuries of local democracy reveal the tenacity of robust democratic institutions and speak to their practicality. In Habicht's words: "Nothing justifies the occasional claim that political participation by Athenian citizens declined in the Hellenistic age. The history of Athens did not end with its military defeats by the armies of Macedonia. Even after these defeats the administration of justice and official cults, the provision of food supplies, the resolution of finances and all the other area of government administration remained the exclusive responsibility of the citizens of Athens."[22]

Athenian democratic roots also extend far into prehistory. The Athenians prided themselves as unique among ancient Greek city-states in having come more or less intact through the Dark Ages between the end of the Bronze Age and the Archaic period, although, perhaps because of foreign threats, they did develop a kingship. An aristocracy of sorts also developed, as elsewhere, though to a lesser extent, it seems. This relative exemption from one of the worse aspects of state society—foreign conquest—may have helped preserve democratic kinship procedures into classical times. Plutarch, in his work on the life of Theseus, credits the semilegendary founder of Athens with instituting a democracy in mythical times, at the very founding of the city.[23] And Solon's famous reforms, around 594 BCE, not only expanded popular sovereignty at the expense of the nobility, but canceled most debts, suggesting the presence of populist values. Solon did not, however, provide for the distribution of wealth; he left assets largely unchecked in the hands of the rich. The poor got a clean slate, as it were, but no recognition of an inherent claim on common resources.[24] This failure to create a genuine populist state, as we shall see, seriously compromised the democracy. Cleisthenes and Ephiates solidified a democracy in which sigificant discrepancies of wealth were beginning to appear, with the wealthy enjoying their private baths and dinner clubs, while using their resources to support their claims to special status.

Athens was a patriarchal society, to be sure (and one of the most pronounced), yet it preserved many ancient kinship features. It is important to recall that there was no wage labor among kin in ancient societies, only cooperative labor. In ancient Athens, for instance, kinfolk (actual Athenian citizens, or male heads of free households) could only work cooperatively (as neighboring landowners, or business partners, or in the army or assembly), never as wage laborers, or unequals, a situtation we also find in Rome and generally in ancient and medieval societies. As Edward E. Cohen makes clear in his *Athenian Economy and Society*, what today is for us a corporate enterprise like banking, was then necessarily a kin or family matter:

> Functioning within a legal system that did not recognize businesses as autonomous persons for juridical purposes, the Athenian bank was not an institution, but an intensely personalized "operation" (*ergasia*) conducted by individuals having considerable skill in finance…. Banking as an ongoing business necessarily involved a multitude of mundane functions. The bankers could not employ free Athenians to handle these tasks. Although individual citizens might undertake specific, limited assignments—representation in a particular commercial dispute, expedition of a financing through provision of a guarantee, and the like—societal values inhibited citizens from working on a continuing basis under another person's control.[25]

Citizens were free, however, to engage in business enterprises; most were small independent farmers. But they could engage in commerce only as individuals, or more technically, as heads of independent households, or else as free partners, but never as bosses and workers in the modern sense, where some would consistently be dominated by others. Women, children, and slaves were totally subordinated to the heads of households, and could be delegated many tasks. Any emancipation of noncitizens would have consisted in giving them what the male heads of household already enjoyed: full autonomy in politics and property. This full autonony—in which citizens are precluded from putting one another in subservient roles—was no doubt an important bulwark of the ancient democracy. Further, the material as well as spiritual achievements of the Athenian state—a concentration of human achievement in science, philosophy, literature, and the arts perhaps not equalled in the West until the European Enlightenment, if then—suggest that a democratic society cannot only provide more than adequately for its own needs, but can also be capable of a stupendous flowering of fine art, literature, architecture, philosophy, and science.

The power of the ancient Athenian assembly in the classical period was absolute, with rich and poor on an equal political footing but increasingly on an unequal social and economic footing. Individuals could be ostracized for ten years and could be held liable in the courts for proposals of theirs adopted by the assembly. Citizenship was hereditary, exclusive to freeborn male Athenians, though it is interesting that Aristotle, in *The Constitution of Athens*, writes of both parents as "citizens," and of "citizen wives."[26] Freedom for individual citizens was given a wider scope and greater public responsibility, however, than anything we can find in modern representative goverments. Abuses that did occur tended to be exceptions that proved the rule. Most stemmed from the malfunctioning of the democracy, particularly during wartime crises when the absence of significant prodemocracy groups serving in the army and navy allowed their aristocratic opponents to carry measures in the assembly that otherwise likely would not have passed. This was particularly true at the time of the short-lived oligarchic coups in 411 and 404 BCE, toward the end of the Peloponnesian War.

***

There has been a long tradition of criticism of the Athenian experience by antidemocratic writers; it is important to review these criticisms. One of them is likely little more than a myth, as I. F. Stone argues in *The Trial of Socrates*. Most modern scholars have accepted that the anti-impiety law of Diopeithes was passed around 430 BCE and invoked against Anaxagoras, Alcibiades, Socrates, and perhaps other prominent Athenians. It was long thought to represent a telling early example of a

McCarthyist assault by mob democracy against freedom of thought and expression. If such a law was indeed pased around 430 BCE it would have been carried out at a time when the democratic elements in the assembly were below their normal strength, deployed at war in the field or in the fleet, or coping with the plague Athens then suffered. But it is not even clear that any such law was passed at all. Stone traces assumptions of its existence to a confusion in later writers like Plutarch, who were drawing from literary as well as historical sources. If Stone is right, Diopeithes turns out also to have been a character used in Attic comedies by several playwrights, with no evidence that he was a real person. Interested in moral fiction perhaps more than historical veracity, as most classical writers were, it would appear that various writers picked up this imaginary dramatization, which came to be read retrospectively by later historians as a fact about the Athenian democracy.[27]

The reputation of the assembly as a mob, fostered by antidemocrats from Plato and Xenophon down to James Madison and Leo Strauss, may be seriously exagerrated. The coups, plots, and individual persecutions came primarily from the antidemocratic, elitist dining clubs and other associations of Athens' wealthier citizens, who were able to act in concert to push through their policies when attendance in the assembly was reduced, allowing antidemocrats to muster temporary majorities. As M. I. Finley points out in *Democracy Ancient and Modern*, Athenian elitists in these circumstances were able to use fear-mongering propaganda, unconstitutional violence, and terrorist tactics, such as the infamous mutilization of the herms (sculpted busts of gods, mostly Hermes, on top of stone posts scattered throughout the city) to foment conflict and gain their ends.[28] But when the assembly was able to function—as it did most of the time—with most citizens free to participate, toleration, not persecution, was the rule. After the democratic restorations in 411 BCE and 403 BCE, the assembly acted with noted magnanimity. Even Plato notes that "the restored democratic exiles exhibited considerable decency."[29] On each occasion, only a few oligarchs were brought to trial for treason, with a general amnesty declared for the rest.

There are other important examples of the wisdom and prudence of the Athenian democracy. As Stone points out, it was among the prodemocracy sophists that slavery was perhaps first called into question. He cites an ancient note in Aristotle's *Rhetoric* quoting an obscure Alcidamas, a pupil of Gorgian, as saying, "God had left all men free; Nature has made none a slave."[30] Alcidamas, like Phaleas, seems otherwise unknown. In the *Lysistrada*, Euripides opens a door to the empowerment of women and questions the virtue of war and violence. The democratic impulse, even then, may have been pushing already for the univeralization of democracy. It has been a tragedy for the democratic tradition in the West that its ancient champions were largely silenced in favor of oligarchic and aristocratic writers, although, as we have seen, we can find a thorough presentation of democracy in Aristotle's *Ethics* and *Politics*.

But there is more to this important story. There are at least three other eposides of apparent irresponsible democracy in Athens that call for closer examination: the assembly's condemnation and execution of its generals after the naval battle of Arginusae, the genocide at Mylos, and the attempted genocide at Mytilene. In the first case, after an impressive Athenian victory over a Spartan-led fleet in 406, near the end of the Peloponesian War, Athenian naval commanders failed to retrive survivors and the bodies of victims, as prescribed by religous custom, apparently due to pressure to relieve a nearby blockade and bad weather. The assembly, frazzled by a long war otherwise going poorly, was furious at this breech of religious obligation and, overriding precedents and objections, voted to try the generals as a group, in violation of their rights to individual trial. Six of them were executed by what amounted to a kangaroo court. In the second case, the Athenians in 416 overran the island of Melos, oligarchic and sympathetic to Sparta in the Peleponesian War, but officially neutral. The city of the island surrendered, asking for mercy. There was none. The Athenians killed all the men of military age and sold everyone else into slavery, what today would be called acts of genocide. In the third case, the Athenians put down a revolt at Mytilene, on the island of Lesbos, early in the Peloponesian War. The assembly voted to do to Mytilene what they actually did to Melos a decade later, and a ship with these instructions was sent out. But the assembly had a change of heart the next day, and voted to rescind the orders, and sent out another ship that luckily arrived in Mytilene in time to prevent the mass murders and enslavements.

What do these stories tell us? That the Athenians were not immune from violating their own democracy at home, and that they were not above the use of state terror in ruling an imperial empire of some 250 city-states. Does this discredit democracy, as many have argued? Not necessarily. The populist mean was not struck in Athens, or imperfectly so at best, particularly in the imperial period. Political democracy was established, but not economic democracy; the recirculation of resources without which it appears democracy cannot work was imperfectly achieved in Athens. Inequities of wealth, augmented by imperial largesse, began to grow in the decades after the defeat of the Persian empire. A powerful antidemocratic faction of rich families increasingly opposed democracy as the fifth century BCE rolled on. Some citizens came to own thousands of slaves, large estates, and large productive and commercial enterprises, and enjoyed all the trappings of wealth. Others were on the dole, and still others everywhere in between. Their wealth gave the oligarchs the resources and motivation to play a subversive role in the democracy.

The problem in Athens was not too much democracy, but, one could argue, too little. Playing on the insecurities of the lower classes, and using their new economic influence, the oligarchs were in a position to argue for harsh policies, including state terrorism at home and abroad, in times of crisis, to protect the "interests" of Athens, which was argued to benefit even the poorest citizens economically. Cleon was instrumental in the initial decision to crush Mytilene, as Alcibiades was in the later decision to destroy Melos. Both were prominent oligarchic leaders. And it was the demogogery of Alcibiades that persuaded the Athenians to undertake their disasterous invasion of Sicily. Had Athens followed Phaleas and established not only a democracy but also institutionalized in some way the claim of all citizens to their fair share of the wealth of the community, the lower economic orders in Athens would have had more independence and security, and less fear, rendering them more likely to be skeptical of the dubious proposals of the oligarchs, and in a better position to resist them. It is remarkable, however, that they resisted them as well as they did. Nor in a more populist society would the oligarchs have had the resources and prestige to enable their faction to agitate as disruptively as they did for their own interests. Indeed, they would hardly have been oligarchs at all. The Athenian "empire" did foster democratic, as opposed to oligarchic governments in the city-states it included, while Mytilene and Melos were oligarchic holdouts, it may be worth noting. But a more populist Athens might have pursued a more thorough and humane democratic policy toward these cities and avoided the excesses it committed, as it tended to do anyway in its better nature, as we see in the amnesty given the oligarchs after the failed coups at the end of the Peloponnesian War.

The Athenian experience suggests that maximizing participation by individuals who are cooperative but independent of one another—again, the populist balance—is no idle fantasy or irresponsible exercise, but a practical lesson that can be drawn for resolving the problem of how best to conduct politics. The Athenian assembly as a whole held absolute power. Yet, precisely because it was an independent body of free citizens still largely economically independent of one another, if not yet economically independent enough to act together cooperatively on all occasions, the assembly, for the most part, did not succumb to faction, or consistent concentration of power. Indeed, the longer it lasted, the more established the democracy became. The loss of the Athenian empire no doubt had a leveling effect on the distribution of wealth, and likely contributed to the greater stability of the democray from the fourth century on. The free Athenian citizen in the end remained typically a property owner, usually a small farmer, even though there continued to be propertyless citizens as well.

One last example of mob action by a democratic state, this time not Athens, is worth noting. It is found in the account given by Thucidydes in the third book of his *Peloponnesian War*, where he describes the brutalities, including wholesale massacres, exercised by the democratic party and its oligarchic opponents in their civil conflict in the city of Corcyra, on the present-day island of Corfu. Both sides engaged in a destructive spiral of violence. He comments: "Human nature, always ready to offend even when laws exist, showed itself proudly in its true colours, as something incapable of controlling passion, insubordinate to the idea of justice, the enemy to anything superior to itself; for, if it had not been for the pernicious power of envy, men would not so have exalted vengeance above innocence and profit above justice."[31] But resentment and envy surely have their causes as well, which Thucydides does not examine; they need not be presumed to be the "true colors" of human nature. It is those who deprive many citizens of their property, of their natural right to resources, it could just as well be argued, who create the conditions of envy and resentment, and must bear the subsequent responsibility. The frenzies of the mob, *pace* Thucydides, can just as well be read to show, not the shortcoming of democracy, but that democracy requires the general distribution of property, not its concentration in a few hands, in order to be worthy of its promise.

It is sometimes argued that we need representative government in order to foster leadership. Pure democracy, its critics say, following Thucydides, Plato, and Madison, leads only to sophistry, contentiousness, mob rule, and anarchy. Yet it can be argued that leadership is nowhere fostered more than in pure democracy, where the ability to persuade one's fellow citizens, and to be corrected by them, is what really counts. One can lead a democratic society—as Pericles did—not by holding office (as would be a requirement for us) but by being free to persuade the assembly or council of one issue or another (something we do not have the opportunity to do). Pericles did not have to hold office (though he was in fact repeatedly elected as general, or *strategos*) because the democracy automatically gave him and any other citizen access to full participation. Yes, there will be demagogues who will feed on ignorance, but a people seasoned in democratic practice may be the least rather than the most likely to remain ignorant for long. Over time, it is in a better position to judge all comers more or less accurately in real, face-to-face encounters; our judgments, by contrast, are in terms of the virtual creations of a mass media full of spin. Indeed, demagogues can be understood to be not so much the creatures of genuine democracy, where they are subject from the start to examination and criticism, but primarily of representative governments, where they are in a position to manipulate a mass electorate using all the techniques of propaganda that money can buy.

The condition of dehumanizing evil is no doubt as rare as superhumanizing sainthood. Only a collective trauma (such as the Germans suffered in World War I, or as Athens suffered in the Peloponnesian War) perhaps can create for a time the mass hysteria necessary to make scapegoating fantasies credible enough to feed an out-of-control tyranny of the majority. The Germans, unfortunately, had only a limited tradition of democracy to check their excesses. But the Athenian oligarchs, even in the absence of their major opponents, still had to persuade a conflicted and intimidated rump-assembly to abolish democracy in 411. It would be foolish to think there could be any absolute assurance against tyranny of the majority. The point, however, is that democracy can just as plausibly be considered the antidote, not the cause, of such tyranny. Similarly, probably only a collective epiphany (such as followed the Greeks' unlikely victory over Persia) can both create and express the confidence necessary for radical democratization. But no epiphany alone will secure lasting results unless the ground for democracy is already prepared (as many democratically inclined young Americans learned in the 1960s, with the failure of the antiwar and countercultural movements to secure more democratic means to social and environmental justice).

***

Democracies like those of Greek and other ancient cities were based on direct participation—not mere representation—by ordinary citizens by their own choice. The citizens met in a committee of the whole, representing only themselves. This committee of the whole, or assembly, was the source of all authority. The Roman Republic, by contrast, was a modified democracy, where powers were split, and citizens meeting in assembly were only part of the story. The Republic is significant for the role it subsequently played as a political model in the West, especially in the United States. It is important, therefore, to appreciate its genuinely democratic elements, often overlooked. The locus classicus of the Roman system is the description offered by Polybius, a Greek historian of the second century BCE, found in book 4 of his *Histories*.[32] He famously describes the Roman government in the second century BCE, at the time of its triumph over Carthage, as divided into three parts, roughly corresponding to what we would call the executive, legislative, and judicial branches of government. The two consuls, elected for yearly terms by popular vote of the people, held the executive power. The consuls were in charge of public administration and all the other magistrates; they had a hand in foreign policy, and they commanded in war. They executed the decrees of the senate and of the popular assemblies, which they summoned and chaired. The senate constituted the aristocratic power, its main authority lying in its control of state finances, including military affairs, public contracts, and so forth. The senate also enjoyed a privileged voice over foreign affairs.

Subsequent scholarship has mostly confirmed and deepened Polybius's account. The popular assemblies, the *comitia centuriata* and the *comitia tributa*, acting as juries, held the power of justice over most disputes; they elected the magistrates, including the consuls, and most important had the final yea or nay over any legislation. The consuls depended both on the senate and popular assemblies for support. The senate could cut off funds for the consuls, and the popular assemblies could refuse to ratify treaties with foreign powers, or fail to approve laws or the accounting consuls had to make to them at the end of their term of office. The senate needed the popular assemblies to ratify its decisions, and the tribunes of the people—officials representing the sentiments of the popular assemblies—could nullify decisions of the senate, and even forbid the senate to meet. The popular assemblies could not initiate legislation, though, and many citizens were dependent upon government contracts, particularly for public works, controlled by the senate. Individual citizens were also under the authority of judges, who were often senators, and of the consuls in time of war. Most power lay in the hands of magistrates and other officials—consuls, praetors, censors, pontiffs, and others—elected by male citizens meeting in the popular assemblies. The competitive system of campaigning for public office—as later in modern Western countries—became increasingly corrupted in the Late Republic by money lavished by wealthy candidates on clients and supporters. Still, the Roman Republic was not merely a oligarchic representative system, as are most modern states, but at the same time in important respects a functioning democracy.

The arguments that turned out to be decisive for adopting the Roman rather than the Greek system of politics for America (but not including its democratic component) were developed primarily in *The Federalist*, written by Alexander Hamilton, James Madison, and John Jay at the height of the debate over the new Constitution. Madison's principal concern in "Federalist No. 10" was to combat the "violence of faction," whose "instability, injustice and confusion ... have, in truth, been the mortal diseases under which popular governments have everywhere perished."[33] The worst expression of faction, he thought, was the tyranny of the majority over the minority he saw manifest in popular assemblies. Although admitting that "the most common and durable source of factions has been the various and unequal distribution of property," Madison traced this unequal distribution not to tyranny and conquest but to nature, to "the diversity in the faculties of men."[34] The result of this line of thought was to remove the issue from the political agenda. Madison was particularly deaf to any sense of Phaleas's insight. He was willing to tolerate a degree of faction only because it seemed to him the price necessary to pay for liberty, understood as freedom of property. The only question was how to mitigate its excesses. The Roman system of the separation of powers as advocated by him might just as well be described as the institutionalization of antidemocratic forces, particularly the privileging of an aristocracy of wealth, and the executive, judicial, and financial instruments supporting that aristocracy.

We should understand, however, as Fergus Millar makes clear in his *The Crowd in Rome in the Late Republic*, that the Roman popular assemblies were in fact direct democratic bodies, with individual citizens voting not only on candidates, but on laws and all other proposals.[35] No such provision survived in the U.S. Constitution, which created entirely representative bodies. Millar reminds us that Roman citizens in the Late Republic—numbering close to a million in all of Italy—could exercise their right to vote in the city of Rome, which many seem to have done. Legislation was put out to the people in assembly in what we would call a binding referendum. Prior to voting on legislation, the issues normally would be presented and debated at open-air meetings called *contiones*.

The senate was never a legislative body, but technically an advisory one, though of enormous importance and prestige. Its decrees did not have to be obeyed, did not have the force of law, yet the prestige of the senate gave them de facto force. Even if enacted by the consuls, senatorial decrees could be challenged by tribunes, the courts, or the popular assemblies. Laws—which did have to be obeyed—were proposed by consuls and tribunes to the people by public announcement and discussion, involving varying degrees of public response, in the forum and other public meeting places, after which citizens lined up to vote. Of the two main assemblies, the comitia centuriata and the comitia tributa, the former was a version of the latter weighted by property qualifications, though not excluding any citizens. Most voting for public office (over fifty offices yearly) was done by the comitia centuriata. The comitia tributa divided Roman citizens into thirty-five arbitrary tribes (similar to the artificial tribes of Athens) on a one-man, one-vote basis within each tribe, and it was this assembly, voting by tribes, that had to pass any measure for it to become law. Millar has documented the vigor and scope of the comitia tributa, especially in the Late Republic, arguing persuasively that it was the focus of power and authority in the state. It is worth remembering that the Romans were unusual in the ancient world as a city founded by refugees, with little carryover of ancient kinship ties—almost the opposite of Athens in this regard. The Romans also were perhaps unique in giving citizenship to manumitted slaves often as a matter of course. Rome is famous as a slave society; but it was perhaps easier in Rome than in any other major slave society to be released from slavery.

Madison's fear of the tyranny of the majority—the main criticism directed at radical democracies like Athens and modified democracies like the Roman Republic—is the nightmare myth of democracy perpetrated by its opponents. It is apparently ill-informed, as our discussion of ancient Athens and Rome suggests, and largely the product of antidemocratic ancient writers like Thucydides and Plato, whose appeal to oligarchs has continued undiminished down through the centuries. The evidence suggests otherwise: a tyranny of the majority is unlikely as long as citizens come to the assembly mainly not as masters and servants, patrons and clients, employers and employees, and so on, but more or less as equals, not just in theory or even in law, but in substance, in their personal command of resources. A majority will tyrannize a minority only when it feels that its own material independence and identity is at stake. It is representative government and other forms of oligarchy, rather than democracy, that arguably pose the greater danger of tyranny, as Aristotle pointed out.

It would be going too far to claim that ancient Rome, especially in the Late Republic, came anywhere near to equality of personal wealth, but the Early Republic was likely more equalitarian, and the struggle to reduce extremes of wealth long contined in Rome with some success. One example, by recent historian Klaus Bringmann, gives a sense of some degree of progress achieved in mitigating disparities of wealth and power: "A consular law of the year 326, the *lex Poetelia Papiria* (named after its two proponents Gaius Poetelius Libo Visolus and Lucius Papirius Cursor), mitigated the harsh debt laws of the Twelve Tables by prohibiting creditors from imprisoning debtors privately for non-payment. Thirteen years later the dictator Gaius Poetelius Libo Visolus continued the reforming work of his father by introducing a law according to which only the goods and no longer the person of the debtor could act as security for the repayment of borrowed capital and interest."[36]

Clearly the lower orders in Rome had enough power to push back, to a significant degree, the predatory debt system of wealthy creditors. That debt system intensified, however, when the state decided to go into debt in the difficult time of the Punic wars. In Bringmann's words:

> We are told that the construction of large fleets in the First Punic War was financed by private contributions and on credit. And after the battle of Cannae supplies to the armies operating in Spain could only be ensured when three groups of private entrepreneurs, who had already earned handsomely from their deliveries to the state, declared themselves ready to supply clothing and grain on credit and to transport them to Spain on condition that the state bear the transport risk…. The state accumulated a huge debt. Between 215 and 187 it amounted to twenty-five and a half times the ordinary revenue of the property tax of 150 talents or 3.6 million sesterces.[37]

The upshot was the creation of a national debt, a privatized financial engine in which the benefits of interest payments and contracts associated with the military went disproportionately into the hands of wealthy private investors, who in turn funded and profited further from vast public works projects, developed what we would call agribusiness in large latifundia with intensive slave labor, and generally employed their new wealth to ensure its perpetuation (for example, in buying lucrative tax farming contracts, etc.). Although the debt was eventually paid down, it provided for a massive and permanent shift in wealth to the elites. (We shall see below, in England in the eighteenth century, the reappearance of a national debt as a key element of modern plutocratic power.) Small landowners, the backbone of the Roman Republic, were exhausted and depleted by lengthy military service. A shrinking independent middle class, rural and urban, led to political instability. In the second century, the reformist Gracchi brothers, Tiberius and Gaius, fought to redistribute land and reduce the power of the Roman plutocracy; although they achieved some limited success, such as the secret ballot and some land distribution, they were unable to overturn the new concentrations of wealth and power. Their efforts were the last gasp of the populist impulse in antiquity.

***

Whatever the virtues of the Roman Empire, successor to the republic, there was little scope within it for the further development of populist ideas and practices. After the fall of the empire, however, with the retribalizations and relocalizations of what used to be called the Dark Ages, conditions in many areas became more favorable to a sort of natural populism.[38] The tribal assemblies of the barbarians, as described by Tacitus, suggest populist values, and incipient city-states like Venice embodied elements of democratic self-rule. A sixth-century Byzantine historian, Procopius, writing of the Slavic tribes of Eastern Europe of that period, tells us that they were "not ruled by one man, but they have lived from old under a democracy, and consequently everything which involves their welfare, whether for good or for ill, is referred to the people."[39] Yet in most places after the fall of Rome political and economic power tended to become hierarchical under the rule of chiefs and princes or else the church. It was not until the rise of new city-states and the major rediscoveries of ancient literature in Europe, beginning in the twelth and thirteenth centuries, that the ancient classical republican tradition began to be revived.

By the fifteenth century, particularly in Florence, ancient notions of civic virtue were once more widely circulated, particularly by Guicciardini, Machiavelli, and others. J. G. A. Pocock has argued for the importance of this revival in *The Machiavellian Moment*, particularly for subsequent British and American constitutional history. The Florentine focus was not, however, on the populist point of the necessity of property as well as democracy to foster virtue, but on the possibilities for the cultivation of virtue in *any* of the traditional political systems (monarchy, oligarchy, democracy).[40] Our populist tradition, with its locus classicus in Aristotle's *Politics*, is properly a subset of classical republicanism; it is that version of it that argues that access to ownership of resources is the key to democracy, and that democracy so founded is superior to oligarchy or monarchy. The populist point, however, is missed or underrated by most republicans thinkers after Aristotle, from Cicero to Machiavelli and beyond, including most Renaissance thinkers, who do not privilege democracy nor recognize the importance of property to democracy, but at best seek to balance democracy against oligarchy and monarchy. It is plain that Machiavelli, for instance, is no populist when he states flatly in *The Discourses* that "in well-regulated republics the state ought to be rich and the citizens poor."[41]

Phalean populism resurfaces somewhat later, in James Harrington's *Commonwealth of Oceana*, published in 1656. Harrington appreciates what he calls the "invention" of Phaleas, and makes it plain that Aristotle fails to give Phaleas the credit that is his due, while eventually coming to essentially Phalean conclusions: "Nor is Aristotle so good a commonwealthsman for deriding the invention of Phaleas, as in recollecting himself, where he saith that democracies, when a lesser part of their citizens overtop the rest in wealth, degnerate into oligarchies and principalities."[42] Harrington is alive to the shift in Aristotle's *Politics*, discussed above, where the philosopher "recollects" himself back to a Phalean notion of society, a shift missed or dismissed by most other readers, then and now. Harrington was an English gentleman and courtier to Charles I, but also something of a democrat who had studied republics, including Venice. He influenced Locke, Hume, and the American founding fathers. John Adams compared Harrington's appreciation of the connection between power and property to Harvey's discovery of the circulation of the blood, and the constitutions of several American colonies (Carolina, New Jersey, Pennsylvania) exhibited Harringtonian features, including separation of powers and limits to landholdings.[43]

Harrington's version of the revived classical republican tradition makes central the populist connection between property and democracy, and promotes the superiority of a populist polity, which he calls a commonwealth. For Harrington, the principal form of property is land. He writes:

> If one man be sole landlord of a territory, or overbalance the people, for example, three parts in four, he is grand seignior; for so the Turk is called from his property, and his empire is absolute monarchy. If the few or a nobility, or a nobility with the clergy, be landlords, or overbalance the people to the like proportion, it makes the Gothic balance … and the empire is mixed monarchy, as that of Spain, Poland, and late of Oceana [England]. And if the whole people be landlords, or hold the lands so divided among them that no one man, or number of men, within the compass of the few or aristocracy, overbalance

them, the empire (without the interposition of force) is a commonwealth.[44]

Harrington elaborates on how the most desirable of states, a commonwealth, can be constituted. His gothic prose, uncongenial perhaps to many modern readers, is worth the effort:

> An equal commonwealth is such a one as is equal both in the balance or foundation, and in the superstructure; that is to say, in her agrarian law [how land is distributed] and in her rotation [of offices]. An equal agrarian is a perpetual law, establishing and preserving the balance of dominion by such a distribution, that no one man or number of men, within the compass of the few or aristocracy, can come to overpower the whole people by their possessions in lands. As the agrarian answers to the foundation, so does rotation to the superstructures. Equal rotation is equal vicissitude in government, or succession to magistracy conferred for such convenient terms, enjoying equal vacations, as take in the whole body by parts, succeeding others, through the free election or suffrage of the people.[45]

Harrington's commonwealth, like Aristotle's, is built upon the radical populist vision that seeks to accommodate the variety of human talents and ambitions in a productive democratic meritocracy based on widespread private ownership of resources.

Far from endorsing the prerogatives of privilege in monarchy or oligarchy, Harrington insists that any true commonwealth requires that "the whole people be landlords, or hold the lands so divided among them, that no one man, or number of men, within the compass of the few or aristocracy, overbalance them."[46] Democratic government cannot succeed when animated by an impoverished and embittered mob, where some are necessarily servants if not slaves to others, but only when "the whole people be landlords"—that is, be economically self-sufficient. In the pithy words of another populist, Algernon Sidney, one of Harrington's followers, and a man killed by James II for his democratic beliefs,[47] we find perhaps the most succinct statement of the populist attitude: "no man, whilst he is a servant, can be a member of a commonwealth, for he that is not in his own power cannot have a part in the government of others."[48] The key phrase is to be "in one's own power." Only in such a free commonwealth, with property distributed to all in reasonable portion, can democracy function, because only then will all persons be in a position to freely and independently judge the proposals of their peers on their merits. In such a commonwealth, with each citizen being in his or her own power, a natural aristocracy of those more talented than others will be recognized by the body of citizens, Harrington maintains, without fawning or bitterness, solely on their merits. As Harrington colorfully puts it:

> Twenty men, if they be not all idiots—perhaps if they be—can never come so together, but there will be such difference in them that about a third will be wiser, or at least less foolish, than all the rest. These upon acquaintance, though it be but small, will be discovered and … lead the herd; for while the six, discoursing and arguing one with another, show the eminence of their parts, the fourteen discover things that they never thought on, or are cleared in divers truths which had formerly perplexed them; wherefore in matter of common concernment, difficulty or danger, they hang upon their lips as children upon their fathers…. The six then approved of, as in the present case, are the senate, not by hereditary right, nor in regard of the greatness of their estates only, which would tend unto such power as might force or draw the people, but by election for their excellent parts, which tendeth unto the advancement of the influence of their virtue or authority that leads the people. Wherefore the office of the senate is not to be commanders but counsellors of the people.[49]

Harrington was also a proponent of what we now call the separation of powers. He did not separate functions of government as we do, however, among legislative, judicial, and executive, but rather he separated, to use his language, the proposing from the disposing of policy. Social decisions rising above special interest and faction to do justice to common concerns, to create just social orders, he thought should be made as follows:

> that such orders may be established as may, nay must, give the upper hand in all cases unto common right or interest, … is known even unto girls, being no other than those that are of common practice with them in divers cases. For example, two of them have a cake yet undivided, which was given between them. That each of them therefore may have that which is due,

"Divide," says one unto the other, "and I will choose; or let me divide, and you shall choose." If this be but once agreed upon, it is enough; for the divident dividing unequally loses, in regard that the other takes the better half; wherefore she divided equally, and so both have right."[50]

Just so, the natural aristocrat who rises to propose policy in a democratic assembly—a Pericles or a Patrick Henry—can only lay his or her plans before the public, suggesting that such-and-such a division of the social cake, so to speak, be made. For he or she has no other power, no special office or privilege, to effect policy. It is up to the people to carry out the process, and accept or reject or refine the proposal in question. The responsibility is divided, but mutual, and entirely democratic. If there must be representatives of the people in any democracy, they must be their agents, not their rulers.

***

In the eighteenth century, the "county" opposition to the "court" in English politics recognized the populist need in a healthy polity to balance property and democracy, but faced a new challenge in doing so. In *Cato's Letters*, published serially between 1720 and 1723 in a London newspaper by John Trenchard and Thomas Gordon, a new threat to liberty was identified in the corruption of public credit by private interests. From this time on the nature of wealth begins a fundamental shift from ownership of land to ownership of capital. The assumption of public debt by private corporations, most notoriously by the South Sea Company, had led to a speculative bubble whose collaspe left many in ruins.[51] Trenchard and Gordon in an early letter invoked the sentiment if not the name of Phaleas: "A free people are kept so, by no other means than an equal distribution of property; every man, who has a share of property, having a proportionable share of power; and the first seeds of anarchy (which, for the most part, ends in tyranny) are produced from hence, that some are ungovernably rich, and many more are miserably poor; that is, some are master of all means of oppression, and others want all the means of self-defence."[52] Trenchard and Gordon went on to advocate a system of public credit based on stable money and low interest,[53] but provided few details as to how this might be achieved. We shall pursue the important question of credit and interest rates, and of finance and monetary systems in general.

At least Trenchard and Gordon saw the new problem. As J. G. A. Pocock puts it, by the eighteeenth century "it was no longer possible to believe with Harrington that an agarian law might equalize in perpetuity the distribution of the material foundations of virtue. Land could not be freed from its dependence on trade, or trade from its dependence on credit; and the equivalent of an agrarian law for a speculative society was unknown and perhaps unthinkable. Men had therefore to be better than their circumstances."[54] From this time on, land and privileged commodities like gold were steadily displaced as principal expressions of wealth in favor of other more fungible forms, what Pocock calls "credit—" that is, various new financial instruments including bills of exchange, bank notes, fiat money, securities, and other innovative legal claims against public resources. With the eclipse of land as the nearly universal expression of wealth, the populist idea of distributing wealth more equitably became more problematic, given the many complex and elusive forms wealth could now take. The link between personal resources and personal democracy could no longer be addresseed, it seemed, in a simple manner, and democracy, with its stabilizing and legitimizing populist connection with property obscured, continued to be understood mostly in its negative form as rule of the poor, or the mob. We see this modern retreat from the populist insight of Phaleas in one of the last references made to him by a major modern political philosopher. Montesquieu in *The Spirit of the Laws* notes that Phaleas "contrived a very extraordinary method of rendering all fortunes equal"—namely, that "the rich should give fortunes with their daughters to the poor, but received none themselves," and vice-versa for the poor. "But I do not remember," Montesquieu goes on, "that a regualtion of this kind ever took place in any republic. It lays the citizens under such hard and oppressive conditions as would make them detest the very equality which they designed to establish."[55]

Although the rise of new forms of wealth and power in the eighteenth century consigned the Phalean ideal to the margins for most social philosophers, it also presented an opportunity to update the Phalean populist program. The populist call for for a just and ultimately demo-cratic polity based on wide access to capital and economic independence continued to be recognized, and the central challenge of disbursing and distributing the new nonlanded, financial forms of wealth began to be appreciated as offering a solution rather than an obstacle to providing wide distribution of capital. The issue was taken up by George Berkeley, Bishop of Cloyne, otherwise famous among philosophers for his cogent arguments denying the independent existence of the external world. Berkeley was a true polymath, interested in many subjects, including what we would now call political economy, though these apsects of his work have received far less attention. In 1735 he published *The Querist*, a sustained reflection on the political economy of his native Ireland, written as a tour de force of nearly six hundred short, numbered paragraphs, with each proposition in the form of a question.[56] Berkeley recognized the central role that banking, monetary systems, and credit had come to have in modern economies. He recognized how these magnified the evils of the maldistribution of wealth and power, but argued that they might yet be mitigated significantly if not eliminated altogether by the creation of a national bank accountable to the public and dedicated to the circu-lation of sufficient money, or credit, to the general population. The populist program has depended always on securing access by all to capital; Berkeley recognized that what now counted as capital was money, not land.

His queries speak for themselves. The text is aphoristic rather than argumentative; the focus is on public as opposed to private credit as the foundation of a socially just money system, one that ensures that wealth as money circulates through all of society, not just part of it. As with Aristotle, some extended quotation is necessary to bring out the full force of the argument: "Whether power to command the industry of others be not real wealth? And whether money be not in truth tickets or tokens for conveying and recording such power, and whether it be of great consequence what materials the tickets are made of?" [Query 35] Berkeley clearly states the essential Phalean point: "Whether, as seed equally scattered produceth a goodly harvest, even so an equal distribution of wealth doth not cause a nation to flourish? [Query 214]" He is alive to the misuse of money to concentrate wealth:

Whether the real foundation for wealth must not be laid in the numbers, the frugality, and the industry of the people: And whether all attempts to enrich a nation by other means, as raising the coin, stock-jobbing, and such arts are not vain? Whether a door ought not to be shut against all other methods of growing rich, save only by industry and merit? And whether wealth got otherwise would not be ruinous to the public? Whether the abuse of banks and paper-money is a just objection against the use thereof? And whether such abuse might not easily be prevented? [Queries 217–19]

The problem is not money per se, but how it is instituted:

Whether a bank of national credit, supported by public funds and secured by Parliament, be a chimera or impossible thing? And if not, what would follow from the supposal of such a bank? Whether the currency of a credit so well secured would not be of great advantage to our trade and manufactures Whether the notes of such public bank would not have a more general circulation that those of private banks, as being less subject to frauds and hazards? Whether it be not agreed that paper hath in many respects the advantage above coin, as being of more dispatch in payments, more easily transferred, preserved, and recovered when lost? [Queries 223–26]

Berkeley makes it clear that money ought to be a form of public not private credit, issued for the benefit of all: "Whether the total sum of the public treasure, power, and wisdom, all co-operating, be not most likely to establish a bank of credit, sufficient to answer the end, relieve the wants, and satisfy the scruples of all people? [Query 432]" "Whether there be any difficulty in comprehending that the whole wealth of the nation is in truth the stock of a national bank? And whether any more than the right comprehension of this be necessary to make all men easy with regard to its credit? [Query 438]" "Whether a national bank be not the true philosopher's stone in a State?" [Query 459]. Subsequent, shortened editions of *The Querist* omitted a number of more detailed but significant queries about the national bank found in the first edition: "But whether a bank that utters bills, with the sole view of promoting the public weal, may not so proportion their quantity as to avoid several inconveniencies which might attend private banks? [Query 83]" "Whether the stock and security of such bank would not be, in truth, the national stock, or the total sum of the wealth of this kingdom? [Query 120]" "Whether the sole proprietor of such bank sould not be the public, and the sole director the legislature?" [Query 123]

Berkeley's queries represent the kernal of the modern populist response to the problem of distributing wealth in the context of a modern finance-driven economy. Again, the key is the monetary system, not land or any other factor. The issue of money and banking came to be a central issue in eighteenth- and nineteenth-century America, and its key role in distributing wealth was recognized by a number of influential figures, including Benjamin Franklin, Thomas Jefferson, Tom Paine, Edward Kellogg, and many others in the republican, greenbacker, and populist traditions, as we shall see. The themes they later developed are found in embryo in Berkeley. As *The Querist* shows, they include the mutuality of production between labor and capital, money as a social convention rather than a commodity, the power of money to command social resources, the importance of the "equal distribution" of wealth, the idea of money as "national credit," the accountability of the money system to the public via their representatives, the importance of the circulation of money, the central danger of usury, and the fundamental notion that the monetary system should serve "all people." Berkeley's queries contrast with the system of private banking and its national monopoly on credit—a system established with the Bank of England in 1694, and continuing down to the modern Federal Reserve in the United States—with the idea of a genuinely public national bank accountable to the people. Berkeley recognizes that credit is the basis of modern economic prosperity, and that it should be publically administered for the private use and benefit of all.

Whatever functions as money in a society (from wampum to gold to paper notes to electronic entries) does so as a legally sanctioned claim, credit, token, or ticket on such outstanding resources of society as are available in the marketplace for consumption or investment. The "national stock" or "sum total of wealth" in a society is what gives the money of that society its value, or backs it up. If the resources of society are to be broadly shared by all, and not monopolized by a few, then money or "national credit" must somehow be available to all. If the creation and distribution of national credit lies in private hands, and if those hands enjoy discretionary power in that creation and distribution, as has been the case in modern capitalistic economies, and if they can privately profit from it, then money and the resources it commands will be controlled by some at the expense of others. However, if money is put in public hands and made accountable for public purposes under a genuinely democratic system of government as described above, then it can be distributed equitably to all. The essentials of this modern populist view are to be found in Berkeley's *The Querist*.

Such a system of public credit is not a giveaway or a free lunch. Because money is a credit against the goods and services available in society, it is a social debit. Money is often confused with wealth, but it is rather a debt, a claim on wealth.[57] In order to get a dollar I must do one of two things: I must sell something I already own in the market, my own labor if I have nothing better, by which I can obtain dollars. Or I can obtain dollars from someone as a loan I am obligated to repay. I can do the latter insofar as I and the lender both believe that eventually I can sell something in the market sufficient to enable me to repay my loan. In the first case, I sell something I already own; in the second, I commit myself to selling something I hope to own in the future by using someone else's money as the capital I employ in the meantime to earn it. Through its money system, a society is able to borrow from itself. For this reason alone, the money system should be a public not a private institution, embodied in a national bank or appropriate institution committed to its equitable distribution. Money should be available on loan from the government to all citizens on the basis of good collateral. And, as we shall see, it should be available at a nominal and not a usurious rate of interest, if we wish to prevent significant concentrations of wealth.

***

Berkeley's views on public credit, however, found little resonance. Most eighteenth-century thinkers abandoned the Phalean equation between capital for all and democracy for all. David Hume displays little if any interest in capital for all, but he does have considerable interest in democracy, or at least decentralized government, and in this regard he makes an important, albeit one-sided, contribution to populist thought. In his 1777 essay, "Idea of a Perfect Commonwealth," Hume dismisses Harrington's "agrarian rotation" or scheme for distributing wealth, saying, "Men will soon learn the art, which was practised in ancient Rome, of concealing their possessions under other people's name; till at last, the abuse will become so common, that they will throw off even the appearance of restraint."[58] Nonetheless, Hume clarifies the nature of accountable government adapted to large states, one that was to prove influential among later populists, particularly via Thomas Jefferson, whose system of ward republics, as we shall see, strongly reflects Hume's scheme.

Although presented merely as a "speculation" that might offer "in some future age, an opportunity ... of reducing theory to practice," Hume develops in considerable detail a scheme of bottom-up confederated government. He may have been inspired by the section of Montesquieu's *Spirit of the Laws* that entertains the possibility of democratic states confederating together, as in ancient times, whereby, Montesquieu tells us, they "contrived a kind of constitution that has all the internal advantages of a republican, together with the external force of a monarchical, government. I mean a confederate republic."[59] Montesquieu does not develop this idea of a confederated republic; his focus is rather on the doctrine of the separation of powers, which, as one scholar puts it, "had [for Montesquieu] definite anti-democratic implications, designed to check the power of elected representatives."[60] Hume, however, took the idea of confederation seriously. He develops a system that allows for all "freeholders of twenty pounds a year" and "all the householders worth 500 pounds in the town parishes" to meet annually in the parish church, where they would choose from their number a representative of the parish to the county. These county representatives would meet in the county town and choose by ballot from their own body "ten county magistrates, and one senator."[61]

The senators, one from each county, would meet in the capital, and "be endowed with the whole executive power of the commonwealth." The county representatives would meet in their respective counties, and "possess the whole legislative power of the commonwealth. . . . Every [proposed] new law must first be debated in the senate," he tells us, and if passed on to the counties, will become law if passed by a majority of the counties. A minority of senators may overrule the majority and have a proposed law sent down to the counties for consideration, and a minority of counties may override the senate and send a law for consideration to the other counties. There are other refinements in this scheme we need not consider here. What is essential is that county governments represent communities—not a mass of individuals—and national governments represent regions of commmunities in Hume's England (counties).

For Hume, it should be noted, the local parishes are not self-governing assemblies or town meetings, but simply districts that hold a yearly election for a county representative. There is no democracy in Hume, strictly speaking, no parish town meeting at the base, but rather a system of accountable, representative government. Hume offers a representative system conditioned by property qualifications, but directly accountable to the grassroots, with yearly elections and face-to-face proximity, with representatives sitting no further away than the county seat. The power of these county assemblies is extraordinary, embodying a decentralized legislative process. Although a national senate has the power of proposing legislation to the counties, it cannot itself establish such legislation, while the counties have the power to take the legislative initiative themselves, if they choose. Hume explains the role of the senate as follows: "All free governments must consist of two councils, a lesser and greater; or, in other words, of a senate and people. The people, as Harrington observes, would want wisdom, without the senate: The senate, without the people, would want honesty." Applying Harrington's metaphor of one girl carving the cake and the other choosing which piece to take, Hume writes: "If the people debate, all is confusion: If they do not debate, they can only resolve; and then the senate carves for them.

Divide the people into many separate bodies; and then they may debate with safety, and every inconvenience seems to be prevented.[62]

"Here is a form of government," Hume writes of his scheme, "to which I cannot, in theory, discover any considerable objection." As we have seen, however, given significant inequalities of wealth among and within the parishes, most of those qualified to vote by virtue of some degree of property would remain clients or dependents of one sort of another. Even a relatively well-off citizen, if dependent on a greater power, falls short of being a free citizen. If we presume a universal franchise, these disparities would further be magnified. The interests of wealth would be served by the inability of the dependents to vote in their own best interests or in the best interests of the community. Concerned with keeping a job, or with gaining some kind of preferment from the powers that be, they could not afford to contradict the rich, even locally. To be sure, Hume's devolution of legislative power to the county level would be unsettling to the wealthy, more difficult for them to control than more remote legislatures chosen not in local parishes or assemblies but in mass elections. Still, such control could be established. On the other hand, Hume's pioneering vision of a decentralized confederated polity, when combined with a circulation of wealth or capital sufficient to erase the economic dependence of citizens on one or another special interest, demonstrates how a responsible democratic polity might be established over a large area. After Hume, it was no longer possible to dismiss democracies solely as local affairs, confined to city-states at best; he shows how there need be no limits of population or geography to the "perfect commonwealth," which is in essence a confederaton of local assemblies.

***

Hume's intriguing vision of political decentralization has remained unrealized in the modern world; similarly the populist precondition, envisioned by Berkeley, for democracy—access to capital by all—has also remained unrealized. Let us look more closely at credit, the modern form of wealth. Money or credit is created in most countries today not publicly by the government in accordance with democratically determined policies in the sense outlined by Berkeley, but privately by central banks on the model of the Bank of England that create and loan money to privileged borrowers largely at their discretion. Ellen Hodgson Brown in her detailed work on privatized modern finance, *The Web of Debt*, puts it succinctly, and in italics: "*What is wrong with the current system is not that money is advanced as a credit against the borrower's promise to repay but that the interest on this advance accures to private banks that gave up nothing.*"[63] Even governments must borrow money from the very central banks to which they have given a monopoly over the creation of the money they borrow. Although some modern central banks are government institutions, and most are perceived as such, some of the most important, like the Federal Reserve Bank in the United States, enjoy at best a kind of quasi-government status, and are in fact comprised of a mix of government appointees and representatives from private banking interests. As a result they are largely controlled by those private interests. Most if not all government banks remain largely autonomous, largely unaccountable to the public for their decision making, and closely tied to the interests of major private financial interests, who act as the conduits of credit and are allowed additional credit creation to serve (or exploit) the general public. The public credit that is the monetary system in major Western countries and elsewhere (for example, Japan) is thereby owed not by the public to the public, but by the public generally to private lenders. These lenders are free to charge interests rates largely as they see fit, giving them rough but effective control over the economy for their own purposes.

The result, from the populist point of view, is a kind of national financial servitude by an economy almost entirely indentured to private financial interests, a system prefigured in the Roman Republic and, in modern times, first established in Britain with the founding of the Bank of England in 1694, and subsequently extended to America and much of the rest of the world. It is important to understand that a new system of political economy was reinvented in Britain at the end of the seventeenth century, in the wake of the Glorious Revolution. That system introduced new financial instruments to control public credit for private benefit by monopolizing public credit in private hands through government sanction. It went a step further than its Roman (or even Dutch and Italian) precedents: the idea was to subscribe a private bank with capital, and then obtain a monopoly for that bank from the government for the issuance of government debt, allowing for usurious rates; such debt was ultimately issued as bills of credit on that bank and circulated as money. This was the plan behind the chartering of the Bank of England in 1694. A privatized central bank of this type creates government debt out of nothing simply by entering a credit in the government account, giving it the money, and simulaneously taking a credit to its own account, counting the debt as an asset. The more government debt is generated, the greater the obligation on the citizens to repay the debt through taxation, a burden that became very significant in Britain and elsewhere, including the

United States, where this "British system" was later adopted. The interest on the national debt goes overwhelmingly to private creditors.

The establishment of the Bank of England marked a fundamental victory of private interests over public credit, after a long struggle. Although prohibitions against usury in England had ended in the sixteenth century, the royal prerogative to control the money and credit system was still affirmed as late as 1604 in the Mixt Moneys case. In the words of Alexander Del Mar, an influential American historian of money and credit in the nineteenth century:

> The Mixt Moneys case decided that Money was a Public Measure, a measure of value, and that, like other measures, it was necessary in the public welfare that its dimensions or volume should be limited, defined and regulated by the State. The whole body of learning left us by the ancient and renascent world was invoked in this celebrated dictum: Aristotle, Paulus, Bodin and Budelius were summoned to its support; the Roman law, the common law and the statues all upheld it: "the State alone had the right to issue money and to decide of what substances its symbols should be made, whether of gold, silver, brass or paper. Whatever the State declared to be money, was money."

But royal control of public credit was not destined to last, as Del Mar goes on to explain:

> This decision greatly alarmed the merchants of London, and for more than a century after it was enunciated they were occupied with efforts to defeat its operation. In 1639 they succeeded in getting the matter before the Star Chamber; but their plans were rejected. The Revolution of 1648 postponed their projects. The Restoration of 1660 revived them. Their final success dates from 1666.... In 1666 was enacted that free coinage law which practically altered the monetary systems of the world and laid the foundation of the Metallic theory of money. The specific effect of this law was to destroy the Royal prerogative of coinage, nullify the decision in the Mixt Moneys case and inaugurate a future series of commercial panics and disasters which down to that time were totally unknown.[64]

Earlier monies, usually coins, were normally issued directly by the state, usually by the monarch, in payment for services, not as loans for interest. As long as the monarch could raise taxes and enjoy a sufficient private income from crown lands, he or she could control the currency. But in England in the sixteenth and seventeenth centuries, the monarchy, for various reasons, lost its economic preeminence.[65] The British monarchy, limited by Parliament in its taxing abilities, gradually found itself unable to maintain its position solely from custom duties, crown lands, and other royal, income-producing prerogatives. Henry VIII was forced to drastically debase the currency in the sixteenth century, initiating a process of fiscal austerity that gradually bled the monarchy dry. The Stuart monarchs found themselves faced with a Puritan opposition enjoying superior financial resources and were eventually caught up in civil war. By the time of the restoration of Charles II, the monarchy had lost fiscal independence. Unable to raise money to fund its expenses, and with Parliament opposed to any attempt to tax the wealthy, the Stuart monarchy foundered and was eventually overthrown.

"After the Glorious Revolution," writes economic historian Larry Neal, "a new financial system based on large-scale use of foreign bills of exchange, easily transferable shares of joint stock companies, and securely serviced long-term government debt grew up to accommodate the government's financial needs."[66] The weakened monarchy under William III agreed in 1694 to give up the monetary power to a new corporation, the Bank of England, subscribed by the wealthiest men of the land and by foreign investors, particularly the Dutch. Ellen Hodgson Brown sums it up this way:

> Before Cromwell's Revolution, *the king did not need to borrow because he could issue metal coins or wooden tallies* [notched wooden sticks, used as money, split into matching payment and receipt portions] *at will to pay his bills.* The Harvard authors [she cites work by J. Lawrence Broz and Richard Grossman] presented a chart showing that in 1693, 100 percent of the government's debt was "unfunded" (or paid in government tallies). "By the 1720s," they wrote, "over 90 percent of all government borrowing was long term and funded." … *In a nutshell, the "Financial Revolution" transferred the right to issue money from the government to private bankers.* [67]

The new central bank, given the power to charge usurious interest rates, proceeded to provide currency for the nation and much needed loans to the king's government, in return for a private, perpetual monopoly over the British monetary system. This process created a national debt and established a class of creditors in Britain who were not only able to skim off the top the interest charged by the bank, leaving it up to ordinary taxpayers to shoulder the burden, but were also able to benefit from the preferential access to credit controlled by the bank. The above description offered by Larry Neal seems perhaps benign enough, even progressive, but the devil is in the details. Christopher Hollis, in his neglected work *The Two Nations: A Financial Study of English History*, goes further and describes just how this system worked in its initial arrangement:

> The plan [of the Bank of England] was that, instead of borrowing from the goldsmiths, the Government should instead borrow £1,200,000, of which it was in need, from a newly formed Corporation called the Bank of England. This corporation promised to collect the required money from the public and to lend it on to the King at 8 per cent plus £4,000 per annum for expenses—a rate considerably lower that that which he would have had to pay to the goldsmiths. In return for lending at this low rate the Bank received a number of privileges of which the most important was that it had the right to issue notes up to the extent of its loan to the Government "under their common seal" on the security of the Government. This is to say, it had the right to issue a £1 note; the holder of that £1 note had the right to demand that the Band give him cash for his note, but, if he made that demand, the Bank had the right to demand that the Government raise £1 by taxation and repay £1 worth of debt to the Bank.[68]

The creation of the Bank of England assured not only that private bankers could mint their own gold, but that henceforth they would be be able to control most forms of public credit, whether based on gold or anything else. It is hard to exaggerate the importance of the establishment of a private rather than public monetary system, beginning in Britain and extending throughout much of the world. As the primary, driving mechanism of the concentration of wealth worldwide, private monetary systems have shaped almost every aspect of modern society. It was this system that Alexander Hamilton introduced in essentials into American economic life. "The Bank of England," he wrote in 1780, "unites public authority and faith with private credit; and hence we see what a vast fabric of paper credit is raised on a visionary basis. Had it not been for this, England would never have found sufficient funds to carry on her wars; but with the help of this she has done, and is doing wonders."[69] Transplanted to America, the system of "private credit" proved adaptable and tenacious, eventually to be institutionalized in the Federal Reserve System, and, after World War II, it found itself the basis of the global economy. But at the same time, as we shall see, populist ideals found root in America, and their advocates resisted the imposition of private credit and usurious interest rates while holding out for the virtues of public credit. That they were not successful does not diminish their importance insofar as some form of public credit remains the fundamental alternative to the private concentrations of wealth and power so evident today in the United States and throughout the world wherever private money reigns.[70] We shall consider American developments in the next chapter.

***

In the nineteenth and twentieth centuries, Phalean populist ideas found less and less resonance in Europe, except among occasional literary writers and idiosyncratic thinkers, such as John Ruskin, C. K. Chesterton, and Erza Pound. The most vocal criticisms of what Americans came to call "the money power" were often superficial and increasingly mixed up with nationalistic and sometimes anti-Semitic agendas. European radical thought in general gravitated to communal solutions, most conspicuously in socialism, communism, and anarchism, but also in nationalism and racism. In these leading political movements of the day, while democracy was sometimes invoked, the idea of private property widely distributed as a right was consistently rejected in favor of one or another kind of system of collective or concentrated ownership of resources. It is not surprising that wherever these modern secular views found practical expression democracy was trumped in the end by state or corporate power.

Nonetheless, populist ideas continued to be reinvented in Europe. Perhaps the most lucid formulation in the European tradition of the economic pillar of populism can be found in the writings of the eccentric thinker Frederick Soddy, especially in his *Wealth, Virtual Wealth and Debt*, first published in 1926. Soddy was a Nobel Prize–winning British chemist who turned his attention to financial and monetary matters later in his life. In these fields he did not find the acclaim he received for his scientific work, but his attack on monetary orthodoxy, though dismissed by the mainstream critics of his day, continues to percolate. Soddy distinguishes carefully between wealth and credit, and argues persuasively (like Berkeley) that money is credit—that is, a claim against resources on the market. Soddy reminds us that the confusion between wealth and money is an old one, already made by Aristotle and the Roman jurists, who defined wealth as what can be bought as sold—as equivalent to money—and that this confusion has been perpetuated by almost all modern thinkers, including such luminaries as J. S. Mill, Karl Marx, and John Maynard Keynes. Soddy observes, "Wealth is the positive quantity to be measured and money as the claim to wealth is a debt, a quantity of *wealth owed to but not owned by the owner of the money.*"[71] Money and wealth are mutually exclusive: money itself being only a *claim* to wealth, and *not* that wealth itself. It is necessary to spend or give up or exchange the money to realize its claims upon wealth. Money is not wealth itself, but a device for transferring its ownership "without an immediate *quid pro quo* in wealth, for the right to a future repayment in wealth."[72]

The difficulty, in Soddy's view, is that money is available only at the price of interest, a situation in which a controlling legal abstraction makes impossible demands on labor and physical resources. "Debts," he points out, "are subject to the laws of mathematics rather than physics. Unlike wealth, which is subject to the laws of thermodynamics, debts do not rot with old age and are not consumed in the process of living. On the contrary, they grow at so much per cent per annum, by the well-known mathematical laws of simple and compound interest."[73] Once made legally binding through debt contracts, simple and compound interest become a compulsory obligation for borrowers and thus perhaps the key factor, generally overlooked, driving economic "growth." Soddy recognizes that there is no need for interest with regard to money as such, as opposed to the lending of money, or credit: "The distinction between money and credit, as purshasing power, is that the use of the former does not leave the user in debt, whilst the use of the latter does. In the case of money the buyer does not have to pay again the wealth purchased, but the seller who receives the money passes on the token, as a legal claim to wealth on demand, indefinitely—that is, the claim circulates and is not cancelled."[74] Or as he puts it in another place:

> In the case of a genuine loan of money from lender to borrower, or creditor to debtor, the borrower who receives the money incurs an equal debt to the lender. In the case of a sale of goods

for money the buyer who receives the goods pays the debt he incurs with money, and so confers upon the seller in exchange for what he has given up an equal credit or right to be repaid in wealth on demand. In the first case the borrower gives his personal promise to repay the creditor; in the second case, the buyer gives money, which is the nation's generalised promise to repay the seller the wealth he has given to the buyer, whenever he pleases. We thus come to look upon money—quite irrespective of whether it is specie or paper—as a token certifying that the owner of it is a creditor of the general community and entitled to be repaid in wealth on demand.[75]

The whole point of the monetary system, the heart of public credit, according to Soddy, is "the power it confers upon individuals not to posses but to be owed wealth."[76] Money, in other words, is the collective but interest-free debt that society has decided to owe to itself as a necessary condition of facilitating the exchanges needed to ensure the ongoing productivity required to satisfy the consumption needs of society. Money is a socially or state-sanctioned token, uniquely designated as an exclusive claim, by whoever holds it, against such goods and services as are available at any time on the market rated at such and such a value of money. Once the bearer of money exchanges it for goods and services, the seller of those goods and services receives the money and can in turn, at a time of his or her choosing, exchange it in turn for further goods and services, and so forth. Since society is an ongoing enterprise, the money can stay in circulation indefinitely; there is no term or limit to the endlessly circulating debt of money, no final need to repay it. This ongoing social debt that does not bear interest nor need to be repaid Soddy calls the "virtual wealth" of society, and it is equal to the purchasing power of the outstanding money supply in any society. When we exchange money for goods and services that we consume, these goods and services must be replaced if society is to continue functioning, and those who are paid for goods and services use a portion of the money they receive to replenish those goods and services in order to sell them again, and so forth.

Soddy concludes that money is a social and therefore public responsibility and ought to be issued by the state on an interest-free basis to facilitate production and commerce. He points out, however, that "in modern times a fundamental change has come over the nature of money. Not only is it now a simple token of the community's indebtedness to the individual owner of it, but it is created not by the national authority, but by private institutions for lending at interest."[77] The coins—both of precious and nonprecious metals—issued in earlier eras by city-states, kingdoms, republics, and empires were interest-free public monies, as was the paper money of China. This public money was often put into circulation as payment for military expenses, including salaries for soldiers and sailors and purchase of their equipment, as well as weapons, transport, provisions, and so on. This was the practice in Rome, which maintained a salaried standing army and navy, and in many early modern European states. This public money (mostly coins) made its way out into the general economy, to be recovered later, at least in part, through taxation. The commodity value of precious metals vis-à-vis other commodities more or less fixed the value of money.

Price inflations like the great inflation of the sixteenth century were tied to fortuitous increases in the supply of precious metals (gold and silver were discovered in great quantities in America) and were relatively gradual though persistent over time. Although this state- or sovereign-issued money based on precious metals was a form of interest-free public credit, it had some serious limitations. Money remained scarce as precious metals were hard to come by and liable to be concentrated into relatively few hands, mostly goldsmiths and traders and their clearinghouses. Most wealth continued to be held in land, under various nonmonetary, quasi-feudal arrangements, and considerable trade in kind among at least semi-self-sufficient households persisted. Economies before the eighteenth century were only partly monetized. Those who had money, given its scarcity, found themselves in a position to charge interest on their loans, including usurious rates of interest, thus further consolidating the concentration of money.

By the eighteenth century, credit had replaced land as the chief form of wealth. Soddy reminds us that credit, once predominately a public function, has become increasingly controlled by private interests. Here's Soddy's observations on the transition from public to private national credit: "The first step on the downward path, from money for use to money for usury, was the power conferred upon the Bank of England to issue bank notes to a limited extent in return for the loan of money to the Government."[78] Today the national and global monetary system is controlled so thoroughly by the private banking and financial system that no alternative seems even conceivable. Money for private usury is now substituted routinely almost everywhere in the world for old-fashioned money for public use: "The old extreme *laissez-faire* policy of individualistic economics," Soddy tells us, "jealously denied to the State the right of competing in any way with individuals in the ownership of productive enterprise, out of which monetary interest or profit can be made, and this was ignorantly extended even to the virtual wealth of the community [the monetary system]. Individualistic economics, regarding money as wealth instead of debt, hands over to individuals the power of issuing money, and leaves to the tax payer the duty of paying interest for the issue."[79]

Soddy advocates a return to public credit money—that is, money for use issued by the state in place of the private issuance of money for debt by the banking system. Acknowledging that past public credit monies—principally the coins of monarchs as well as some controversial experiments, including the French *assignats* and the American continentals—have not been as successful as might have been hoped, Soddy argues for an indexing system run by a neutral government agency to keep the value of the currency stable. In Soddy's view the value of money ought to be standardized in just the same way as weights and measures and other public metrics (e.g., time zones, etc.): "Commerce would be freed from all the legally unrecognized forms of theft attendant upon a variation of the standard of monetary value, which are of much the same nature as would result from fraudulent weights and measures."[80] Soddy envisions a body of government statisticians coming up to an objective measure of the value of money relative to the goods and services for which it can be exchanged.[81] It is doubtful, however, that such an agency could be kept neutral; more likely, it would sooner or later become a political football, subject to the major interests controlling the central government, or a branch of government, independently setting monetary policy. The wisdom of concentrating so much monetary power in any one place, whether public or private, may well be questioned. American populists also struggled with the challenge of figuring out how to provide credit to all in a manner resistant to centralized manipulation, and as we shall see in the next chapter, at least one of them, Edward Kellogg, offered an ingenious solution.

Chapter Four

American Populism

After Harrington and Sidney, Phaleas drops out as an explicit reference for populists. He is not mentioned in Berkeley's *The Querist*; nor is he invoked by any writer with serious populist inclinations. Although his essential insight linking property and democracy is reinvented independently by a number of modern thinkers, this loss of historical memory reflects the fragmented and marginalized nature of modern populism. Insofar as populist ideas coalesced into any sort of modern tradition, it was in America under the successive rubrics of antifederalism, Jeffersonian and Jacksonian democracy, critiques of "the money power," in the efforts of overlooked thinkers like Edward Kellogg, and the later greenbacker and explicitly "populist" movements. A keen appreciation of the importance of national credit became important to American populists aware of the consequences of the privatization of the monetary system in modern economies. The importance of public credit as a basis for fair access to resources was not only widely recognized from the colonial era through the late nineteenth century but was also developed in important and original ways; American populists also created a striking vision of how to establish a bottom-up system of genuine democracy. We shall explore their contributions in this chapter.

Many of the colonies had issued their own paper currencies as a way to circumvent the onerous demands of British credit privately controlled from London. Colonial experiments in public credit, led by the issue of the first paper currency in the West by Massachusetts in 1690, were surprisingly successful. Techniques for establishing a stable paper currency were then untested, but in spite of some excesses, these currencies overall seem to have held their value sufficiently to have played an important role in making possible the widely noted economic prosperity of the American colonies by the mid-eighteenth century.[1] A number of colonies—Pennsylvania, Delaware, New Jersey, and

New York—developed government-run "land banks" that lent farmers and productive landowners money against the collateral of their real estate, with the interest income going to the province and the loan notes circulating as currency. The possibility of an alternative local American source of public credit to the monopoly of British finance from London was one of the key issues that estranged the American colonies from Britain.

It is hard to exaggerate the importance of the new system of political economy invented in Britain at the end of the seventeenth century. That system introduced new financial instruments to control public credit for private benefit. The way this was done, as we have seen, was to subscribe a private bank with capital, and then obtain a monopoly for that bank from the government for the issuance of government debt, allowing for variable and usurious interest rates; such debt was ultimately issued as bills of credit on that bank and circulated as money. Such a bank creates government debt out of nothing simply by entering a credit in the government account, giving the government the money, and simultaneously taking a credit to its own account, counting the debt as an asset. The more government debt is generated, the greater the obligation on the citizens to repay the debt through taxation, a burden that became significant in Britain. The interest on the national debt goes to the creditors, those invested in the bank, rather than to the public, where it would seem to belong.

No one was more aware of this system, and its baleful social consequences, than Benjamin Franklin. In a short essay published in Philadelphia in 1729, "A Modest Inquiry into the Nature and Necessity of a Paper-Currency," Franklin reaches the same conclusions Berkeley did a few years later. Berkeley, who spent three years in Rhode Island in the early 1730s, very likely had direct experience in colonial paper currencies, and could have been influenced by Franklin and other Americans.) Franklin, like Berkeley, calls for a national currency backed by low-interest mortgages on land issued by a government accountable to the people. "For as Bills issued upon Money Security are Money," Franklin writes, "so Bills issued upon Land, are in Effect Coined Land."[2] Franklin's essay, "wrote and published in Haste,"[3] is, like Berkeley's *The Querist*, a polemical piece focusing on the larger question of the role of money in a prosperous economy. Neither man tells us as much as we would like about how such a public system of public credit would work, and the details of colonial currencies remain an obscure subject to most historians. A systematic work by Franklin or Berkeley on public credit might have changed history, but no such work was written.

The most systematic statement by Franklin is as follows, in a passage responding to the objection that falling land prices might cause a land-based currency to fall as well. His eighteenth-century language is worth following in detail:

> If Land in this Province was falling, or any way likely to fall, it would behove the Legislature most carefully to contrive how to prevent the Bills issued upon Land from falling with it. But as our People increase exceedingly, and will be further increased, as I have before shewn, by the Help of a large Addition to our Currency; and as Land in consequences is continually rising, So, in case no Bills are emitted but what are upon Land Security, the Money-Acts in every Part punctually enforced and executed, the Payments of Principal bona fide sunk according to Law, it is absolutely impossible such Bills should ever sink below their first Value, or below the Value of the Land on which they are founded. In short, there is no little Danger of their sinking, that they would certainly rise as the Land rises, if they were not emitted in a proper Manner for preventing it; That is, by providing in the Act That Payment may be made, either in those Bills, or in any other Bills made current by any Act of the Legislature of this Province; and that the Interest, as it is received, may be again emitted in Discharge of Publick Debts; whereby circulating it return again into the Hands of the Borrowers, and becomes Part of their future Payments."[4]

The British government and the private banking interests behind it were not about to tolerate an independent currency in the colonies. The British crackdown on autonomous colonial currencies, manifest in acts of Parliament in 1751 and 1764, contributed greatly to support for the Revolution, and, though omitted or downplayed by the standard narratives of the revolution, might be considered its initial and perhaps deepest cause.[5] Alexander Del Mar, a nineteenth-century populist historian, makes this case:

> Lexington and Concord were trivial acts of resistance which chiefly concerned those who took part in them and which might have been forgiven; but the creation and circulation of bills of credit by revolutionary assemblies in Massachusetts and Philadelphia, were the acts of a whole people and coming as they

did upon the heels of the strenuous efforts made by the Crown to suppress paper money in America, they constituted acts of defiance so contemptuous and insulting to the Crown that forgiveness was thereafter impossible. After these acts there was but one course for the Crown to pursue and that was, if possible, to suppress and punish these acts of rebellion. There was but one course for the Colonies; to stand by their monetary system. Thus the bills of credit of this era, which ignorance and prejudice have attempted to belittle into the mere instruments of a reckless financial policy, were really the standard of the Revolution. They were more than this: they were the Revolution itself![6]

The Revolution was financed on the American side by the issuance of a fiat currency by the continental Congress: the continentals. Historians have criticized it for being overissued, ending up worth only a few cents on the dollar, but the overissuance seems to have been due much more to massive British counterfeiting than to anything done by the Continental Congress, which stayed within its authorized limits.[7] For its part, the British subversion of a responsible form of public credit in the early United States by counterfeiting, though it failed in its purpose to keep the colonies under British rule, did succeed in tarnishing the idea of publicly controlled public credit, and opened the door for an eventual imposition of privately controlled public credit by privately controlled banks and other financial institutions. The United States won its independence, but in the end became saddled with the incubus of a privately controlled system of public credit on the British model largely because of the assault on the continental currency, and its subsequent discredit, rooted in British chicanery. The undermining of the continental currency by British counterfeiting was compounded, it is true, by the excessive issuance of bills of credit by individual colonies unauthorized by the Continental Congress. These abuses, which might have been corrected or avoided, helped give the idea of a publicly controlled central system of public credit a bad reputation. The opportunity to establish a system of responsible, nonusurious public credit was tragically lost. In the end, the interests of creditors in the new United States turned out to be the same as those in London. They, too, wished for private control of public credit if at all possible, not only for their own profits, but to ensure that their interests would become those of the government.

The principal advocate of these views was Alexander Hamilton. Hamilton developed a program to implement what was called "the English system" in the United States, as we have seen. The essence of that

program is nicely summed up by Martin Van Buren in his lively and
revealing *Inquiry into the Origin and Course of Political Parties in the
United States*:

> The power wielded by the English ministry, in Parliament and
> in the country, springs from influences derived from various
> sources, mainly from the funding system, from the Bank of
> England, from connection with the East India Company, and
> from ability to confer government favors on individuals and
> classes. . . . The measures which Hamilton deemed indispens-
> able to the success of the new government, in addition to those
> authorized by the Constitution, consisted of First: A funding
> system upon the English plan, with authority to assume the
> separate debts of the States; Second: A national bank; and Third:
> An unrestricted exercise by Congress of the power to raise
> money, and the employment of the national revenue in patron-
> izing individual, class, and corporate interests, according to the
> plan described in his report, nominally on manufactures, but
> embracing an infinite variety of other concerns.[8]

Hamilton developed, Van Buren tells us,

> a conviction that for the favorable changes, as he regarded them,
> which had taken place in the condition of England she was more
> indebted to the operation of her bank and funding system than
> to any other cause. These, like his corresponding systems, had
> been originally formed for the accomplishment of immediate
> and limited objectives. His were avowedly to revive and to
> uphold our sinking public credit; theirs, to relieve the govern-
> ment established by the Revolution of 1688 from its dependence
> upon the landed aristocracy for its revenues, and to secure the
> acquisition of ample means to defray the expenses of the war in
> which England was at the time involved. From such beginnings
> these principal measures, aided by kindred and affiliated estab-
> lishment of which they were the parents, had with astonishing
> rapidity developed a great political power in the state, soon and
> ever since distinguished from its associates in the government
> of the country as the MONEY POWER,—a power destined to
> produce greater changes in the workings of the English system
> than had been accomplished by the Revolution itself.[9]

Hamilton seems to have hoped that a strong central government would exercise a sort of benign financial despotism in favor of the public good,[10] but his notion that private interests could somehow be contained once given a key role in creating and managing the money system seems to have been the fatal point of naïveté in a thinker otherwise so astute. The eventual victory of private financial interests over the central government led them away from Hamilton's idea of a strong central government into the camp of the free-market, laissez-faire liberalism of the classical British economists. Although the Hamiltonian idea of a strong, central government was later abandoned by the right wing in the United States (except for the military-industrial complex), it came to be embraced, ironically, by later left-wing movements, including progressivism, liberalism, and socialism.

This money power, Van Buren reminds us, was the principle issue informing the politics of his day, particularly in the struggle between Federalists led by Hamilton and Republicans led by Jefferson, just as it remains the principle though largely unconscious issue underlying the politics of our own day. A long quotation from Van Buren is necessary to bring out the deeper argument:

We differed from England in the condition and political aspect of affairs; we had no monarchical institutions, no landed aristocracy to excite the rivalry and opposition of the money power. It was itself, on the contrary, destined, when firmly established, to become whatever of aristocracy could co-exist with our political system. Its natural antagonist would be the democratic spirit of the country. . . . It was to keep down this spirit that he [Hamilton] desired the establishment of a money power here which should stand by the Government as its interested ally, and support it against popular disaffection and tumult. He well understood that, if he accomplished that desire, they would soon become the principal antagonistic influences on our political stage. . . . To be allied to power permanently, if possible, in its character and splendid in its appendages, is one of the strongest passions which wealth inspires. The grandeur of the Crown and of the landed aristocracy affords a fair vent to that in England. Here, where it is deprived of that indulgence, it maintains a constant struggle for the establishment of a moneyed oligarchy, the most selfish and monopolizing of all depositories of political power, and is only prevented from realizing its complete designs by the democratic spirit of the country.[11]

The Republicans opposing Hamilton and the Federalists knew that the new federal government would be controlled either by the people through democratically elected and accountable representatives, or by the money power. As Jefferson put it, writing to John Wayles Eppes in 1813: "In the revolutionary war, the old Congress and the States issued bills without interest, and without tax. They occupied the channels of circulation very freely, till those channels were overflowed by an excess beyond all the calls of circulation. But although we have so improvidently suffered the field of circulating medium to be filched from us by private individuals, yet I think we may recover it in part, and even in the whole, if the States will co-operate with us."[12] Jefferson continues in the same letter to suggest how this might be done: "The States should be applied to, to transfer the right of issuing circulating paper to Congress exclusively, in perpetuum, if possible. . . . This national paper might thus take place even in the non-complying States. In this way, I am not without a hope, that this great, this sole resource for loans in an agricultural country, might yet be recovered for the use of the nation during war; and, if obtained, in perpetuum, it would always be sufficient to carry us through any war."[13] In between wars, Jefferson hoped, circulating coin would suffice in place of paper, but the principle of a publicly controlled national credit currency is plain enough.

***

Some context may be useful here. Attempts to redistribute wealth in the past have almost everywhere foundered on the resistance of the rich, which has been usually if not always effective. Many in the middle class, and those aspiring to the middle class, have also been fearful of proposed redistributions; they have noticed that any taking from the rich might include some taking from them as well, and that they may lose an opportunity of their own to get rich, or at least to prosper. Wealthy elites have argued to the indebted middle class, an argument as common now as in the past, that their real fear should the loss of freedom and opportunity under any left-leaning redistributive government. The American Left, influenced by Marxist ideas imported from Europe, has largely played into the hands of the Right, at least in recent decades, by continuing to advance programs that rely on "big government." Often suffering from resentment and guilt, many on the Left, in their anger at the oppression of the ruling elites, and in their guilt over their own complicity in "the system," have too often reduplicated the authoritarian structures of the Right. Left intellectuals have too often remained top-down in their approach to government, relying on centralized authority to "get things done." Whether under the labels of "progressive," "liberal," or "socialist," the nonrevolutionary Left has accepted "the system"—the pseudo-democracy of misrepresentative government—as the means to establishing and defending what used to be called "the welfare state." Lacking a sense of genuine democracy, and too often letting the ends justify the means, the left has failed to mobilize a sufficient opposition to the rule of finance capital.

For populists, we remind ourselves, the way to reconcile the market's imperatives with unfulfilled human needs is by the deliberate recirculation to labor of enough capital to satisfy the fundamental right to labor for oneself rather than for someone else, to establish in effect a limited but ever renewing grubstake, a right to natural capital. William M. Gouge, a widely read economist of the Jacksonian era, put the issue clearly: "A man has as strong a natural right to the profits which are yielded by capital which was formed by his labor as he had to the immediate product of his labor. To deny this would be to deny him a right to the whole product of his labor. The claims of the honest capitalist and the honest laborer are equally sacred and rest, in fact, on the same foundation."[14] The populist right to labor for oneself is the right *to* property (as a means), not (as in John Locke and subsequent mainstream political economists) the right *of* property (as an end). Locke and his modern successors recognize that "every man has a property in his own person"—that is, in his or her physical body, but not in the bounty of nature of such. If a person can get such bounty—some land or raw materials, Locke doesn't say how— he or she can secure it only by removing it out of the state of nature and transforming it into "something that is his own, and thereby makes it his property."[15] For Locke, property has to be earned, it has to emerge out of a state of nature through labor; but for populists, property is already there, the free gift of nature, the natural capital that is the common inheritance of the earth for every man and woman: the land, air, and water without which one cannot live, let alone labor.

This natural capital is public, not private, but no less convertible into personal property, albeit with community approval. In an earlier day, the ever renewable resources required to meet this ever renewable right to natural capital came from the land, and in the United States this meant preeminently land on the frontier—a resource Jefferson came to appreciate as a young lawyer defending Western settlers against absentee landowners and speculators. With the eventual end of the frontier, natural capital was choked off as a common inheritance. To be restored today, in a world where wealth is a function of credit instead of land, it must be made available (as Berkeley saw) in a new and renewable form of credit, through an intentional restructuring of our political economy, particularly our system of finance, including our monetary system. Wealth in modern times, it cannot be overstated, is rooted in money (that is, credit), not land. We shall consider below how American populists addressed the challenge of making credit reasonably and conveniently available to all.

John Locke long ago wrote of life, liberty, and property as natural rights. By substituting "happiness" for "property" in Locke's formula, Jefferson transformed property (including money, the command of property, as well as land) from an end into a means, and opened the road to American populism. The difference is critical. As an end in itself, money or command of property or any form of wealth can be defended simply on the grounds of possession. But as a means, the role and use of money is (or should be) subject to the will of the community. The common will of the community, in turn, is tempered and balanced by the individual private uses of money. The social justification for command of property does not mean socialism, which demands the surrender of individual ownership in favor of collective property rights. Rather, it means the balance recommended by Phaleas: community affirmation of individual or personal rights to command property on the one hand, with the needs of the community as a whole, the commonwealth, on the other, expressed in democratic self-rule. The point is to make money and thereby the property it commands into a means of individual liberation and fulfillment that is socially justified and available to all, not to treat it as an end in itself to be obtained if necessary at the expense of the rest of society.

Jefferson became the leader of the opposition to Hamilton and the Federalists. This opposition carried on the struggle against the money power the colonists had waged against Britain, but after the revolution it had to face the prospect of a domestic money power ruling the new federal state, replacing the banished British. At the heart of the struggle against "the money power" was the question of direct access by individual citizens to private property, the crucial populist precondition of democracy. Jefferson was very clear about the right of individuals to personal property. Writing from Fontainebleau in France to James Madison on October 28, 1785, Jefferson meditates on the need to distribute wealth widely, and on the right of all to a claim on the "common stock" of the earth. The passage is oft-quoted, but particularly apt in our context. He notes that the property of France is "absolutely concentrated in a very few hands," and "that an equal division of property is impractical, but the consequences of this enormous inequality producing so much misery to the bulk of mankind, legislators cannot invent too many devices for subdividing property, only taking care to let their subdivisions go hand in hand with the natural affections of the human mind." He goes on to add:

> The descent of property of every kind therefore to all the children, or to all the brothers and sisters, or other relations in equal degree, is a politic measure and a practicable one. Another means of silently lessening the inequality of property is to exempt all from taxation below a certain point, and to tax the higher portions or property in geometrical progression as they rise. Whenever there are in any country uncultivated lands and unemployed poor, it is clear that the laws of property have been so far extended as to violate natural right. The earth is given as a common stock for man to labor and live on. If for the encouragement of industry we allow it to be appropriated, we must take care that other employment be provided to those excluded from the appropriation. If we do not, the fundamental right to labor the earth returns to the unemployed. It is too soon yet in our country to say that every man who cannot find employment, but who can find uncultivated land, shall be at liberty to cultivate it, paying a moderate rent. But it is not too soon to provide by every possible means that as few as possible shall be without a little portion of land. The small landholders are the most precious part of a state.[16]

Jefferson's immediate antecedents were the writers of the Scottish Enlightenment, as introduced to him at William and Mary College by a Scottish professor William Small. A key idea derived from the Scottish philosopher Francis Hutcheson was the notion "that moral goodness could be measured by the extent to which one's actions promoted the happiness of others," as Jefferson biographer William Sterne Randall puts it.[17] This suggests the populist point that overall prosperity (goodness, well-being, and happiness, including economic security) is a condition of economic social justice. "In the world of the Scottish Enlightenment," as George McGuire puts it, "society begins with the social contract. But no one can be expected to enter, of their own free will, into a contract that is to their own permanent disadvantage, let alone the disadvantage of their descendants. The rights of property are a part of the social contract and thus the ONLY justification for private property is that ALL members of the society are better off with the institution of private property than they would be without it."[18] Jefferson not only accepted this conditioning of private property upon public benefit, but he saw that the best public benefit would come from fair, direct access by all to private property (that is, productive resources or capital, in Locke's sense).

Jefferson insisted further that resources be held not in exploitive ownership but in accountable stewardship, or "usufruct," for future generations, reserved for private uses, but subject to democratic public accountability. Jefferson saw that the wide and secure distribution of wealth throughout society necessary to a just prosperity could be established and secured only by deliberately phasing out or diluting, through democratic means, politically unaccountable concentrations of wealth and power, including the money power. "I am conscious," wrote Jefferson to Madison in the same letter cited above, "that an equal division of property is impracticable, but the consequences of this enormous inequality producing so much misery to the bulk of mankind, legislators cannot invent too many devices for subdividing property, only taking care to let their subdivisions go hand in hand with the natural affections of the human mind."[19] Jefferson was acutely aware that one of the central "devices" for subdividing property legislators might "invent" was a genuinely accountable public system of money and credit. In his 1813 letter to John Wales Eppes, he notes the importance of "bills without interest, and without tax" issued by the Continental Congress, and expresses his hope that a system of fiat money and public credit may yet be established. He makes it clear in that letter that "Congress exclusively" should have the right to issue circulating paper, or money. Without an adequate public system of money and credit, Jefferson realized, the broader populist vision was probably doomed.

Although he seems to have seen land, particularly on the frontier, as the major resource to be guaranteed to all, Jefferson was very alive to the modern abuses of money, especially usury. In his June 24, 1813 to John Wayles Eppes, Jefferson also states:

> It is a wise rule and should be fundamental in a government disposed to cherish its credit, and at the same time to restrain the use of it within the limits of its faculties, "never to borrow a dollar without laying a tax in the same instant for paying the interest annually, and the principal within a given term; and to consider that tax as pledged to the creditors on the public faith." On such a pledge as this, sacredly observed, a government may

always command, on a reasonable interest, all the lendable money of their citizens, while the necessity of an equivalent tax is a salutary warning to them and their constituents against oppressions, bankruptcy, and its inevitable consequence, revolution. But the term of redemption must be moderate, and at any rate within the limits of their rightful powers."[20]

More dramatically, in his letter of May 28, 1816, to John Taylor, Jefferson states: "And I sincerely believe, with you, that banking establishments are more dangerous than standing armies; and that the principle of spending money to be paid by posterity, under the name of funding, is but swindling futurity on a large scale."[21]

It was Jefferson, more than anyone else, who forged the framework of American populism by uniting his call for distribution of wealth through land and some kind of public credit with a call for radical, direct democracy. Jefferson connected the issue of the wide distribution of money commanding wealth with the issue of direct democracy through his scheme of "ward republics." He gives us not only the idea of a national currency and public credit, but a blueprint for confederated democratic local assemblies. He realized early on that the American revolution was seriously incomplete politically as well as economically. To the end of his life he hoped that the United States might be refounded on a populist basis, with citizens as resource-owning independent producers controlling their system of money and credit and governing themselves through direct democracy in local communities, and indirectly through accountable representatives to broader levels of government. Jefferson developed his views on direct democracy in considerable detail (see the appendix), proposing a revolutionary scheme of local self-government by independent producers in what he called "ward republics," with higher levels of government accountable directly to them.[22]

We shall consider Jefferson's ward republics in more detail below. We find in his scheme a full-blown picture of what a confederated democracy might look like. Every local community would be a direct democracy, and direct democracies would be linked together by regional, national, and state representative bodies. He envisioned these democratic ward republics, or empowered local assemblies or town meetings, as the ultimate repositories of civic virtue and social justice. To this end, he proposed giving them and their accountable representatives power over broader levels of government, sufficient to ensure that the demands of the public good be respected, and that open access to resources be granted. A similar political scheme was endorsed by another populist, Tom Paine, in the second part of *The Rights of Man*, though only in summary outline, as follows: "Referring, then, to the original simple democracy, it affords the true data from which government on a large scale can begin. It is incapable of extension, not from its principle, but from the inconvenience of its form. . . . Retaining, then, democracy as the ground, and rejecting the corrupt systems of monarchy and aristocracy, the representative system naturally presents itself, remedying at once the defects of the simple democracy."[23]

***

Apart from their concern to distribute wealth widely through providing access to credit, American populists not only theorized about democracy but actually cultivated democratic practices. It is worth looking at some of these practices in detail. In much of New England, Pennsylvania, and in other colonies, local self-government was the rule not the exception. Pauline Meier, in "The Revolutionary Origin of the American Corporation," has written of the long battle to resist the incorporation of colonial cities such as Boston and Philadelphia, to preserve the direct democracy they then enjoyed against oligarchic systems of representative government advocated by proponents of incorporation.

> Boston was a "quasi-corporation," since it functioned as a body politic, exercising many of the powers of a corporation, but lacked a charter. Beginning in the seventeenth century, reformers repeatedly proposed that the town should be formally incorporated and replace its town meeting and board of selectmen with a mayor, aldermen, and common council like those of English municipal corporations. That proposal was, however, always defeated, sometimes in extraordinarily tumultuous town meetings, until 1822, when Boston finally . . . became a city. Colonial anticharter spokesmen opposed . . . the abandonment of their traditional democratic town meeting for a government under which only a relatively few qualified freemen would be enfranchised. They also preferred their old political system, in which "Rich and Poor Men" were "jumbled together in Town offices," to one that would probably confine power to the rich.[24]

Democratic critics of corporate power feared not only its oligarchic, aristocratic nature, but argued against its essential unfairness, its granting of exclusive political decision-making rights to some citizens (representatives) at the expense of others.

The reaction of men of substance and property to these early American democratic impulses, when they had to placate them, was to soften the steady loss of democracy by a series of reforms that foreshadowed later progressive responses to corporate power. In Maier's words: "Reformers wanted mayors as well as aldermen and common councilors elected, the principle of separation of powers respected, property-holding qualification for office and the vote abandoned, ward representation adjusted for population changes, and, in general, an urban political system less congenial to 'kingly government' and better adapted to 'the more modern and plain republican institutions of the present day.' In imposing such 'republican' reforms, legislatures firmly established their authority over municipal corporations."[25] These top-down reforms obscured the loss of direct democracy and did not compensate for it. The new monied oligarchy was not titled and hereditary as in Europe but nonetheless elitist, prone to suffer hubris, and just as concentrated in wealth and power. With the disppearance of democracy, where richer and poorer citizens shared power, there was no countervailing power left to challenge the new oligarchy of money. The loss of democracy went hand in hand with the loss of property rights. As Meier notes, it is not a loss that went unnoticed: "the Bank of Massachusetts, as Attorney General James Sullivan explained in *The Path to Riches* (1792), could issue loans with paper money beyond the value of its capital. As a result, it earned a higher rate of return on its assets than the 6 percent limit stipulated by law. . . . 'Whenever the laws . . . give to one man, or one order of men, an exclusive right to acquire property, or a greater and more advantageous opportunity to improve his or their talents, than is given to all,' Sullivan declared, 'there is just cause of complaint.'"[26]

In the interesting case of Vermont, in the face of a larger trend toward oligarchy, a populist community for a time found almost complete realization. Few Americans are aware that Vermont, the fourteenth state, admitted to the Union in 1791, was not a colony at all but a preexisting independent state spontaneously created by its residents who rejected the authority of neighboring colonies, particularly colonial New York, which had the strongest claim to its territory. It's a story worth telling. New York's claim was based on a 1664 British royal charter granting it the lands to the west of the Connecticut River north of Massachusetts. The same British royal government, however, subsequently recognized some authority over the lands of Vermont by the New England colonies of Connecticut, Massachusetts, and New Hampshire. In the 1740s the governor of New Hampshire, Benning Wentworth, began to sell land in what is now Vermont to settlers mostly from New England. Wentworth's "New Hampshire Grants" were sold cheaply, partly because they lay in disputed territory. They were bought by many settlers. New York's titles to the same lands were monopolized by absentee speculators, while Wentworth's cheap titles went mostly to actual residents who moved in and cleared the forests and started farms and towns.

Content with having sold the grants at a profit, Wentworth and New Hampshire showed little further interest in the lands west of the Connecticut River. New York, however, rejected the claims of those holding Wentworth's titles, insisting that its own titleholders were the true owners of the land. In 1770 Vermont settler Ethan Allen, having witnessed the validity of New Hampshire grants denied in a New York court, organized an independent militia to defend the claims of those holding New Hampshire Grants: the Green Mountain Boys. This militia, which later fought heroically in the Revolutionary War—capturing Fort Ticonderoga under Allen's leadership—did so not as part of the colonial union under the Continental Congress, but as independent allies of the American colonists. It was the military arm of the Vermont settlers. Allen's resistance to New York proved, in the end, the vehicle of Vermont independence, which was formally declared at the Westminster Convention in 1777, after the Green Mountain Boys drove off invading New Yorker posses and sheriffs in a series of small hit-and-run battles near Bennington, Vermont.[27]

What is relevant to us in this story is the radical democracy of the Vermont settlers. Unlike the neighboring American colonies, with their links to Europe and their increasing hierarchical power structures rooted in the commercial seaport centers, Vermonters in their hills were able to achieve widespread ownership of land as independent farmers and artisans without reckoning with an established wealthy elite in control of most resources, especially financial ones, and the government. Vermont came into existence from the ground up, wholly on the local level, farm by farm, and town by town—almost a textbook case of a free society founded in a state of nature. Without any superstructure of preestablished authority controlling land grants, Vermonters were able to realize the populist vision, reconciling freedom and property in a locally rooted radical democracy. Nearly all settlers were, or soon became, landowners, usually controlling less than three hundred acres. The economy operated on barter and personal credit, enforced by local courts presided over by locally elected judges and constituted by juries of local citizens. Chronic debtors ultimately had to forfeit real property, which functioned as reserve wealth in place of gold or currency (some Vermont coins were minted in the 1780s).

The center of life and the ultimate sovereign authority in Vermont was the town meeting, open to all resident adult males, where all aspects of public life were debated and decided. As in ancient Athens, meetings were lively and occasionally contentious; officials seldom held office for more than a term. Official positions of authority were discounted; and the officers of the local militia were elected. This radical democracy obviated the need for the traditional separation of powers. Separation of powers as normally conceived is designed to check each of the major branches of government—legislative, executive, and judicial—by providing recourse to any one of them against the others. It was developed by Madison and other founders as a way of controlling oligarchy while avoiding democracy. But it also has the less noticed effect of confirming a considerable amount of unaccountable power in each branch of government (and its divisions). By contrast, a decentralized system of local democracies provided for another kind of separation of power, its breakup into numerous local governments. The basis of Vermont democracy, made clear in the works of Ethan Allen, is the doctrine of natural rights (not revealed religion or state authority). The essential natural rights for Allen, as for Phaleas, are the rights of each individual to freedom *and* property.

As Michael A. Bellesiles puts it in *Revolutionary Outlaws*:

> Vermont's constitution [of 1777] demands attention for the way it lived up to its theoretical assertions, creating the most democratic structure of its time. It clearly established and protected certain basic rights: freedom of speech, print, and public assembly, a modified freedom of religion, the right to a fair and open trial before a jury, and the people's right to form new governments as they saw fit. . . . The state's voters controlled every branch of government, electing the state's executive officers and judges, as well as representatives to the unicameral legislature. Vermont failed to institute a separation of the branches of government. . . . The governor and council of Vermont could not veto legislation. . . . To maintain civic participation, the constitution required public legislative sessions and forbade the passage of any bill into law the same year it was proposed, mandating its printing for the public's information. . . . A septennial Council of Censors was to review all legislative and executive acts to ensure that the constitution was being fulfilled. . . . The

Council of Censors could amend the constitution by calling a popularly elected convention allowing "posterity the same privileges of choosing how they would be governed" without resort to "revolution or bloodshed."

Bellesiles then adds the crucial point: "Vermont's leadership did not seek the approval of the people as an undifferentiated mass. Sovereignty lay in the distinct townships, which held the 'unalienable and indefeasible right to reform, alter, or abolish government, in such manner as shall be, by that community, judged most conducive to the public weal.'" Finally, "Vermont's Declaration of Rights proclaimed 'that private Property ought to be subservient to public uses.' . . . And to make certain that the state never got out of hand, the Declaration of Rights stipulated that the people reserved the right of review over every action of the state and its police." As Bellesiles nicely puts it: "The people of Vermont interacted with their state government through their community, not as isolated individuals."[28]

Here was grassroots democracy, or community-based democracy, in actual practice. It was democratic communities that were represented at broader levels, *not* individuals, a fundamental distinction that separates confederalized democracy from our misrepresentative government. Each community or town with less than eighty free citizens got one representative to the unicameral state legislature, or general assembly, and towns over eighty got two representatives (the largest town had less than two thousand in population). The Windsor Convention, which ratified the existence of Vermont, had fifty delegates from thirty-one towns. Vermont may be the only non-kinship example of a system of direct representation grafted onto local assemblies, namely, the combination of direct local democracy with accountable representative bodies, something Jefferson envisioned and Paine thought actually happened, or would happen, throughout the United States.

Vermont, we should not be surprised, was unable to maintain the radical degree of democracy it developed in relative isolation. If it had supported Shay's Rebellion in Massachusetts in the 1780s, it might have sparked a second American revolution, this time directed not against the economic elites of London but those of the American coastal cities. And it might have preserved its own radical democracy. In return, however, for considering an offer of statehood from the United States, the Vermont legislators by a narrow vote rejected Shay's overtures, and Allen, who had been offered command of a revolutionary army by Shay, elected to stay in retirement at his farm.[29] Under pressure, Vermont caved in, and gained symbolic recognition from the top down in 1791 as the fourteenth state, from a national government and federal constitution seriously in conflict with the principles of its democracy. It conceded that its experiment in democracy would henceforth be limited, and no threat to the larger monied interests of the land in their increasingly successful attempts to disassociate free individuals from their property. Still, Vermont has retained a degree of democratic spirit absent in most other states of the union, a spirit reflected in its election to the United States Congress in recent years of its only independent member, and in a number of environmental, civil, and other reforms, as well as in a continued strong tradition of town meetings.

* * *

Although widespread access by most people to resources, particularly land, created in early America the populist conditions necessary for genuine democracy, which indeed blossomed in many places and approached fulfillment in independent Vermont, antidemocratic interests, though vigorously opposed, gradually gained the upper hand over the course of the nineteenth century. The prodemocracy antifederalists and their populist successors were unable in the end to establish the link between the spontaneous democracy of local communities and the higher levels of government. This failure to develop a scheme for confederating communities and states into more inclusive, accountable structures proved fatal to the future of democracy in America. State and federal governments came to be controlled mostly by the concentrated property interests centered in the urban commercial centers: Boston, New York, Philadelphia, and other cities. State constitutions, like the national constitution, increasingly came to follow the aristocratic Madisonian principle of large election districts, with its mass of undifferentiated voters, ensuring that only the rich or those funded by the rich could afford to run for office. The representation of thousands and later millions of voters by individual persons had the effect of disenfranchising local communities, the strongholds of democracy. A state legislator or congressman, by playing the game of divide and conquer, could thwart the organized efforts of democratic communities to promote their interests. His first alleigance, if he was to survive, would be to his coalition of supporters.

The Jacksonian era brought greater political participation in the form of expanding the number of those eligible to vote; but there was no movement to strengthen local democracy or to make elected officials represent local communities. Mass election districts were confirmed as the units of representative government, leaving local communities isolated and unrepresented. The increased importance of political parties in the Jacksonian era did provide opportunities for enhanced grassroots activity, particularly with urban political clubs, but the parties remained one step removed from the actual process of government, and in a sense deflected the democratic impulse to the side. Yet populist attitudes remained strong. Probably the most important instance of resistance to "the money power" in antebellum America was Andrew Jackson's 1832 veto of the bill that would have renewed the charter of the Bank of the United States. Jackson famously promoted political participation by the common man, as well as public control over the money system. In his veto message of the bill that would have extended the national bank, he wrote:

> Congress have established a mint to coin money and passed laws to regulate the value thereof. The money so coined, with its value so regulated, and such foreign coins as Congress may adopt are the only currency known to the Constitution. But if they have other power to regulate the currency, it was conferred to be exercised by themselves and not to be transferred to a corporation. If the bank be established for that purpose, with a charter unalterable without its consent, Congress have parted with their power for a term of years, during which the Constitution is a dead letter. It is neither necessary nor proper to transfer its legislative power to such a bank, and therefore unconstitutional."[30]

The bank, described by historian Jack Beatty as "an 80 percent privately owned franchise corporation awarded the keeping of government deposits and protected from competition by government fiat,"[31] was a key institution of "the money power." Its defeat was perhaps the greatest political victory ever achieved by populist forces in the United States.

But the populists won only a battle and not the war. The private financial interests, smarting over their defeat over the national bank, may in retaliation have provoked and certainly benefited from the crash of 1837, which led to what was perhaps the most serious economic depression before 1929. Previous to the crash, large capital outlays required for massive projects such as the Erie Canal were typically financed largely by taxpayers through state-sponsored corporations, while private capital remained skeptical of such untested large projects. These government projects successfully provided widespread and low-cost public benefit in the form of cheap transportation for the products of farmers and other small producers. One of the most significant results of the post-1837 depression was to undermine these public corporations. As Jack Beatty puts it: "With their tax receipts plummeting, state and local governments were left holding a profoundly empty bag. They could neither afford to finish the improvements nor pay interest on the tens of millions borrowed to make them. Five states defaulted on interest; one on principal. Publically financed improvements fell from public favor."[32] As a result, an opening was created for private corporations, who now appreciated the profits to be made from large-scale projects. The subsequent railroad boom gave an important impetus to large private corporations, which worked increasingly with the private financial interests of Wall Street, while the idea of publically funded and accountable public works remained discredited. Where government support was sought, it was on terms favorable to private interests.

Populists continued to fight back. In the 1840s populist opposition flared up in the Anti-Rent Wars of upstate New York. According to one Anti-Rent tract, "In all free governments, it is essential that the people themselves be free. They cannot be free unless independent. . . . To be completely sovereign, they must individually be the lords of the soil they occupy, and hold it freely, subject to no superior but the people themselves."[33] The difficulty, as Reeve Huston goes on to note in *Land and Freedom: Rural Society, Popular Protest, and Party Politics in Antebellum New York*, is that these rural populists failed to integrate the concerns of propertyless urban workers into their program. The Democratic Party, through which they tried to work, remained opposed to their populist impulses. As Huston puts it: "the anti-renters directed the Jeffersonian tradition against existing concentrations of property, raising fears of an all-powerful state disturbing existing social relations and trampling on the rights of property. If successful, they might set a precedent that could be used against slave property; their movement thus posed a potential threat to intersectional harmony within both parties. Nor did it help that most landlords were Democrats."[34]

Like earlier populist revolts, including Shay's Rebellion, the Anti-Rent resistance was eventually put down. With the gradual decline of Jeffersonian America in the course of the nineteenth century, the very real democracy apparent in Vermont and elsewhere in the old colonies turned out to be the exception, not the rule. Ignorant as Madison and his compatriots were of the degree of success and relative stability of direct democracy in Athens, and even in Rome—and as most political thinkers since have remained—he and other early leaders of the new republic remained prone to a fear of democracy and intent on developing not only the separation of powers (following Montesquieu), but also representative government as a "cure" for the ills of democracy. The idea was to use representation not to reflect the voice of the *demos*, but to substitute for it. There would be no connection between local assemblies, such as town meetings, and broader representative governments. Election districts would be established essentially as fiefdoms, prizes to be won by competition among regional notables for passive ratification by voters. The various communities among which those voters were distributed could safely be ignored. As Ellen Meiksins Wood puts it in "Demos vs. 'We the People'": "the point is not simply that direct democracy has been replaced by representation. The point is rather that the form of representation espoused by Hamilton, et. al. was intended not to give the demos a voice but to speak in its stead."[35] The Roman popular assemblies were democratic bodies open to all citizens, as we have seen, though limited in their powers. But even the most "democratic" of the new national institutions of the United States, the House of Representatives, was not at all a democratic body, but a representative one in the elitist Federalist sense, a kind of vulgar senate.

Although the new United States of the 1780s was probably smaller than ancient republican Rome in population if not territory, Madison and his colleagues held that its legislative bodies would have to be representative and not democratic. Madison reserved the word *democracy* for a government in which the citizens "assemble and administer the government in person," and the word *republic* for "a government in which the scheme of representation takes place."[36] Madison thought that the number of representatives in proportion to their constituents ought not to be so small as to encourage "the cabals of the few," nor so large as to encourage the "confusion of a multitude." He writes: "As each representative will be chosen by a greater number of citizens in a large than in the small republic, it will be more difficult for unworthy candidates to practice with success the vicious arts by which elections are too often carried."[37] That even more unworthy candidates might practice with even greater success the devious arts by which mass elections are too often carried—the arts of propaganda and vote buying—was a possibility that Madison and the Federalists left unmentioned. The constitutional system he largely created has been taken over by the very "cabals" he feared, for there is no contradiction between the cabals of the few and the confusions of a multitude. It is in fact in the interest of the former to foster the latter.

Again and again populist resistance to private finance came up against the antidemocratic Madisonian system, where the special interests were able to control the political process to frustrate the kind of fundamental reforms advocated by populists.

Populism had yet another cross to bear. In nineteenth-century America, populist ideas tragically became entangled with the sorry history of slavery and racism. Although Paine was no slaveholder and opposed slavery and was probably as free of racism as anyone of his time, other populists—most conspicuously Jefferson, the slaveholder—were compromised by these issues. Yet Jefferson, unlike Aristotle, fought slavery on some occasions, and ambivalent though he may have been about the capacities and status of blacks, he recognized their equal claim to democratic rights under his universalizing logic. Doubting the prospects for their assimilation in white society, he called for their resettlement as "free and independent people" in some separate land.[38] Jefferson failed to free his own slaves, except for a few, or to take his own hand to the plow of Monticello like one of the small freehold agriculturalists he apotheosized so eloquently as the essence of a free society. For him to have done away with slavery would have meant not only his own but his family's economic ruin, a fate he choose to avoid. In the event, the persistence of slavery in the United States in conjunction with the anti-Federalist and later republican and populist traditions allowed the language of democracy to be co-opted by generations of reactionary racists, mostly but not all from the South, who insisted on states' rights no longer as a key item in a system of confederal accountability to local democratic assemblies, but mainly as a stopgap against the intrusion of a central government increasingly hostile to slavery and, later, to the Jim Crow segregationist culture.

The American radicalism that crystallized around Jefferson and his successors, both North and South, postulated direct democracy and access to resources, though in practice only for white males; it was a radicalism suspicious of representative government, and opposed to what we would now call corporate power, and other concentrations of property. There is evidence that northern Jeffersonian democrats, linked economically to the South through the cotton trade, infused the new German and Irish immigrants in New York with their antiblack racism.[39] When the antidemocratic Federalist party—the party of centralized representative government, of Hamilton, Adams, and others—evolved into the antislavery Republican Party, democrats found themselves outflanked. The result, decided by the Civil War, was the triumph of what might be called progressive antidemocracy, the two-party duopoly that freed the slaves, derailed democracy, and opened the path to corporate rule, to the plutocratic system that has endured down to the present.[40]

The founding fathers who wrote the Constitution structured a political economy favorable to corporate power, and a monetary and financial system designed to promote the transfer of resources and assets from debtors to creditors, from the many to the few. When Jeffersonian democrats proved unable to free themselves of the incubus of slavery, their party was fatally split. After the Civil War, the Democratic Party had to accept the key assumptions of the Republican Party to survive, and give up any dream of direct democracy in a republic of independent producers. It choose to "work within" the new plutocratic dispensation, accepting its policies and hoping to modify but not overturn them. Indeed, Democrats steadily moved to endorse state power as a remedy to corporate power, just as Republicans steadily moved away from earlier Federalist reliance on state power toward libertarian, laissez-faire, antigovernment doctrines—a little noticed but fundamental reversal of views. Modern Republicans and Democrats nonetheless follow the same prorich policies; they differ perhaps only in that Republicans don't feel guilty about it and Democrats do. The former are more willing to take private interests at face value; the latter accept the centrality of such interests, but recognize abuses they hope to modify. By joining the new plutocratic establishment as the loyal opposition after the Civil War, the Democratic Party sacrificed populism—democracy and the personal right to resources—as the price of its political and military defeat, and has been doing so ever since. The Republicans, not dependent on the slave economy, were able to denounce slavery without personal penalty and gain the moral high ground; hence, perhaps, their lack of guilt. The result was not only the emancipation of the slaves, a fundamental social breakthrough, limited though it was in practice, but the repression of democracy, the rise of corporate power, and the loss of any immediate hope for a populist political economy in the United States. Even the high-water mark of the postbellum Democratic Party—Franklin Delano Roosevelt's New Deal—did not overcome these limitations.

***

Combining direct democracy with representative government is the structural challenge of politics, in the populist view. It has yet to be addressed in practice on a large scale—examples such as early Vermont notwithstanding—yet the populist democratic promise is worth considering in detail. The modern solution was suggested, albeit in passing, by

Montesquieu in *The Spirit of the Laws*, as noted in the previous chapter. Thinking of ancient confederations, he argued that local democracies can find security only by associating together into a "confederate republic . . . a kind of assemblage of societies, that constitute a new one, capable of increasing by means of further associations, till they arrive at such a degree of power as to be able to provide for the security of the whole body."[41] In the last chapter we also considered David Hume's detailed presentation of a confederal system in his essay *The Idea of a Perfect Commonwealth*. In *The Rights of Man*, Tom Paine succinctly develops the idea of confederal democracy, anticipating Jefferson's scheme of ward republics:

> The case, therefore, is not that a republic cannot be extensive, but that it cannot be extensive on the simple democratical form; and the question naturally represents itself, What is the best form of government for conducting the res-publica, or the public business of a nation, after it becomes too extensive and populous for the simple democratical form? . . . Simple democracy was society governing itself without the aid of secondary means. By ingrafting representation upon democracy, we arrive at a system of government capable of embracing and confederating all the various interests and every extent of territory and population; and that also with advantages as much superior to hereditary government, as the republic of letters is to hereditary literature. It is on this system that the American government is founded. It is representation ingrafted upon democracy. It has fixed the form by a scale parallel in all cases to the extent of the principle. What Athens was in miniature, America will be in magnitude.[42]

Paine does not reject the "simple democratical form" that characterizes local assemblies; he rather presupposes its continuance. His concern is to blend or "ingraft" democratic local assemblies with an accountable system of broader, representative bodies, not to replace the former with the latter as Madison advocated and which came to pass. Paine's view was the vision of the radical anti-Federalists, who did not prevail, as Paine in his enthusiasm thought they had. Having left America for revolutionary France, his hopes for the American Revolution continued to run high, even as the Federalist reaction of the 1790s set in in the United States. Only later, after his return to America, did he appreciate the degree to

which the Constitution frustrated and ultimately denied the kind of confederal democracy widely practiced in early America.

The whole point of a confederated democracy is to insure that
"higher" levels of government remain accountable to "lower" levels (with
recallable representatives, etc.), while at the same time—in a kind of
positive feedback effect—the "higher" levels provide the "lower" levels
with the minimum procedural standards necessary to check abberant
local dysfunction. Power flows up from the bottom, then down again, in
a kind of ladder of recirculation as described by Hume. Imagine local
assemblies composed of citizens; county assemblies composed of representatives from local assemblies; state assemblies or legislatures composed of representatives from county assemblies; and a national assembly
or Congress composed of representatives from state legislatures. At the
foundation of this system, in the populist view, stands the local
assembly—the public meeting in each neighborhood. The distinguishing
feature of the local assembly is that it is not a representative but a primary
body, a collection of community residents, meeting officially as citizens,
open to all, a town meeting. In the local assembly, citizens enjoy full and
direct rights of political participation, with the assembly functioning in
effect as a committee of the whole for the community. No adult resident
of any precinct would be denied any right of political participation consistent with parliamentary procedures: voting, speaking, making and
seconding motions, nominating, being nominated, raising points of order, and so forth. In a number of remarkable letters in his later years,
Jefferson developed just this kind of a system of grassroots, bottom-up
democracy, based on what he called local "ward republics," his term for
neighborhood assemblies, or town meetings. Jefferson's detailed comments flesh out the system outlined by Montesquieu and Paine; and he
expands on Hume by insisting that the local level of government is a direct
democracy, not a representative body. Such a system—the whole series
of his letters on bottom-up democracy is presented in the appendix
to this work, along with a projection of what his system might look
like in modern America—he thought essential to completing the
American Revolution.

Consider here just a couple of these letters, first one written by
Jefferson to Samuel Kercheval on July 12, 1816:

> The organization of our county administrations may be thought
> more difficult. But follow principle, and the knot unties itself.
> Divide the counties into wards of such size as that every citizen
> can attend, when called on, and act in person. Ascribe to them

the government of their wards in all things relating to themselves exclusively. A justice, chosen by themselves, in each, a
constable, a military company, a patrol, a school, the care of
their own poor, their own portion of the public roads, the choice
of one or more jurors to serve in some court, and the delivery,
within their own wards, of their own votes for all elective officers
of higher sphere, will relieve the county administration of nearly
all its business, will have it better done, and by making every
citizen an acting member of the government, and in the offices
nearest and most interesting to him, will attach him by his
strongest feelings to the independence of his country, and its
republican constitution. The justices thus chosen by every ward,
would constitute the county court, would do its judiciary business, direct roads and bridges, levy county and poor rates, and
administer all the matters of common interest to the whole
country. These wards, called townships in New England, are the
vital principle of their governments, and have proved themselves the wisest invention ever devised by the wit of man for
the perfect exercise of self-government, and for its preservation.
We should thus marshal our government into, 1, the general
federal republic, for all concerns foreign and federal; 2, that of
the State, for what relates to our own citizens exclusively; 3, the
county republics, for the duties and concerns of the county; and
4, the ward republics, for the small, and yet numerous and
interesting concerns of the neighborhood; and in government,
as well as in every other business of life, it is by division and
subdivision of duties alone, that all matters, great and small, can
be managed to perfection. And the whole is cemented by giving
to every citizen, personally, a part in the administration of the
public affairs.[43]

Jefferson outlined the relationship between local direct democracies and
representative assemblies in an 1816 letter to I. H. Tiffany. Jefferson, like
Paine, makes it clear not only that the word *republic* for him means a
system in which representatives are directly accountable to local assemblies, but that such a system ought to be established in America. Speaking
of the ancient Greeks, Jefferson wrote: "They knew no medium between
a democracy (the only pure republic) and an abandonment of themselves
to an aristocracy or a tyranny independent of the people. It seems not to
have occurred that where the citizens cannot meet to transact their business in person, they alone have the right to choose the agents who shall

transact it; and in this way a republican, or popular government, of the second grade of purity, may be exercised over any extent of country. The full experiment of government democratical, but representative, was and still is reserved for us."[44] (The ancient confederacies are passed over by Jefferson, perhaps because they never, or only partly, developed into the fully functioning representational governments they seemed to suggest.)

We know that city-state Greek assemblies and New England town meetings—our most familiar examples of direct democracy—were far from wholly inclusive bodies, yet as far as they went they embodied the ideal of democracy. In their broadest expressions, they consisted, particularly in their earlier periods, in large qualifying populations of economically more or less independent individuals (usually male heads of households) carrying on the business of government directly in open committees of the whole according to procedures more or less like those described in Henry M. Robert's *Rules of Order*.[45] In a genuine democratic face-to-face assembly, any citizen can take the floor, state opinions, introduce business, make and second motions, amend motions, nominate candidates, vote, raise points of order, and otherwise generally and repeatedly and fully participate in the free and open proceedings. These standards of self-democracy Jefferson applied to his ward republics, or local assemblies, and they would apply within the representative bodies built up on the basis of local assemblies. Almost nowhere today do citizens practice this kind of self-democracy. Almost nowhere do they govern themselves simply as citizens by meeting directly in a committee of the whole.

America still awaits its populist democratic apotheosis in a confederal system. More recent efforts in this direction have not been lacking. An interesting thought experiment seeking to work out the details of confederal democracy, echoing Paine and Jefferson, can be found in Frank Bryan and John McClaughry's *The Vermont Papers*.[46] They outline how one small state—again, Vermont—might be entirely reorganized politically on the basis of local assemblies confederated together. On a broader scale, Gary Hart, former U.S. senator and one-time presidential candidate, in his 2002 book *Restoration of the Republic: The Jeffersonian Ideal in 21st-Century America*, advocates the application of the "Jeffersonian pyramid of republics" to modern America.[47] Hart, despairing of "the Hamiltonian vision in the form of a corrupt national state,"[48] aims to introduce Jefferson's confederal system to a wider audience as an alternative to the Madisonian representative system. His work is perhaps the first to place Jefferson's system—otherwise noted by scholars more or less in passing—at the center of an effort to rethink the structure of

American politics. Hart's emphasis is on the benefits of civic virtue that ward republics would encourage. The business of ward republics, however, seems to remain primarily local in his view, with the higher levels of Madsonian representative government left intect: "For democratic republicanism to flourish and to assume greater influence in citizen self-governance, it is not required for federal authority to diminish."[49] In Hart's view, ward republics would invigorate citizenship by providing a space for its public realization, but would remain disconnected from higher levels of government. The larger question Jefferson, Paine, and other populists posed concerned the role of local assemblies as the basis of broader levels of accountable representational government in place of the kind of centralized authority they already recognized and feared, and would no doubt be shocked by today.

***

To appreciate real or full democracy, we need to understand the faux-democracy under which we live. With the interesting but highly limited exception of local town meetings still functioning in New England, America is ruled on all levels by representative bodies closed to full public participation with little or no grassroots accountability. We have broadened citizen access to participation, to be sure, successively including all males (whether propertied or not), slaves and their descendents, immigrants, and, lastly, women, but at the same time the scope of citizenship has been kept surprisingly narrow. We have restricted the nature of participation from direct and full access by all citizens to all decision-making functions to the occasional and very limited function of periodic voting in mass elections. At the grassroots level in our misrepresentative system you can often (but not always) watch the proceedings and sometimes be recognized to speak, at least at the local level, but otherwise participation is not allowed. What you cannot do is set an agenda, introduce business, vote on motions, and so on. Our governments—local, state, and national—are literally closed oligarchies established through so-called free elections based on "popular sovereignty" mediated by political parties. The only participatory right held by the ordinary modern citizen (in contrast to a citizen of ancient Athens, or an early New England town, or a member of a kinship tribe) is the meager (indeed, literally self-alienating) right to vote for others to represent him or her.

The right to vote is not currently exercised by ordinary citizens in any actual deliberative assembly, but only on those rare special occasions (namely, elections) set apart from government, when prechosen lists of candidates (and occasional issues) are presented to the citizens for a passive yes or no judgment. Voting has become the title and badge of modern representative governments, widely called "democracies," even though it is profoundly divorced from the actual face-to-face government that defines genuine democracy, and is hardly efficacious without the other rights of direct participation found in a committee of the whole. Voting in the modern sense is largely, if not wholly, meaningless as a political act. Indeed, delegating one's political rights to someone else, to a representative, is the very antithesis of democracy, unless that elected representative be directly accountable to constituents on a face-to-face basis. Only in the crudest and most desperate sense—as in the opportunity to choose the "lesser evil"—does voting serve as the roughest of checks on otherwise unaccountable government. It is true that anyone can register in any established political party, or try to start a party of their own, or write in anyone's name at the polls, or collect signatures to put candidates and (sometimes) issues before the voters, and so on. None of this, however, adds up to anything remotely close to democracy; these important but very limited rights serve mainly as escape valves for venting frustrations while securing the imprimateur of public legitimacy.

Representative government and voting as we know them not only have nothing to do with democracy, they actually stand in opposition to it. As Ellen Meiksins Wood points out in her essay "Democracy: An Idea of Ambiguous Ancestry," the novelty of the American idea, particularly in the Federalist form adopted in the Constitution, fosters "not the exercise of political power but its relinquishment, its transfer to others, its alienation."[50] She is acute on the shift in the modern meaning of the word *democracy*: "The identification of democracy with the formal and procedural principles of 'toleration,' the rule of law, civil liberties, constitutionalism, 'limited' or 'responsible' government, representation, 'pluralism,' and so on—in place of its essential association with popular power—has, if anything, become dominant."[51] The perverse genius of the American system, Wood goes on to assert, is to substitute a sort of human rights paternalism for democracy. The people give up their actual right to direct participation in government in return for the mostly symbolic privilege of electing representatives pledged to honor human rights. Real representation, by contrast, must be an "ingrafting" to democracy, as Paine put it, accountable to the democratic grassroots, and an extension of it, and not a substitute for it. Representatives ought to be understood as instruments of the citizens' will, and so directly accountable to fully democratic local assemblies.

At best, we find in our system a recognition of universal human rights and the theoretical right to struggle for democracy, mostly for the symbolism, not the substance, of popular sovereignty. In America, as in most other so-called modern democracies, to actually get into government it is necessary to get elected or appointed to public office. Relatively few citizens have the leisure or resources necessary to contemplate such an ambition. Even where it is most possible, at the local level, only a handful out of hundreds or thousands can hope to be elected. Those not elected to office are reduced to being petitioners, even with their own local government. As a result government on all levels stands apart from and opposed to its own citizens. It should not be necessary, in a genuine democracy, to run at all for local office. Citizenship itself should be the embodiment of local office. Any citizen should be able to go to local precinct meetings armed with full rights of participation, already, in every sense, a public official, if he or she chooses to to do so. But few such local assemblies, or Jeffersonian ward republics, exist, and none that do send representatives to broader bodies in the accountable, bottom-up sense populists insist upon.

Elections at all levels of American government are almost always ratifications of slates of candidates privately preselected by largely self-perpetuating party committees. Candidates for any significant office require large sums of money and a political organization to run effectively. The parties—Republicans, Democrats, and the minor parties—provide both. Party membership is normally open to all comers, but decision making is strongly conditioned by the wishes of large contributors and party "insiders" devoted to their service. Freedom of speech, since the Supreme Court *Buckley v. Valleo* decision of 1976, has been confused with the right to spend unlimited monies to advertise any particular point of view, thus ensuring that political debate is mainly controlled by private interests who are big enough drown out any opposition. Political struggles—for example, between conservatives and liberals—reflect the struggles between various competing special interests, national and regional, and not the "will" of the people. Rarely has there been a place in recent American politics for the general interest; rarely can we find today any binding nonpartisan forum in which the people and/or their direct representatives can meet, discuss, and act upon the challenges confronting their communities.

Democracy cannot be reduced to the pursuit of self-interest, individual happiness, consumerism, or nationalism. Democracy is not a naive illusion; nor is it the symbolic but all-too-hollow right to vote; nor is it somehow part of the marketplace. Democracy is the deliberate pursuit of the public good by citizens themselves and their direct representatives, in binding, face-to-face public assemblies conducted openly as committees of the whole and by subcommittees. It is at once a practical necessity of decent public life, the precondition of public virtue, and a path to self-knowledge and liberation. To liberate itself from the evils of special interests, corporate influence, usury, greed, and traditional power-brokered government, modern society in America and elsewhere where "the money power" rules need's to radically reform and democratize its political system, its government, at all levels. The public realm—never very large in our pseudorepresentative system of government—has very nearly eroded away in recent decades. In the early twenty-first century, as people increasingly retreat to their private affairs, less and less is left to bind Americans together as one people. The idea of America has become largely a negative idea, a vacuum to be filled by the hidden hand of selective self-interest. The danger is one of anarchy, of an out-of-control struggle of individuals and groups bent on survival and success for themselves at the expense, if need be, of anyone or everyone else.

Democratizing America, by contrast, depends upon the reestablishment of a common cultural realm, a physical place to cultivate civic virtue, a space for Americans to come together as citizens of the same community, and to take up their common responsibility for their own public decisions. Democratic grassroots government would provide a natural school for civic virtue. A public realm where individuals and special interests are subject to the direct judgments of fellow citizens in the service of common goals would help check excessive ambitions and destructive interests. The public becomes a mob only when its oppressions and resentments at perceived elitist rule boil over. But this cannot happen if elites do not rule, if such a perception seems preposterous, if the public openly and democratically sets the rules, and has the opportunity to develop democratic practices into a stable and tested set of institutions.

To contemplate genuine democracy is to reveal the depths of antidemocracy we tolerate. Far from being aware of the liberties that should be ours, we are largely ignorant of them. Americans think they are free whereas they are lucky, for the most part, to be left alone. Even today, the largess of a rich continent and relative geographical isolation helps to temper the struggle for power and to soften its worse abuses. Americans are free more by circumstances than by virtue of their institutions, although the principles of human rights enshrined in the Declaration of Independence and the Bill of Rights provide valuble standards of public behavior. In its separation of powers, its separation of church and state, its enunciation of human rights, its respect for private property, and in its basis in popular sovereignty, the American constitutional system was a vast improvement over its feudal and monarchical predecessors. It remains, however, seriously and perhaps fatally incomplete in its deliberate antidemocracy, leaving too many opportunities for gross concentrations of wealth and power at the expense of the general public and the environment. Without being rooted in direct democratic practice, our constitutional protections and liberties will continue to remain vulnerable to serious abuse and even rollback into tyranny.

***

Democracy for all, as I have been insisting, is only one side of the populist coin—the other being property for all. Populist views on the wide distribution of property were held not only by visionaries, agrarians, and small producers, but by some elitist thinkers as well. Francis Bowen of Harvard College pursued broadly populist themes in his widely read *American Political Economy*, published in 1870. But like most other nineteenth-century Jeffersonians, he advanced no comprehensive remedy to forestall the concentration of capital in the hands of the investing few at the expense of the laboring many, much as he deplored it. Bowen wrote in an era when it was still possible to believe in what he called "our disposition to manage our own affairs in our own town-meetings, and there to allot the greatest trust to him who is distinguished above all others by this very American trait, this disposition to toil, and to save be his race or parentage what it may."[52] He is alive to the populist conviction that any laboring person has the right to such capital as necessary to sustain his or her labor. He is very clear about the importance of a publicly controlled monetary system, accountable to a democratic government, as an alternative to a privately controlled monetary system, accountable only to private financial interests: "I insist that the whole people, who consent thus to use paper instead of specie, are entitled to the whole profit or saving thereby effected; that the Banks have no claim whatever to this profit, and do not need it; and that the people ought also to be fully protected against loss by fluctuation in the value of this paper, or by failure to redeem it on demand in coin or bullion. These ends can be secured only through its issue, under proper precautions, by the government for the common benefit."[53] Bowen is also alive to the evils of what he calls "the vicious methods of the English funding system."[54] But he offers no clear prescription to deal with these issues, and offers only vague hopes for public credit publicly controlled.

If Bowen had known of the work of an earlier American thinker, Edward Kellogg, he would have found a clear prescription for dealing with the vexed questions of currency, banking, and so forth. Indeed,

Kellogg was a remarkable populist, far too neglected then and now, a thinker who took the problem of providing capital to labor perhaps further than any other populist thinker before or since. We shall examine his work in some detail. Kellogg was a New York City businessman who in the years before the Civil War developed a theory of money designed to produce a system of wealth distribution, mainly in two works, *Labor and Other Capital*, published in 1849, and *A New Monetary System*, posthumously published in 1861. Though Kellogg is perhaps the most neglected of nineteenth-century American populist thinkers, in the decades after his death in 1858 he was for a time important enough to be an inspiration for the greenback and populist movements. According to historian Mark A. Lause, Abraham Lincoln "had his own copy of Kellogg's book, *Labor and Capital* [*sic*] advocating the government issuance of paper currency as a just means of redistributing wealth, and he corresponded with the author's son-in-law."[55] What if anything came of this contact, we know not.

His book *A New Monetary System*, largely a restatement and expansion of *Labor and Other Capital*, was edited by his daughter and published after his death and appears to be his most comprehensive work, and I shall rely on it in what follows. In *A New Monetary System* Kellogg makes the populist point connecting property for all with democracy for all by invoking, as the link between them, the nature of money and interest: "If the people desire a more rapid centralization of wealth and power, and to increase the depression and poverty of the producers, let them annul all Usury Laws, and they will be sure of success. But if they wish to perpetuate a democratic government, and elevate the producing classes, they must reduce the present power of money, or it will surely make this nation a practical aristocracy, even though we professedly continue to be a democracy."[56]

Central to Kellogg's thinking is his insistence on public—meaning democratic—control over the monetary system. His solution to the populist problem of circulating capital is to be found in fundamental monetary reform. To understand it, we need to be clear about our current monetary system. In it the creation of money is a monopoly held by a privately controlled central banking system—the Federal Reserve—following the pattern set by the Bank of England. The government borrows back the money (with interest paid by taxpayers) that it allowed the private banks it sanctioned to create in the first place. This kind of modern money is produced on the condition that it function as a debt to be repaid to its issuers by its users, with the income going to private banks and other lenders. We have a system of fully developed private fiat money issued for public purposes, for private profit, through interest charges, with central banks and their client banks as the principal beneficiaries. It doesn't have to be this way. Private money controlled by bankers, Kellogg argues, can just as easily be replaced with public money controlled by democratic governments. We could decentralize the monetary system and put the power to exercise it and the wealth it can create into the hands of citizens. We could replace the private top-down money system with a public bottom-up money system, and thereby make possible, as we shall see, a satisfaction of populist claims in a novel way.

These ideas, anticipated by earlier populists, were systematically developed by Kellogg. His work remains, as far as I know, the best and fullest statement we have for a democratic system of public credit. The economic situation he describes, writing before the Civil War, has only expanded and intensified in our own day: "Our government professes to establish laws for the benefit of the whole people; and such laws, if justly administered, should secure to every individual a fair equivalent for his labor; yet probably half the wealth of the nation is accumulated in the possession of but about two and a half per cent. of the population, who to say the most, have not done more labor toward the production of the wealth than the average of the ninety-seven and a half per cent., among whom is distributed the other half of the wealth."[57] Kellogg traces the chronic maldistribution of wealth and attendant economic booms and busts neither to "overproduction," as was claimed even in his day by capitalists, nor to the forceful expropriation of labor, as claimed by socialists, but to something completely different: the monetary system, the rules of which ought to form "a national standard of value."[58] Kellogg (nearly a century before Soddy) identifies money as a national standard of value, literally like feet and yards and other such uniform measures (pounds, miles, gallons, etc.), money in some ways being the most general standard of them all. Kellogg is very clear that money is not to be confused with any commodity (e.g., gold or silver), that it is a legal creation, a binding definition, what the philosophers call a "performative act," maintained either by social consensus, or, in postkinship societies, by law. In other words, according to Kellogg, all money really is fiat money—that is, money by official sanction; even a commodity money like gold exists only because it is given the stamp of public approval, insofar as, say, gold coins (foreign or domestic) are legally accepted for the payment of debts and other transactions by common agreement.

Money for Kellogg has "four properties, or powers, viz.: power to represent value, power to measure value, power to accumulate value by interest, and power to exchange value."[59] The most important and problematic of these is the power to accumulate value by interest, a power that "is essential to the existence of money," he tells us, "for no one will exchange productive property for money that does not represent production."[60] The accumulation of interest is possible, he points out, only because of the legal obligation to pay back debts contracted according to some rate of interest. "Money," Kellogg tells us, "is valuable in proportion to its power to accumulate value by interest. A dollar which can be loaned for twelve per cent. interest, is worth twice as much as one that can be loaned for but six per cent., just as a railroad stock which will annually bring in twelve per cent., is worth twice as much as one that annually brings in six per cent."[61] He encapsulates the value of money very neatly according to the relative burden of repayment over time: "If the borrower . . . pay interest half yearly at the rate of seven per cent. per annum, he must double the lump in about ten years. If he pay interest half yearly at the rate of six per cent. per annum, he must double the lump in less than twelve years; at three per cent., in less than twenty-four years; and at one per cent., in about seventy years."[62] Kellogg here anticipates what has become a common accounting formula: "the rule of 72." If one divides 72 by the interest rate, one arrives at the number of years it takes for the investor to double his or her money. At 1 percent interest, it takes the investor 72 years, or a lifetime, to double his or her money; at 2 percent, it takes 36 years; at 3 percent, 23.5 years; at 4 percent, 18 years; at 5 percent, 14.4 years; at 6 percent, 12 years; at 7 percent, 10.3 years; at 8 percent, 9 years; at 9 percent, 8 years; at 10 percent, 7.2 years, and so on. At 20 percent interest—a rate actually seen in the United States in the late 1970s—it takes only 3.6 years to double one's money.

The rule of 72 dramatizes both the extraordinary gains and the extraordinary burdens generated by usurious interest rates. It makes plain that in real time it takes a lifetime for an investor to double his or her money—72 years—at a nominal or 1 percent interest rate. From the point of view of the borrower, however, the prospect for repaying a loan with a 1 percent or nominal interest rate is a burden eased by being stretched over a lifetime, and must seem less onerous than any higher rate. As rates rise, the time required to double the initial principal decreases exponentially, quickly compounding both the return to the lender and the burden on the borrower. If it costs $250,000 to build a house, and a builder takes out a loan for that amount for fifteen years at 6 percent—a common figure, rate, and term for mortgages in recent years in the United States—then to discharge his debt the borrower will in effect labor to repay approximately twice the value of the house over fifteen years. He or she will have paid over that period for the building of two houses in order to be able to own one.

Of course it does not take fifteen years to build a house, but perhaps only one year. At 6 percent for one year, the builder pays to the lender an extra $15,000. To break even (other costs aside) he or she must sell the new house at the end of the year for at least $265,000. The interest cost is passed on to the consumer, the purchaser of the new house, who is likely to take out a similar mortgage to pay for the house. The new basis, however, will be $265,000, and more if the builder is to make any profit. We see in this example—and it applies to virtually any example of commercial activity using borrowed money—how interest rates are the principal engine of economic growth. It is arguably not technology, innovation, human desire, or direct exploitation that drives the need to *increase* production, but rather the legal obligation to repay not only the principal borrowed, but the significant additional burden of interest. Many earlier economic systems were highly exploitive, but until the advent of finance capitalism none was able to generate economic growth on an ongoing basis. For that, it seems, the compulsion of usury is needed. Only in modern times has usury been made the basis of the monetary system; in earlier eras it was present but constrained by religious prohibitions and the limited liquidity of independent state coinage. In a usurious system such as ours, creditors not only have the power of the state at their disposal to enforce contracts with debtors; they have the power to create money. Debtors, laboring under this financial peonage, must go out and produce not only what's needed to serve their purposes, but the additional amount required to cover the interest. Hence the economy, fueled by borrowed money in the absence of natural sources of capital, must grow rather than stand still, and indeed grow quickly.

Kellogg brings out the destructive burden of even modest interest rates. Here is one of his more homely but revealing examples:

> Suppose G. owns a farm of one hundred acres of well improved land worth $100 per acre. H. rents this farm at seven per cent. interest on its cost, and consequently must pay to G. $700 a year. If the land produce twenty-five bushels of wheat to the acre, and wheat be worth $1 per bushel, H. must sow, reap, and sell the products of twenty-eight acres, and pay the whole proceed to G. as the rent of one hundred acres for the year. If interest were at one per cent. instead of at seven, the rent of the farm, or of the $10,000 for the year would be $100, instead of $700; and H. would be obliged to cultivate and sell the products of four acres only to procure one hundred bushels of wheat, or $100 to pay

the rent. If he performed the same labor when interest was at one as when it was a seven per cent., he would retain the products of twenty four acres—i.e., six hundred bushels of wheat as the surplus earnings of his labor, instead of paying them to G. for the use of capital. The reduction of the rate of interest would not lessen the quantity of products, not decrease their value; it would only give a larger proportion to producers.[63]

This transfer of wealth, over time, can be enormous. Kellogg applies the rule of interest—the rule of 72—against what labor needs to produce to meet its contractual obligation to discharge the loan. The 7 percent interest rate in Kellogg's example would require, taken on a national scale, that the actual physical (not "paper") wealth of the nation be doubled every ten years. This means that the creditor has ten years to earn, not only enough to repay the principle, or the original amount borrowed, but twice that amount, in order also to cover the accumulated interest, and all of this before he or she can gain any income for himself or herself from the loan. For small amounts of money, the burden is trivial. But as the labor time required to repay a loan expands with the size of the loan, the burden mounts dramatically. In Kellogg's example of the farmer, the labor required to service his debt at 7 percent was 28 acres out of 100, or 28 percent of his effort. This amounts to working more than a quarter of his time, more than a day of the normal work week, to labor for someone else, with no return to one's self at all. This extracted labor compares unfavorably to the feudal dues of peasants. Of course the burden will vary given the other factors involved, including the fluctuating nature of interest rates, the inflation rate, and so forth.

The crux of the matter, Kellogg tells us, is a faulty financial system that permits by law either ruinous rates of interest or rates still so high as to prevent an adequate return to labor, in effect disallowing labor any ability to accumulate capital for itself, and condemning those who labor, the vast bulk of the citizenry then as now, to economic servitude:

> The law of interest, or percentage on money, as much governs the rent or use of all property, and consequently the reward of labor, as the law of gravitation governs the descent of water. If the interest on money be too high, a few owners of capital will inevitably accumulate the wealth or products of the many. With the present accumulative power of interest, there is no more chance of the laboring classes gaining their rights by combining their labor to increase production, than there would be hope of

success that by combining their labor they could reverse the course of the rivers, and make them run to the tops of the mountains, and pile up the waters on their summits.[64]

"If the producers ever gain their rights," he adds succinctly, "it will be by legally controlling the power of money, and not by any combinations of labor."[65] Labor unions may and have struck effectively for higher wages and other benefits from time to time, but lacking any control over the power of money, and particularly of interest rates, these measures have been palliative rather than substantive, and subject to rollback. "If farmers, manufacturers, and mechanics and merchants," on the other hand, "were compelled to pay only a just rate of interest, they could devote the labor now expended in the payment of high rates to nonproducers, to the supply of their own wants and of general comforts and conveniences."[66]

Kellogg's rule of the interest on money is comparable to Malthus's theory of population growth: "The centralizing power of money increases in geometrical proportion to the rate of interest. This is a practical as well as a mathematical truth or law; which is constantly operating to centralize wealth in the hands of a few at the expense of the producers."[67] The key is always the time required to double an initial investment at varying rates of interest, just as the key for Malthus is the time required to double any population. Even 2 percent interest is usurious according to Kellogg: "A rate of interest of even two per cent. per annum, would put it out of the power of the people to fulfill their contracts. The establishment of this rate of interest would be equivalent to the passing of a law, compelling the laboring classes to double the capital of the nation, in favor of capitalists once in thirty-four and a half years, besides producing their own support … would not a tribute or tax like this keep us forever in poverty?"[68] In an economy operating at 2 percent, in other words, half the capital or additional productivity created over thirty-four years, or close to half a lifetime, would be placed not in the hands of the indebted producers who created it, but in the hands of their creditors. This is not a marginal skim, or merely the price of risk, but a massive and ongoing transfer of wealth, one that keeps most laborers and producers or anyone relying on borrowed money, in perpetual debt, while constantly concentrating wealth. It requires doubling the economy every thirty-four and a half years, a rate unsustainable not only in terms of the individual burden of labor for most, but ecologically for the economy as a whole in terms of real resources and production.

Kellogg compares the ability of individuals (or institutions) to set interest rates at what the market will bear to lotteries and other kinds of gambling. Such activities, he points out, are generally illegal, or heavily circumscribed by law, since gambling contracts, though voluntary, enshrine the antisocial principle that "no equivalent is rendered to losers for what is gained by winners." He asks if "wealth is the product of labor, and it passes into the hands of a few capitalists by agreements less voluntary than betting and buying lottery tickets, is not the former even more contrary to justice than the latter?"[69] To allow interest rates to fluctuate is to allow a kind of gambling with the monetary system where those in a position to raise and lower interest rates (governments, bankers, financiers) are in a position, like a casino taking its "house" percentage, to gain unearned profit from a largely gullible public—except the exploitation of the monetary system is much worse. Gambling is a vice that can be avoided; the money system is a reality that cannot be escaped.

***

Kellogg's critique of usury is unusually clear, if perhaps not unique. What is unique is the systematic alternative he provides to the now dominant privatized monetary and financial system. Let us consider it in some detail. Kellogg proposes to establish local public credit banks, and we might imagine one in each county. These local, public, credit banks would be part of a national banking system Kellogg called the Safety Fund. These banks, federally authorized and regulated but locally run, would offer low-interest loans to individual citizens, at a fixed rate he determined to be 1.1 percent. They would be the only source of money; there would be no central bank in the modern sense. Kellogg lived in a precorporate world, compared to what we have today, and he presumed that only flesh-and-blood persons could borrow money from public credit banks. Reserving the initial borrowing of money for real persons would not preclude corporate borrowing in secondary debt markets (should there be such), but it would seem to provide a powerful instrument for ensuring that the benefits of credit go first to the public, and to other interests only secondarily.

Although Kellogg envisioned land as collateral for his loans, credit worthiness presumably could just as well be based, as it is today, on one's general potential earning power. The eligibility criteria used today by banks, credit card companies, and so son, could be applied as standards of public credit. Indeed, at 1.1 percent interest, such loans would seem to be the most likely to be repaid. Once lent out, Kellogg's public credit dollars would flow into circulation, providing the basis of a new currency backed by the assets and productive labor power of individual borrowers. The beauty of Kellogg's system lies in its decentralized but standardized nature. Instead of money being issued as it is now through a centralized money management system on a top-down basis primarily as loans from a central bank to national banks, and then to regional and local banks, and then to the public on the basis of fractional reserve lending, money instead would be issued by independent, decentralized, local federal banks as loans directly to citizens under uniform standards at nominal interest on the basis of the economic prospects of those citizens.

A centrally issued national currency in Kellogg's system would be replaced by thousands of local sources of the same currency, but these would be subject to common national standards ensuring that each local public credit bank reliably issues equivalent units of currency—that is, dollars. A dollar issued by one local public credit bank, Kellogg intended, would be worth the same as and interchangeable with one issued by any other. The independence of local branches would be guaranteed by the discretionary power reserved to them to actually loan money; the compatibility of their monies would be ensured under federal law, according to Kellogg, by fixing the value of the dollar by law at 1 percent per year—that is, by lending money to citizens at that rate everywhere. Kellogg's system is designed for local control of capital and resources. "The Safety Fund will lend money at a low rate of interest to all applicants," he tells us, "furnishing the requisite landed security; hence every town, county, and State, which has the power to perform the necessary labor, can make internal improvements without pledging its property to large cities or to foreign nations to borrow money."[70] Amounts of money lent in Kellogg's system would vary considerably from place to place, with some areas needing and creating (and extinguishing) more currency than others. The money supply would be stabilized by repayment of loans as they came due. The interchangeability of public credit bank notes would ensure a wide circulation for the new money. Kellogg's public credit banks can be understood as a form of free banking, but done as a regulated nonprofit public service rather than as an unregulated private, for-profit enterprise.

On the national level, we would no longer find a central bank in the modern sense, but something functioning much like the Bureau of Standards, defining but not creating money. Kellogg says that "the Safety Fund may consist of a Principal Institution with Branches," and that "the Principal Institution should issue money only to the Branches."[71] The issuance of currency to the branches, as they request it, would enable the principal institution to monitor local practices and enforce the law. A branch found in violation of national monetary standards (perhaps by charging illegal interest rates or otherwise defrauding its clients) could be deprived of new currency to issue and perhaps otherwise penalized.

Without this provision, we would have an unregulated system of free banking. But, unlike a central bank, the principal institution would not lend at interest at all, nor would it lend preferentially to some borrowers rather than others; nor would it have any discretionary power to manage the system, apart from enforcing uniform legal standards. Nor would there be any need for fractional reserve lending. In Kellogg's words: "It is not intended that the Safety Fund and its Branches shall be made offices of discount and deposit. If they should be made such, they would more than double the amount of their loans but the increase of loans would not augment the amount of money. They would lend the money left on deposit, and thus increase their income, as banks now lend their deposits and gain the interest."[72] Kellogg presumes that nothing would be served by the safety fund engaging in fractional reserve lending. Lenders would already have their money, and anything they put on deposit would remain there for withdrawal. Fractional reserve lending by banks serves only their private interest, in Kellogg's view, not the public interest. The principal institution, in short, would have no control over the money supply.

Borrowers would be able to defer payment of the principal indefinitely, as long as they paid the interest: "Whenever a mortgagor shall have the means, he can pay off any part of the mortgage, and stop the interest. But he will never be compelled to pay the principal as long as the interest shall be regularly paid."[73] Kellogg further suggests that individuals be allowed to purchase public interest bonds from the branches of the safety fund, thus providing what he thought in his system would be a safe haven for investors. To keep money in circulation rather than in bonds, he suggests that local, federal, public interest loans be put out at a slightly higher rate of 1.1 percent, and bonds at 1 percent. A 1.1 percentage rate for public credit loans allows for the interest to equal the principal in sixty years. Although somewhat less than the seventy years required to do so by 1 percent loans, it remains sufficiently close to the sustainable criterion of a human lifetime, and indeed it more closely approximates a working lifetime. National standards, in sum, would determine for the safety fund—beyond the fixed 1.1 percent interest rate—uniform rules of creditworthiness, rules of local public management, and other technical matters. A local federal credit bank issuing too many bad loans, or refusing loans to otherwise credit worthy citizens, would be subject to legal penalties, including closure and reorganization.

In the plan we are about to propose for the formation of a National Currency by the General Government, all the money circulated in the United States will be issued by a national institution, and will be a representative of actual property, therefore it can never fail to be a good and safe tender in payment of debts. It will be loaned to individuals in every State county, and town, at a uniform rate of interest, and hence will be of invariable value throughout the Union. All persons who offer good and permanent security will be at all times supplied with money, and for any term of years during which they will regularly pay the interest. Therefore, no town, county, or State, need be dependent upon any other for money, because each has real property enough to secure many times the amount which it will require. If more than the necessary amount of money be issued, the surplus will be immediately funded, and go out of use without injury. It will be impossible for foreign nations, or any number of banks, or capitalists, to derange the monetary system, either by changing the rate of interest, or by inducing a scarcity or a surplus of money. It will be the duty of the Government to ascertain as nearly as possible what rate of interest will secure to labor and capital their respective rights, and to fix the interest at that rate.[74]

The money will bear no interest, but may always be exchanged for the Safety Fund Notes, which will bear interest. Those who may not wish to purchase property or pay debts with their money, can always loan it to the Institution for a Safety Fund Note, bearing an interest of one per cent. per annum. Therefore the money will always be good for it will be the legal tender for debts and property, and can always be invested to produce an income. The money being loaned at one and one-tenth per cent., and the Safety Fund Notes bearing but one per cent., the difference . . . will induce owners of money to lend to individuals, and thus prevent continual issuing and funding of money by the Institution.[75]

Insofar as the value of money is a function of the interest it can command, Kellogg maintains, then the definition of a dollar is the interest rate it can command. It is worth quoting at greater length from a passage quoted above:

The worth and amount of the interest on the dollar constitute and determine the value of the dollar. . . . Demand and supply are sometimes said to give value to money; but it would be as reasonable to assert that demand and supply fix the length of the yard, the weight of the pound. . . . Money is valuable in proportion to its power to accumulate value by interest. A dollar which can be loaned for twelve per cent. interest, is worth twice as much as one that can be loaned for but six per cent., just as a railroad stock which will annually bring in twelve per cent., is worth twice as much as one that annually brings in six per cent.[76]

A dollar of fixed value would be one with a fixed interest rate. Once fixed at 1.1 percent, the rate would remain unchanged in perpetuity, just as inches and ounces and meters and liters remain unchanged in perpetuity.

To achieve its purpose of a stable sustainable currency, Kellogg insists that the rate be fixed by law—just like other standard measurements—at an invariable, sustainable rate of interest of 1.1 percent: the rate that allows for the replacement of debt over a lifetime. "A rate of interest of even two per cent. per annum," to repeat his observation, "would put it out of the power of the people to fulfill their contracts," leaving them deprived of the capital that is their birthright as laborers.[77] If I am lucky enough to borrow money to buy a house and repay it at 1.1 percent, I have sixty years, essentially a lifetime, to pay the interest on that loan equivalent to buy a second house. In effect, I am replacing the value of the house I use up or consume over a lifetime, leaving another one in its place. But if I borrow the money at 2 percent, I must replace the value of my house not once, but nearly twice over sixty years; at 7 percent I would have to replace the value of my house every ten years, which would be the equivalent of committing myself to building seven houses in return for the use of one house over my lifetime. These additional houses, of course, are not mine to own and enjoy, but must instead be turned over to my creditors for their benefit. And the same applies to the economy as a whole.

A sustainable or steady-state economy is no more or less than a replacement economy over the course of a lifetime, which, following Kellogg, can be defined in monetary terms at 1.1 percent interest on money, the rate that allows a population to reproduce over a lifetime the goods and services it consumes, leaving to posterity not a debt but a material legacy equivalent to that with which it began. Holding to this standard for the succeeding lifetimes of succeeding generations would establish, it seems, an indefinitely sustainable financial system. An unsustainable or "growth" economy by contrast requires the debtor to repay the lender at rates not only exceeding the replacement value of the population, but often even the rate at which an economy is able to grow by maximizing its labor and resources without depleting its natural capital. In a developed economy growth rates of 3 or 4 percent historically have not been uncommon and seem increasingly unsustainable. We see the disastrous results increasingly in the strained global economy and ecology and resource scarcities of the early twenty-first century.

That debt burden on the economy is eliminated with Kellogg's public credit funding at 1.1 percent interest. His 1.1 percent loans would put capital into people's pockets and encourage a personal but sustainable productivity hitherto unknown in his experience. In Kellogg's words:

> In the United States, if interest were reduced to one, or to one and one-tenth per cent., useful productions would probably increase from twenty-five to fifty per cent. The wealth, instead of being accumulated in a few hands, would be distributed among producers. A large proportion of the labor employed in building up cities would be expended in cultivating and beautifying the country. Internal improvements would be made to an extent, and in a perfection unexampled in the history of nations. Agriculture, manufactures, and the arts would flourish in every part of the country. Those who are now non-producers would naturally become producers. The production would be owned by those who performed the labor, because the standard of distribution would nearly conform to the natural rights of man.[78]
>
> The per centage income upon capital can only be paid with the proceeds of labor; therefore this reduction of the per centage income would be equivalent to the distribution of several hundred millions of dollars among the producing classes, according to the labor performed. The effect of so large an annual distribution among this class would be to diffuse, in a few years, competence and happiness where now exist only poverty and misery.[79]

Of course, in Kellogg's day, resources were abundant and population low by comparison with today, when population is high and resources are increasingly scarce and further growth is increasingly checked by the limits of nature. This abundance of capital in his day would have allowed producers under his system to maximize the return on their labor. Today limits of population and nature will likely not allow such rich returns, but his system will still allow producers to maximize what returns they can earn and to do so fairly.

***

Kellogg, it should by now be clear, envisions a very different kind of money from that with which we are familiar:

> Now if money were properly instituted and regulated there would never be such a thing as a money market. There would be a market for the productions of labor; and these would doubtless vary more or less in their market value or price, but there would be no variation in the market value of money. It is as unreasonable for people to gain great wealth by fluctuations in the market value of money as it would be for them to grain great wealth by fluctuations in the length of the yard. Money is as much a standard of value as the yard is of length; and deviations in the market value of money are as much a fraud upon the public as deviations in the length, weight and size of other measures. No matter how long this gross wrong has been practiced upon all nations, it is no less an evil; and it has shown itself to be such by the centralization of wealth in every nation, and the poverty of the people whose labor has produced the wealth.[80]

If creditors are allowed, as they have been in recent times, to raise and lower interest rates more or less freely, they have it in their power to favor some debtors and punish others, and to maximize their own profit by optimizing interest rates at what the money market will bear: lower rates to stimulate borrowing and the economy, and higher rates to do the opposite.

Kellogg intends his fixing of the value of money at 1.1 percent to be a universal law, with no one anywhere allowed to charge more than 1.1 percent for money loaned out. He writes of banks "closing up their business," but being allowed nonetheless the full value of their assets, insofar as "no injustice will be done to them, for the law making paper money [safety fund dollars lent at 1.1 percent] a tender in payment of debts, gives to it a value equal to that possessed by gold and silver money regulated at the same rate of interest. While the establishment of the Safety Fund can do no wrong to the banks, it will greatly benefit those engaged in production and distribution."[81] Kellogg refers here to the specie-backed banks of his day, but his argument applies just as well to the fiat money of Federal Reserve notes in today's banking system. Capital under his system would become cheaply and widely available at local, public credit banks to anyone minimally credit-worthy. Students, for instance, could take out public credit loans instead of student loans. Public credit banks could offer 1.1 percent interest credit cards. Homebuyers could take out public credit loans instead of mortgages. Small business (sole proprietorships and partnerships) could take out public credit loans instead of borrowing money from commercial banks. Corporations presumably would not be able to borrow from public credit banks. Kellogg is not explicit about this, but he speaks throughout his work only of individual citizens as borrowers. Corporations as we know them played a growing but still limited role in his day. Insofar as the corporate system is rooted in private finance, Kellogg's Safety Fund would undercut much of its rationale, perhaps preparing the way for a revocation or disappearance of corporate personhood in favor of flesh-and-blood partnerships enjoying the full benefit of public credit.

Notice the profound implications of Kellogg's money system. There would be *no* controlling central bank in the modern sense, no discretionary central issuance of currency by behind-the-scenes decisionmakers. The banking system would be set on its head. A bottom-up system of capital creation by demand would replace the old top-down system of privileged dispensation. Most fundamentally, credit would be made available to the general public on clear terms at a perpetually fixed and sustainable 1.1 percent interest rate on good collateral, instead of being made available selectively to large commercial banks at higher rates, who in turn lend it at their discretion to others at even higher rates. With interest eliminated as a factor in monetary policy, the principle engine of wasteful and compulsive economic growth would be eliminated. There would be no need to labor frenetically to overcome the interest burden. Economic investment would be possible on the merits of the situation, not on an abnormally forced rate of return. A sustainable economics would become possible, perhaps for the first time. And, not least, the widespread availability of capital to individuals (unknown since the closing of the Western frontier in America in 1890) would do much to overcome the vast and growing discrepancies of wealth that exist because of usurious interest rates.

Kellogg's model of a decentralized but democratically regulated monetary system is worth pondering not only for financial and economic reasons, but for political ones as well. Democracy is necessarily a decentralized, face-to-face affair, and it cannot be successful, populists since Phaleas have argued, unless its citizens personally enjoy relative economic independence in a relatively decentralized economy. For only then can they come together as equals in a free community. Providing capital directly to the people promises, over time, to reduce economic inequality. Most citizens today, by contrast, are economic dependents, having been forced into debt peonage by usurious interest rates for most of the necessities of life (education, housing, transportation, etc.). Not being free economic agents, they cannot afford to oppose the harsh and destructive economic system that oppresses them, nor the policies of those who control it. A key step in making possible greater political freedom is the realization that a decentralized, self-regulating, nonusurious monetary system, of the sort outlined by Kellogg and advocated in part by greenbackers and populists later in the nineteenth century, can provide the basis for widely distributing and conserving wealth, making possible a more sustainable and fulfilling way of life.

One may be tempted to dismiss Kellogg's ideas as remote, even utopian. Yet Kellogg was no idle dreamer, but a practical man who made his own way in the world, raised on a farm, largely self-educated, successful in business. He took the long view and refused to conclude that the practical unlikelihood of ideas otherwise compelling was a fatal disqualification. In his words:

> It may be admitted that the theory of the Safety Fund is good, but impracticable at present; it is calculated for some future generation, when men shall have become more intelligent and virtuous. If the same faith shall be held by the generations which are to follow us, it will be difficult to point out at *what* period this desirable reformation will occur, because the evil of our present system will always be in the present, and the good of the plan proposed in the future. We are, however, persuaded that a large majority of the people are aware that their present depressed condition may and should be exchanged for something better, and the safety Fund will be regarded by them as neither too Utopian nor visionary to be made immediately operative for their benefit. All the objections to the proposed currency, upon the ground that it will lessen the incomes of capitalists who are supported by the labor of others, only serve to show the true working of the Safety Fund system; for its object is to furnish a standard of distribution which will cause men to sustain such mutually just relations as to render it generally

necessary for all to render an equivalent in useful labor for the labor received from others.[82]

Kellogg offers us the American dream in its populist essence: every person a property owner, with productive capital at his or her disposal. If the populist precondition of a democratic society is that citizens must be property owners, the question since Phaleas has been how to create a society in which private property is very broadly and more or less equitably distributed. Phaleas suggested that the rich in a city give and not receive dowries, and that the poor receive but not give them, and most approaches since his day to the question of ensuring a just distribution of resources among citizens have presumed that we must take from the rich and give to the poor. Aristotle, we have seen, advocated taxing the rich to help relieve the poor. Even taxing inherited wealth, as Tom Paine suggested we do, violates the natural affections and, as we have seen, encounters fierce resistance. The long history of class warfare between rich and poor suggests that taking directly from the rich, or threatening to do so, has the effect of galvanizing the rich to protect their advantages. And since the rich have the advantage of greater means to ensure their ends, they have by and large been able to resist major encroachments on their disproportionate control of resources.

There have been times in all periods and all countries when circumstances have made it prudent for the rich to offer greater concessions to the poor and in effect to share more of the wealth with them. And there have been times when the rich could appropriate vast amounts with apparent impunity, impoverishing their neighbors. The rich have been actually defeated only in communist states, where unfortunately the resources confiscated from them were not distributed on a personal basis to the general public as populists advocate, but concentrated in powerful state bureaucracies run by a privileged party elite. One form of tyranny was replaced by another and cruder one, but here too the resentment of the displaced rich has been implacable, even in defeat. It takes the genius of a Kellogg to demonstrate how an equitable social mechanism (the National Safety Fund) could ensure that, over time, virtually everyone could receive reasonable and fair access to credit, and so to the means necessary to secure their own welfare, not as a mere possibility, but as a likely eventuality. Safety fund loans would cost 1.1 percent, it is true, but they would be voluntary and no taking would be required of anyone to issue them. The rich would not be one bit poorer if the Kellogg money system were established. Good investments in productive enterprises could even enhance their wealth. They could not, however, expect any longer to loan out their capital hoping for preferential and usurious returns. They would be constrained, like every one else, by the prevailing low interest rates, while being as free as anyone else to put their private resources to productive use. Over time, some would succeed in preserving and perhaps increasing their fortunes, while others would dissipate them. But the proverbial playing field would at last be a level one.

With easy access to credit, or money, no able-bodied person need be poor. Being able to find credit at the 1.1 percent rate established by the national currency, ordinary citizens ought be able to invest in and for themselves. And since easy credit is pegged to the nonusurious 1.1 percent, human lifetime rate for the doubling of capital, and not to any demands upon existing private capital, the rich need not fear that their property will be taken away; they will also have the security of a stable money supply, with financial speculation removed. The poor, in Kellogg's view, can hope actually to earn and maintain their own property for they will not have to share more than 1.1 percent of their earnings with their creditors. High interest rates have put the bulk of the citizenry into debt peonage; releasing them from that bond, relieving them of high interest rates so they can keep a vastly greater share of what they produce, would allow them better to contribute such support as they decide, collectively and individually, to give to those members of the community unable to labor.

***

Kellogg's ideas were an inspiration, in part, for the greenback and populist movements that followed the Civil War. To finance that war, the federal government issued several hundred million dollars worth of fiat currency, the greenbacks. But the issuance of greenbacks was under the central control of the Treasury Department, and no effort was made to set up anything like Kellogg's decentralized safety fund. Nonetheless, this public currency posed a direct challenge to the private banking system and its control of credit and the money supply. Eventually, after the war, "the money power" was able to phase out the greenbacks and reestablish its control, but not without a struggle. Populist forces supporting public credit and money fought against bankers and wealthy creditors. The 1876 Independent or "Greenback" Party called for "a United States Note, issued directly by the Government, and convertible on demand into United States obligations bearing a rate of interest not exceeding one cent a day on each $100, and exchangeable for United States notes at par." It went on to quote Jefferson approvingly, that "'bank paper must be suppressed and the circulation restored to the nation, to whom it belongs.'"[83] The *Omaha Platform* of the Peoples' Party of 1892, the high-water mark of the populist movement, called for "a national currency, safe, sound, and flexible, issued by the general government only, a full legal tender for all debts, public and private, and that, without the use of banking corporations, a just, equitable, and efficient means of distribution direct to the people, at a tax not to exceed two per cent per annum."[84] The concept of abundant credit guaranteed by the government through a new monetary system was at the heart of the populist movement.[85]

The history of late-nineteenth-century American populism— perhaps the largest mass movement in American history—has been told elsewhere, perhaps most fully by Lawrence Goodwyn in his *Democratic Promise*.[86] Still something of the post-Kelloggian story needs to be noted here. The most important populist thinker after Kellogg was probably Charles Macune, a Wisconsin native who emigrated to Texas, where he practiced law and medicine. He became a leader in the Farmers' Alliance in the 1880s, a widespread populist organization, where he developed what he called the Sub-Treasury Plan, presented in the Alliance publication, the *National Economist*, in 1889. Lawrence Goodwyn, in his *Democratic Promise*, describes Macune's plan:

> Macune's sub-treasury concept was the intellectual culmination of the cooperative crusade and directly addressed its most compelling liability—inadequate credit. Through his sub-treasury, Macune proposed to mobilize the currency-issuing power of the government in behalf of the agricultural poor: the federal government would underwrite the cooperatives by issuing greenbacks to provide credit for the farmer's crops, creating the basis of a more flexible national currency in the process; the necessary marketing and purchasing facilities would be achieved through government-owned warehouses, or "sub-treasuries," and through federal subtreasury certificates paid to the farmer for his produce—credit which would remove furnishing merchants, commercial banks, and chattel mortgage companies from American agriculture. The sub-treasury "certificates" would be government-issued greenbacks, "full legal tender for all debts, public and private."[87]

The key point of Macune's scheme is that fiat currency (greenbacks) would be issued not by private banks as a debt on the government, and therefore on taxpayers, but directly by the government to ordinary producers on the collateral of actual goods and services that have been and are likely to continue to be produced. Yet Macune seems not to have followed Kellogg closely, with unfortunate consequences. "As for Edward Kellogg's influence," Goodwyn points out, "Macune's problem was that he did not respond to this soft-money advocate as much as he should have. Macune concentrated with such single-mindedness upon commodity loans (the only negotiable asset Southern farmers possessed) that he failed to see the merit of land loans until Kansas Alliancemen point it out to them."[88] Kellogg presupposed land as the principal (if not exclusive) collateral for his system; Macune proposed a range of agricultural products, but excluded land. Eventually land loans were incorporated in the Alliance program, but Goodwyn suggests it came too late: "The immediate incorporation of land loans in his [Macune's] system might have made his plan more persuasive to the hesitant spokesmen of the Nebraska Alliance, thus speeding up by two years the eventual absorption of the Nebraskans into the organized agrarian movement, and, conceivably, fatally undermining the development of the shadow movement of Populism."[89] This "shadow movement of populism," which eventually swept over the Democratic Party with the nomination of William Jennings Bryan in 1896, was distinguished from the stronger Alliance version of populism by its abandonment of any notion of a national fiat currency in favor of easy credit based on silver coinage. By this point almost nothing was left of Kellogg's program. The very characterization of Kellogg as a "soft money" man is misleading; low interest rates are "soft" only by comparison to the usurious "hard" money of the private bankers. Kellogg points out that interest rates need not only be low, but also that they be fixed (and in that sense "hard").

The triumph of "the money power" over "the democracy" in the 1890s depended upon preventing any alternative from replacing the monetary system run by and for private finance capital. Kellogg's decentralized system was truly revolutionary, but even the idea of centralized public credit on the greenback model was too much for "the money power." The distractions of the call for "free silver" turned out to be sufficient to smother any talk of public credit. The populist voices promoting public money (some form of the Kelloggian system, however watered down, or fiat money like greenbacks) were at a disadvantage from the start, and their campaign turned out to be the last major effort in American history to strike at the heart of "the money power," a battle going back to colonial times against British financial interests. But it was too little, too late. America returned to the grip of private finance capital on January 1, 1879, when by congressional action signed into law some years earlier the United States government committed itself to once more redeem greenback notes in gold, ending its limited experiment with publicly accountable fiat money. By the 1890s, after the death throes of populist resistance, private finance capital had confirmed its victory, ensuring its lock on lending money at high and fluctuating interest rates,[90] and the relative impoverishment and depoliticization of the many and the enrichment and empowerment of the few. The rights of capital since then have been increasingly institutionalized and legalized, and the rights of persons have been increasingly discounted and marginalized. In the decades since the 1890s, there have been ups and downs, periods of relative prosperity (the 1920s, '50s, '60s, and '90s) and of relative impoverishment (the 1930s, '70s, '80s, and the first decade of the twenty-first century). But even in the best of these times, vast and overwhelming discrepancies of power and wealth remained, with political power highly concentrated throughout.

Isolated voices reintroducing populist ideas continued to be raised, of course, though they gained little traction. The efforts of Alfred Lawson deserve note. Lawson (1869–1954) was an eccentric American original, a professional baseball player, a pioneer in early aviation, a social thinker, and self-made philosopher and religious prophet who independently reinvented many of the insights about money and credit first advanced by Kellogg. His populist political economy is briefly stated in his 1931 tract, *Direct Credits for Everybody*. He criticized economists for failing to distinguish between finance and capital. Wealth is the production of society, but finance is the "system whereby privateers are allowed to legally collect a tax from everybody in the form of interest charged on money loans."[91] He argued that money has no intrinsic value except as endorsed by governments in the name of the people in order "to give equal benefit to everybody."[92] Lawson, like Kellogg, called for the abolition of the private system of money and credit, and for its replacement by a public system of money and credit, though with a somewhat different emphasis. He summarized his new system in a fourteen-point program.[93] Unlike Kellogg, Lawson would have the government issue credits, or loans, directly to individuals without any collateral requirement. The amount issued would be equivalent to the annual income from the products of the industries of the nation, an amount Lawson estimated in 1931 at $100 billion, about a quarter of the total wealth of the nation that he estimated at $400 billion, which would work out to about $1000 per capita. This would become the basis of a new currency, and Lawson went so far as to envision the abolition of all taxes insofar as the government might fund itself by issuing loans to itself on the same basis as it issued loans to others. Unlike Kellogg, Lawson, who started out as a socialist, seems to have presumed that the government could issue loans to large corporations, thus controlling the evolution of the national economy. The Kelloggian vision of a decentralized, natural, steady-state, individual entrepreneurial economy funded by local loans rooted in local collateral recedes here before a vision of a government-controlled loan system in which benefits are directed at the judgment of central authorities.

More recent critiques of "the money power" suffer from similar limitations. Even authors as highly aware of the privatized, usurious money system as Stephen Zarlenga, in *The Lost Science of Money*, and Ellen Hodgson Brown, in *The Web of Debt*, miss the ingenious resolution of national monetary standards with local issuance of currency offered by Kellogg. They, like most critics of the plutocracy, see the solution in the direct issuance of money: preferably by the treasury on the model of Lincoln's greenbacks, or perhaps by a Federal Reserve somehow made accountable to the federal government. In doing so they fall back on what we might call Hamiltonian progressivism, the idea that a centralized state is the ultimate vehicle for reform of the financial system. Authority and policy making are reconcentrated, not dispersed. We see here the mind-set of progressive antidemocracy at work, well intentioned as it might be. For it is hard to see how a centralized federal issuance of money could—in the absence of any effective political accountability to the people—avoid being a political football, or why there should be confidence that anything like our current misrepresentative government could provide the kind of accountability necessary to put credit directly in people's hands efficiently and fairly. More likely, any federally run system would be top down, with money issued to government contractors and others on a preferential basis, according to the desires of special interests. Even the issuance of direct credits as Lawson suggested would be subject to the whims of Congress and, these days, an increasingly powerful executive.

At the other extreme from the neo-Hamiltonians, with regard to money, we find the ecocritics discussed in chapter 1, who promote decentralization and tend to favor local alternative currency initiatives, such as Ithaca Hours, the LETS (Local Employment and Trading System) associations, and other decentralized, labor-time denominated clearinghouse exchange systems. As a clearinghouse system of credits, such local currencies are limited to functioning as media of exchange among voluntary participants. They suffer from a lack of standardization (there being competing variations) and they vary widely in performance and efficiency. They remain parasitic on the usurious national currency. They are not fully fledged monies in Kellogg's (or Soddy's) sense, where money is a the noninterest debt a community issues to itself not only to purchase goods and services, but to make capital investments. In a clearinghouse system—perhaps best developed by Thomas H. Greco Jr.[94]—credits are issued by, say, local merchants to pay workers, who can then use those credits at local shops, and so on. There is no way in such a system for anyone to borrow significant sums at low interest to use as capital investment; a system of exchange credits is not a loan system, and the latter is what is required if we are to have real money—that is, credit. To be able to exchange goods and services for local currency does not enable anyone to acquire in advance capital for investment; that requires going into debt—that is, getting money *without* first laboring for it. Recent critics of our privatized usurious system suggest either a centralized government-run fiat currency, or a plethora of decentralized but variable and inadequate clearinghouse currencies. Neither seems adequate. Kellogg by contrast offers a spontaneous, self-correcting, decentralized monetary system providing significant credit to individuals, and yet standardized so that local issuers everywhere follow the same rules. There is no need for central control of issuance, since local conditions of borrowing and repayment will automatically adjust the money supply to the needs of commerce.

In any event, the marginalization of Jeffersonian democratic, redistributive populism by the triumphs of Hamiltonian corporatism and later laissez-faire financial corporatism has put it more or less off the political agenda for well over a century now. The post–Civil War populist movement that culminated in the Farmers' Alliance and the Peoples' Party was the last serious expression of populist principles in the United States. Populism as a political movement was decisively co-opted and defeated by the time of the 1896 election; it was pushed back to the margins of national politics where it has uneasily remained ever since. Progressive antidemocracy has kept political power firmly in the hands of the wealthy, even during the Progressive, New Deal, and Great Society eras, though not without a struggle. Populist rhetoric continued to be employed by a variety of public figures—from Thomas Edison and Henry Ford to Huey Long, Jerry Voorhis, and Wright Patman—but to diminishing effect. Progressive antidemocracy managed to establish and maintain a program favorable to concentrations of property, with most citizens in most places effectively cut off from direct democracy and meaningful access to capital. The deep populist idea of democratic decentralization of both politics and economics was obscured by the progressives relying on big government to balance big business in their opposition to the worst of finance capitalism. Even perhaps the most formidable challenger to the status quo in twentieth-century America—Huey P. Long—relied in his "share our wealth" program on centralized state power to redistribute wealth by taxing the rich and limiting their incomes and assets.[95] As far as the political side of populism is concerned—local grassroots democracies confederated into larger inclusive assemblies accountable to the grassroots—little more is heard after the Civil War. The Jeffersonian democratic vision finds fewer and fewer defenders. Instead, the antidemocratic politics of plebiscitary plutocracy (under various labels: progressivism, liberalism, conservatism, etc.) has become the norm.

In the face of war and depression, there have been various reforms of the plutocratic "money power" system, but they have remained top-down and elite-controlled. Progressive antidemocracy enshrined in the party duopoly has given the cloak of legitimacy to corporate powers not recognized in the Constitution. Over the years, the Madisonian representative system—with its large electoral districts requiring expensive, privately funded campaign organizations—has triumphed, underwriting oligarchic power while confusing democracy in the public mind with the largely symbolic right to vote in general elections. The collapse of socialism in the last decade of the twentieth century in the Soviet Union, and its transformation into state capitalism in Communist China, has left private finance capitalism dominant globally and prone to unchecked excess. For those who are distressed at the political, social, and ecological prospects of finance capital, including progressive antidemocracy, the populist alternative remains to be taken more seriously.

Appendix

Jefferson's Ward Republics

The first part of this appendix contains a compilation of passages from Jefferson's correspondence outlining his notion of ward republics. The second part offers a brief projection of how a confederal system based on ward republics might look if implemented in the United States today.

I quote from Jefferson's letters, written between 1800 and 1824, to Joseph Priestly, John Tyler, John Adams, Peter Carr, Joseph C. Cabell, Samuel Kercheval, and Major John Cartwright. Collectively they describe Jefferson's system of ward republics. The passages are sometimes repetitious, but with interesting shifts in emphasis and detail. The ward republics, born out of Jefferson's interest in education, became the centerpiece of his revolutionary program, which also included the abolition of entails and primogeniture, universal education, religious freedom, the periodic review of laws, the abolition of public debt, and periodic constitutional conventions. Parts of that program—religious freedom, and the abolition of entails and primogeniture—were wholly adopted. Other parts—universal education and a constitutional convention—have been adopted or recognized to limited degrees. Still other parts—self-government, the ward republics, the periodic review of laws, the abolition of public debt—have not been adopted at all.

The wards were the most important plank in Jefferson's revolutionary platform. They were to be the "keystone of the arch of our government." "Begin them only for a single purpose," Jefferson wrote of the wards, and "they will soon show for what others they are the best instruments."[1] For him, the wards were the necessary means by which the other goals of good government could be obtained and sustained. The behavior of New England townships and committees of correspondence in the wake of the British embargo of Boston in 1774, and perhaps some sense of community self-government gleaned from Native Americans, provided for Jefferson the key example of the potential of ward republics. Here the people, gathered together in local assemblies, were able to act justly and decisively. By institutionalized ward republics as the basis of political activity throughout the nation, Jefferson intended to secure for posterity the benefits of free and direct political action.

***

To Joseph Priestly, Philadelphia, January 27, 1800:

> About 20. years ago, I drew a bill for our [Virginia] legislature, which proposed to lay off every county into hundreds or townships of 5. or 6. miles square, in the center of each of which was to be a free English school; the whole state was further laid off into 10. districts, in each of which was to be a college for teaching the languages, geography, surveying, and other useful things of that grade; and then a single University for the sciences.[2]

To John Tyler, Monticello, May 26, 1810:

> I have indeed two great mesures at heart, without which no republic can maintain itself in strength. 1. That of general education, to enable every man to judge for himself what will secure or endanger his freedom. 2. To divide every county into hundreds, of such size that all the children of each will be within reach of a central school in it. But this division looks to many other fundamental provisions. Every hundred, besides a school, should have a justice of the peace, a constable and a captain of militia. These officers, or some others within the hundred, should be a corporation to manage all its concerns, to take care of its roads, its poor, and its police by patrols, &c., (as the select men of the Eastern townships [New England].) Every hundred should elect one or two jurors to serve where requisite, and all other elections should be made in the hundreds separately, and the votes of all the hundreds be brought together. Our present Captaincies might be declared hundreds for the present, with a power to the courts to alter them occasionally. These little republics would be the main strength of the great one. We owe to them the vigor given to our revolution in its commencement in the Eastern States, and by them the Eastern States were enabled to repeal the embargo in opposition to the Middle, Southern and Western States, and their large and lubberly division into counties which can never be assembled. General

orders are given out from a centre to the foreman of every hundred, as to the sergeants of an army, and the whole nation is thrown into energetic action, in the same direction in one instant and as one man, and becomes absolutely irresistible. Could I once see this I should consider it as the dawn of the salvation of the republic, and say with old Simeon, "nunc dimittas Domine." But our children will be as wise as we are, and will establish in the fulness of time those things not yet ripe for establishment. So be it, and to yourself health, happiness and long life.[3]

To John Adams, Monticello, October 28, 1813:

At the first session of our legislature after the Declaration of Independence, we passed a law abolishing entails. And this was followed by one abolishing the priviledge of Primogeniture, and dividing the lands of intestates equally among all their children, or other representatives. These laws, drawn by myself, laid the axe to the root of Pseudo-aristocracy. And had another which I prepared been adopted by the legislature, our work would have been compleat. It was a Bill for the more general diffusion of learning. This proposed to divide every county into wards of 5. or 6. miles square, like your townships; to establish in each ward a free school for reading, writing and common arithmetic; to provide for the annual selection of the best subjects from these schools who might receive at the public expence a higher degree of education at a district school; and from these district schools to select a certain number of the most promising subjects to be compleated at an University, where all the useful sciences should be taught. Worth and genius would thus have been sought out from every condition of life, and compleatly prepared by education for defeating the competition of wealth and birth for public trusts.

My proposition had for a further object to impart to these wards those portions of self-government for which they are best qualified, by confiding to them the care of their poor, their roads, police, elections, the nomination of jurors, administration of justice in small cases, elementary exercises of militia, in short, to have made them little republics, with a Warden at the head of each, for all those concerns which, being under their eye, they would better manage than the larger republics of the county or state. A general call of ward-meetings by their Wardens on the same day thro' the state would at any time produce the genuine sense of the people on any required point, and would enable the state to act in mass, as your people have so often done, and with so much effect, by their town meetings. The law for religious freedom, which made a part of this system, having put down the aristocracy of the clergy, and restored to the citizen the freedom of the mind, and those of entails and descents nurturing an equality of condition among them, this on Education would have raised the mass of the people to the high ground of moral respectability necessary to their own safety, and to orderly government; and would have compleated the great object of qualifying them to select the veritable aristoi, for the trusts of government, to the exclusion of the Pseudalists: and the same Theognis who has furnished the epigraphs of your two letters assures us that ["Curnis, good men have never harmed any city"]. Altho' this law has not yet been acted on but in a small and inefficient degree, it is still considered as before the legislature, with other bills of the revised code, not yet taken up, and I have great hope that some patriotic spirit will, at a favorable moment, call it up, and make it the key-stone of the arch of our government.[4]

To Peter Carr, Monticello, September 7, 1814:

The mass of our citizens may be divided into two classes—the laboring and the learned. The laboring will need the first grade of education to qualify them for their pursuits and duties; the learned will need it as a foundation for further acquirements. A plan was formerly proposed to the legislature of this State for laying off every county into hundreds or wards of five or six miles square, within each of which should be a school for the education of the children of the ward, wherein they should receive three years' instruction gratis, in reading, writing, arithmetic as far as fractions, the roots and ratios, and geography. The Legislature at one time tried an effectual expedient for introducing this plan, which having failed, it is hoped they will some day resume it in a more promising form.[5]

To Joseph C. Cabell, Monticello, February 2, 1816:

My letter of the 24th ult. conveyed to you the grounds of the
two articles objected to the College bill. Your last presents one
of them in a new point of view, that of the commencement of
the ward schools as likely to render the law unpopular to the
country. It must be a very inconsiderate and rough process of
execution that would do this. My idea of the mode of carrying
it into execution would be this: Declare the county ipso facto
divided into wards for the present, by the boundaries of the
militia captaincies; somebody attend the ordinary muster of
each company, having first desired the captain to call together
a full one. There explain the object of the law to the people of
the company, put to their vote whether they will have a school
established, and the most central and convenient place for it;
get them to meet and build a log school-house; have a roll taken
of the children who would attend it, and of those of them able
to pay. These would probably be sufficient to support a common teacher, instructing gratis the few unable to pay. If there
should be a deficiency, it would require too trifling a contribution from the county to be complained of; and especially as
the whole county would participate, where necessary, in the
same resource. Should the company, by its vote, decide that it
would have no school, let them remain without one. The advantages of this proceeding would be that it would become the
duty of the alderman elected by the county, to take an active
part in pressing the introduction of schools, and to look out for
tutors. If, however, it is intended that the State government shall
take this business into its own hands, and provide schools for
every county, then by all means strike out this provision of our
bill. I would never wish that it should be placed on a worse
footing than the rest of the State. But if it is believed that these
elementary schools will be better managed by the governor and
council, the commissioners of the literary fund, or any other
general authority of the government, than by the parents within
each ward, it is a belief against all experience. Try the principle
one step further, and amend the bill so as to commit to the
governor and council the management of all our farms, our
mills, and merchants' stores. No, my friend, the way to have
good and safe government, is not to trust it all to one, but to

divide it among the many, distributing to every one exactly the functions he is competent to.

Let the national government be entrusted with the defence of the nation, and its foreign and federal relations; the State governments with the civil rights, laws, police, and administration of what concerns the State generally; the counties with the local concerns of the counties, and each ward direct the interests within itself. It is by dividing and subdividing these republics from the great national one down through all its subordinations, until it ends in the administration of every man's farm by himself; by placing under every one what his own eye may superintend, that all will be done for the best. What has destroyed liberty and the rights of man in every government which has ever existed under the sun? The generalizing and concentrating all cares and powers into one body, no matter whether of the autocrats of Russia or France, or of the aristocrats of a Venetian senate. And I do believe that if the Almighty has not decreed that man shall never be free, (and it is a blasphemy to believe it,) that the secret will be found to be in the making himself the depository of the powers respecting himself, so far as he is competent to them, and delegating only what is beyond his competence by a synthetical process, to higher and higher orders of functionaries, so as to trust fewer and fewer powers in proportion as the trustees become more and more oligarchical.

The elementary republics of the wards, the county republics, the States republics, and the republic of the Union, would form a gradation of authorities, standing each on the basis of law, holding every one its delegated share of powers, and constituting truly a system of fundamental balances and checks for the government. Where every man is a sharer in the direction of his ward-republic, or of some of the higher ones, and feels that he is a participator in the government of affairs, not merely at an election one day in the year, but every day; where there shall not be a man in the State who will not be a member of some one of its councils, great or small, he will let the heart be torn out of his body sooner than his power be wrested from him by a Caesar or a Bonaparte. How powerfully did we feel the energy of this organization in the case of embargo? I felt the foundations of the government shaken under my feet by the New England townships. There was not an individual in their States whose body was not thrown with all its momentun into action; and although the whole of the other States were known to be in favor of the measure, yet the organization of this little selfish minority enabled it to overrule the Union.

What would the unwieldy counties of the middle, the south, and the west do? Call a county meeting, and the drunken loungers at and about the court houses would have collected, the distances being too great for the good people and the industrious generally to attend. The character of those who really met would have been the measure of the weight they would have had in the scale of public opinion. As Cato, then, concluded every speech with the words, "Carthago delenda est," so do I every opinion, with the injunction, "divide the counties into wards." Begin them only for a single purpose; they will soon show for what others they are the best instruments. God bless you, and all our rulers, and give them the wisdom, as I am sure they have the will, to fortify us against the degeneracy of one government, and the concentration of all its powers in the hands of the one, the few, the well-born or the many.[6]

To John Taylor, Monticello, May 28, 1816:

Witness the self-styled republics of Holland, Switzerland, Genoa, Venice, Poland. Were I to assign to this term a precise and definite idea, I would say, purely and simply, it means a government by its citizens in mass, acting directly and personally, according to rules established by the majority; and that every other government is more or less republican, in proportion as it has in its composition more or less of this ingredient of the direct action of the citizens. Such a government is evidently restrained to very narrow limits of space and population. I doubt if it would be practicable beyond the extent of a New England township. The first shade from this pure element, which, like that of pure vital air, cannot sustain life of itself, would be where the powers of the government, being divided, should be exercised each by representatives chosen either pro hac vice, or for such short terms as should render secure the duty of expressing the will of their constituents. This I should consider as the nearest approach to a pure republic, which is practicable on a large scale of country or population. And we have examples of it in some of our States constitutions, which, if not poisoned by priest-craft, would prove its excellence over all mixtures with other elements; and, with only equal doses of poison, would still be the best. Other shades of republicanism may be found in other forms of government, where the executive, judiciary and legislative function, and the different branches of the latter, are chosen by the people more or less directly, for longer terms of years or for life, or made hereditary; or where there are mixtures of authorities, some dependent on, and others independent of the people. The further the departure from direct and constant control by the citizens, the less has the government of the ingredient of republicanism; evidently none where the authorities are hereditary, as in France, Venice, &c., or self-chosen, as in Holland; and little, where for life, in proportion as the life continues in being after the act of election.[7]

And further from the same letter:

On this view of the import of the term republic, instead of saying, as has been said, "that it may mean anything or nothing," we may say with truth and meaning, that governments are more or less republican as they have more or less of the elements of popular election and control in their composition; and believing, as I do, that the mass of the citizens is the safest depository of their own rights, and especially, that the evils flowing from the duperies of the people, are less injurious than those from the egoism of their agents, I am a friend to that composition of government which has in it the most of this ingredient. And I sincerely believe, with you, that banking establishments are more dangerous than standing armies; and that the principle of spending money to be paid by posterity, under the name of funding, is but swindling futurity on a large scale.[8]

To Samuel Kercheval, Monticello, July 12, 1816:

The organization of our county administrations may be thought more difficult. But follow principle, and the knot unties itself. Divide the counties into wards of such size as that every citizen can attend, when called on, and act in person. Ascribe to them the government of their wards in all things relating to themselves exclusively. A justice, chosen by themselves, in each, a constable, a military company, a patrol, a school, the care of their own poor, their own portion of the public roads, the choice of one or more jurors to serve in some court, and the delivery, within their own wards, of their own votes for all elective officers of higher sphere, will relieve the county administration of nearly all its business, will have it better done, and by making every citizen an acting member of the government, and in the offices nearest and most interesting to him, will attach him by his strongest feelings to the independence of his country, and its republican constitution. The justices thus chosen by every ward, would constitute the county court, would do its judiciary business, direct roads and bridges, levy county and poor rates, and administer all the matters of common interest to the whole country. These wards, called townships in New England, are the vital principle of their governments, and have proved themselves the wisest invention ever devised by the wit of man for the perfect exercise of self-government, and for its preservation. We should thus marshal our government into, 1, the general federal republic, for all concerns foreign and federal; 2, that of the State, for what relates to our own citizens exclusively; 3, the county republics, for the duties and concerns of the county; and 4, the ward republics, for the small, and yet numerous and interesting concerns of the neighborhood; and in government, as well as in every other business of life, it is by division and subdivision of duties alone, that all matters, great and small, can be managed to perfection. And the whole is cemented by giving to every citizen, personally, a part in the administration of the public affairs. The sum of these amendments is, 1. General Suffrage. 2. Equal representation in the legislature. 3. An executive chosen by the people. 4. Judges elective or amovable. 5. Justices, jurors, and sheriffs elective. 6. Ward divisions. And 7. Periodical amendments of the constitution.

I have thrown out these as loose heads of amendment, for consideration and correction; and their object is to secure self-government by the republicanism of our constitution, as well as by the spirit of the people; and to nourish and perpetuate that spirit. I am not among those who fear the people. They, and not the rich, are our dependence for continued freedom. And to preserve their independence, we must not let our rulers load us with perpetual debt. We must make our election between economy and liberty, or profusion and servitude. If we run into such debts, as that we must be taxed in our meat and in our drink, in our necessaries and our comforts, in our labors and our amusements, for our callings and our creeds, as the people of England are, our people, like them, must come to labor sixteen hours in the twenty-four, give the earnings of fifteen of these to the government for their debts and daily expenses; and the sixteenth being insufficient to afford us bread, we must live, as they now do, on oatmeal and potatoes; have no time to think, no means of calling the mismanagers to account; but be glad to obtain subsistence by hiring ourselves to rivet their chains on the necks of our fellow-sufferers. Our landholders, too, like theirs, retaining indeed the title and stewardship of estates called theirs, but held really in trust for the treasury, must wander, like theirs, in foreign countries, and be contented with penury, obscurity, exile, and the glory of the nation. This example reads to us the salutary lesson, that private fortunes are destroyed by public as well as by private extravagance. And this is the tendency of all human governments. A departure from principle in one instance becomes a precedent for a second; that second for a third; and so on, till the bulk of the society is reduced to be mere automatons of misery, and to have no sensibilities left but for sinning and suffering. This begins, indeed, the *bellum omnium in omnia*, which some philosophers observing to be so general in this world, have mistaken it for the natural, instead of the abusive state of man. And the fore horse of this frightful team is public debt. Taxation follows that, and in its train wretchedness and oppression.[9]

And further from the same letter:

> This corporeal globe, and everything upon it, belong to its present corporeal inhabitants, during their generation. They alone have a right to direct what is the concern of themselves alone, and to declare the law of that direction; and this declaration can only be made by their majority. That majority, then, has a right to depute representatives to a convention, and to make the constitution what they think will be the best for themselves. But how collect their voice? This is the real difficulty. If invited by private authority, or county or district meetings, these divisions are so large that few well attend; and their voice will be imperfectly, or falsely pronounced. Here, then, would be one of the advantages of the ward divisions I have proposed. The mayor of every ward, on a question like the present, would call his ward together, take the simple yea or nay of its members, convey these to the county court, who would hand on those of all its wards to the proper general authority; and the voice of the whole people would be thus fairly, fully, and peaceably expressed, discussed, and decided by the common reason of the society. If the avenue be shut to the call of sufferance, it will make itself heard through that of force, and we shall go on, as other nations are doing, in the endless circle of oppression, rebellion, reformation; and oppression, rebellion, reformation, again; and so on forever.[10]

To Major John Cartwright, Monticello, June 5, 1824:

> Virginia, of which I am myself a native and resident, was not only the first of the States, but, I believe I may say, the first of the nations of the earth, which assembled its wise men peaceably together to form a fundamental constitution, to commit it to writing, and place it among their archives, where every one should be free to appeal to its text. But this act was very imperfect. The other States, as they proceeded successively to the same work, made successive improvements; and several of them, still further corrected by experience, have, by conventions, still further amended their first forms. My own State has gone on so far with its premiere ebauche; but it is now proposing to call a convention for amendment. Among other improvements, I hope

they will adopt the subdivision of our counties into wards. The former may be estimated at an average of twenty-four miles square; the latter should be about six miles square each, and would answer to the hundreds of your Saxon Alfred. In each of these might be, 1. An elementary school. 2. A company of militia, with its officers. 3. A justice of the peace and constable. 4. Each ward should take care of their own poor. 5. Their own roads. 6. Their own police. 7. Elect within themselves one or more jurors to attend the courts of justice. And 8. Give in at their Folk-house, their votes for all functionaries reserved to their election. Each ward would thus be a small republic within itself, and every man in the State would thus become an acting member of the common government, transacting in person a great portion of its rights and duties, subordinate indeed, yet important, and entirely within his competence. The wit of man cannot devise a more solid basis for a free, durable and well administered republic.[11]

***

Imagine, as a hypothetical exercise or thought experiment, an instantiation of Jefferson's ward republics, or grassroots citizens' assemblies, in every existing voting precinct throughout the United States: in rural townships, suburban districts, and urban neighborhoods. Begin with the election district or precinct in which we vote; this small geographical territory defines our local and most immediate public spaces, the familiar natural environment we call home, the community where our everyday activities normally take place. Precincts are small, usually including a few hundred voters, and so (unlike say, zip codes) are roughly equal in population. In Canada, no voting precinct has more than 500 voters. Nearly every precinct in the United States includes some of the following: stores and shops, workplaces, a post office, a school, civic organizations, a library, religious centers, streets and roads, not to mention the land, the waters, houses and buildings, the natural flora and fauna, and so on. Here citizens could meet together to conduct local affairs, to govern themselves, and to select directly from among themselves officials, including representatives to broader levels of government, to conduct such business as they cannot do for themselves.

Consider further how such ward republics might be confederated together, presuming a two-year term of office at all levels. In Otsego County, New York, where I live, the fifty-eight precincts in the county (called "electoral districts" in New York State) would constitute fifty-eight ward republics. If each one sent one delegate to the county assembly, that assembly would have fifty-eight members. My current county board of representatives, based on large election districts, by contrast has only fourteen members. A much larger county assembly, we may presume, would better reflect the general population of the county, and be less dependent on a few individuals. My county had over 63,000 citizens in the last census. By contrast, the largest county of New York State, Kings County (Brooklyn), had a population in the last census of 2,300,664. It is divided into 1,923 precincts, which would translate into a county assembly of 1,923 delegates. That number, interestingly, falls well short of the quorum of six-thousand required by the ancient Athenian assembly. But if it proved too unwieldy a number, as seems likely, the county could split into two or more separate counties as noted above, so that, instead of Kings County, we might have Park Slope County, Flatbush County, Brooklyn Heights County, and so on. A county with a population of 100,000, assuming one-hundred precincts with one-thousand people on rough average in each precinct, would have a county council of one-hundred members, one with a population of 500,000, would have five-hundred members, and so on.

The same procedure, reduplicated on the next level in New York State, could provide for a single unicameral state legislature, replacing both the current state Assembly and Senate, often deadlocked and paralyzed. While precincts, varying roughly in population between 500 and 1,500, are more or less equivalent, or equivalent enough, to effect more or less equal representation in their various county assemblies, the same is not true of counties in New York State, and in most states, which vary widely in population. Representation from counties to a state legislature would have to be proportional. Say that each county sent one delegate each, chosen from among their members by the county assembly, for every 10,000 of population, and any additional fraction thereof. If a county had fewer than ten thousand citizens, it would send only one delegate to the state legislature.

New York State's smallest county, Hamilton County, in the rural Adirondacks, had a population in the last census of 5,279; under this system, it would send one delegate to the state legislature. My county, Otsego County, with over 63,000 in population, would send 7 delegates to the state legislature. Kings County, as currently constituted with its 2,300,664 people, would send 230 delegates to the state legislature. If it, like other large countries, were divided, the same number of representatives would still be sent from what used to be Kings County, but now they would be representing two or more new counties at the state level.

With a population of approximately eighteen million, a New York State legislature constituted under this system would have a legislature of 1,080 members. These is a large but hardly prohibitive number; the U.S. House of Representatives, by comparison, has 435 members. Similarly, the same system could be applied in turn to the various states that would send representatives to a unicameral national Congress. This exposition, of course, is intended only to suggest the plausibility of a confederal democratic system. Many questions of detail necessarily remain.

Imagine nonetheless a representative named Jane Doe elected by her local assembly in November for a two-year term on the county assembly. At the end of her term as a member of the county assembly, after the experience of serving jointly in direct face-to-face contact with her fellow county representatives for two years, she would be eligible (along with the rest of them) to be elected by that county assembly to represent her county at the state legislature for the following two years. If elected, she would be obliged to report back to county assembly meetings, though someone else would now replace her in the new term as a voting representative of her home precinct. Further, following the same pattern, after another two years, she would be eligible for election by her peers in the state assembly to represent the state in the House of Representatives for two years. At all times, Jane Doe would retain full citizen rights in her local assembly. This system no longer requires—indeed rejects—large electoral electoral districts, but otherwise it makes no change in the traditional internal political boundaries (precincts, counties, states) of the nation. Indeed, it promises to simplify and reintegrate for the first time traditional American political units into a coherent whole, reconnecting the different levels of politics hitherto deliberately separated from one another.

At each level in such a confederal system, a stream of representatives would be rising to the top and then retiring from the system, to begin again, if they wished, at the bottom by accepting office once more as representatives, from their precincts, to their county. If elections for representatives were held at the end of each term of office, one could be elected to represent one's local assembly at the county assembly, then be elected at the end of two years to represent the county assembly at the state assembly, and then be elected at the end for two more years to represent the state assembly in the national Congress, or House of Representatives. This bottom-up confederal system of direct representative democracy would prevent representatives from perpetuating their incumbency, but it would give them invaluble experience, and allow them to serve again in due course. It would ensure a steady infusion of ordinary citizens into the highest levels of government, and create a body of knowledgeable citizen legislators.

In a confederal democracy there would be no professional politicians, no mass political campaigns, but there would be citizen politicians, and over time a large body of citizens well experienced in politics. At each level representatives would be elected on the basis of personal contact and judgment by their peers. Party bosses and campaign contributors, unable to control nominations to office or legislative agendas, would fade away. It would be more difficult for special interests to gain control over distinct and independent precinct meetings, or over higher legislative bodies composed of delegates originating from and responsible to such local meetings. It would be hard to bribe the large numbers of citizen-politicians involved, whose honesty would be reenforced by their direct accountability to the bodies they represent, something conspicuously absent in our current, indirect, money-and-media-dominated electoral system.

A further way to reenforce the popular accountability built into the confederal system would be to allow legislation at representative levels to originate not only from within each level itself, but also from the level immediately below it. The idea that legislation could work its way up in a confederal system would help secure a bottom-up flow of power. If approved by at least one precinct, say, a proposal could thereby automatically be placed by that precinct's representative on the agenda of the county assembly, where it would have to be acted upon. It would be even more important, following Hume, that all bills (or at least controversial ones) that passed the county assembly be returned to the precinct assemblies in the county for final approval, requiring, say, approval by a majority of precinct assemblies to become law. Counties also might function similarly with regard to the state legislature—proposing and approving (at least some) state legislation—and the state legislature, too, might function this way with regard to the national Congress.

A state legislative bill, for instance, would have to originate either in the state legislature or in one of its constituent bodies—that is, in one of the state's county assemblies. A national legislative bill similarly would have to originate in the Congress or in some state legislature. But any controversial bill passed by the Congress, no matter how initiated, perhaps if some of its opponents desired, could be returned for the approval of at least enough states to constitute a majority of the nation's population. And state legislative bills similarly could similarly be returned for the approval of counties representing a majority of the state's population; and similarly county legislative bills also could be returned for the approval of a majority of that county's local precinct assemblies. In such a confederal scheme, local affairs are mediated between precinct assemblies and county assemblies; state affairs are mediated between county assemblies and state legislatures; and national affairs are mediated between state legislatures and the national Congress. The up and down ladder of power is not continuous, but overlapping; local, state, and national politics are distinct, but mutually conditioning.

If all this sounds daunting, it is also simplifying. The only legislation to be passed would far more likely be legislation desired by those who are represented; the whole process would be bound closely to the people and their direct representatives. It would lock in accountability at the grassroots, and be far more transparent than our semiclosed system. Representatives at all levels would be denied their current monopoly on making decisions for their constituents; they would become the instruments of their constituents but without losing their own ability to initiate action. Representatives would either be voting on measures they introduced, including those forwarded by their constituent bodies, or they would be introducing and voting on proposals to send on to the body of which they are constituents. The legislative power would be dispersed among levels of representative bodies, not concentrated, as in our system, in the hands of legislators at each level, with their districts as fiefdoms.

More benefits might be enumerated, but perhaps enough has been said to indicate at least the plausibility of confederal democracy in a large and complex society. Any such confederal system of democracy, of course, is a problem in collective intelligent design, as is its sister notion of public credit; both necessarily require long and full debate, and finally a public consensus, only after which might a populist convention be in a position to draft a satisfactory populist constitution. In the meantime, we continue to live in a nonpopulist world, in which populists can only continue to make their case for decentralizing political and economic power.

Notes

Notes to Chapter One

1. Cf. Arthur C. Parker, *The Constitution of the Five Nations, or the Iroquois Book of the Great Law* (Ohsweken, ON: Iroqrafts, 1991 [1916]).
2. On ancient confederations, see J. A. O. Larsen, *Greek Federal States: Their Institutions and History* (Oxford: Clarenden Press, 1968).
3. On Swiss democracy see Gregory A. Fossedal, *Direct Democracy in Switzerland* (New Brunswick, NJ: Transaction, 2002).
4. The earliest proposal this writer has been able to find for confederate democracy as a solution to the problem of extending democracy over larger areas is David Hume's 1777 essay, "Idea of a Perfect Commonwealth," in David Hume, *Essays Moral, Political, and Literary*, ed. Eugene F. Miller (Indianapolis: Liberty Fund, 1987).
5. Aristotle, *Politics*, vol. 2, bk. 4, sec. 2, trans. H. Rackham, Loeb Classical Library (Cambridge, MA: Harvard University Press, 1990), 111.
6. By a "corporation" I mean any legal entity—business as well as government, profit as well as nonprofit, private as well as public—organized by law under a constitution or charter or legal filing, as an abstract body, independent on its individual members, potentially immortal, and capable of controlling property and otherwise functioning under the legal fiction of a person before the law.
7. Cf. William G. Roy, *Socializing Capital: The Rise of the Large Indusrial Corporation in America* (Princeton, NJ: Princeton University Press, 1997), 280–81; David C. Korton, *When Corporations Rule the World* (West Hartford, CT: Kumarian Press, 1995), 53–68; and Carroll Quigley, *Tragedy and Hope: A History of the World in Our Time* (New York: Macmillan, 1966), 69–77.

8. On the nature and rise to power of private finance, see Ellen Hodgson Brown, JD, *The Web of Debt: The Shocking Truth about Our Money System—The Sleight of Hand that Has Trapped Us in Debt and How We Can Break Free* (Baton Rouge, LA: Third Millennium Press, 2007) and Steven A. Zarlenga, *The Lost Science of Money: The Mythology of Money—The Story of Power* (Valatie, NY: American Monetary Institute, 2002).

9. Ferdinand Lundberg, *The Rich and the Super-Rich* (New York: Lyle Stuart, 1968), 21.

10. Kevin Phillips, *The Politics of the Rich and Poor* (New York: Random House, 1990), 8–10.

11. Kevin Phillips, *Wealth and Democracy* (New York: Broadway Books, 2002), 129–30.

12. Edward Kellogg, *A New Monetary System* (New York: Burt Franklin, 1970 [1861]), 21–22.

13. Here are some representative works by these authors: C. Wright Mills, *The Power Elite* (New York: Oxford University Press, 1959); Ferdinand Lundberg, *The Rich and the Super-Rich* (New York: Lyle Stuart, 1968); Herbert Marcuse, *One Dimensional Man: Studies in the Ideology of Advanced Industrial Society* (Boston: Beacon Press, 1964); Barry Commoner, *The Closing Circle: Nature, Man, and Technology* (New York: Alfred A. Knopf, 1977); Richard J. Barnett and Ronald E. Muller, *Global Reach: The Power of the Multinational Corporations* (New York: Simon and Schuster, 1974); David Noble, *America by Design: Science, Technology, and the Rise of Corporate Capitalism* (New York: Alfred A. Knoph, 1977); William Grieder, *Who Will Tell the People: The Betrayal of American Democracy* (New York: Simon and Schuster, 1992); Howard Zinn, *A People's History of the United States* (New York: Harper and Row, 1980); Noam Chomsky, *The Prosperous Few and the Restless Many* (Berkeley, CA: Odonian Press, 1993); David C. Korton, *When Corporations Rule the World* (San Francisco: Berrett-Koehler, 1995); Jeremy Rifkin, *Biosphere Politics: A New Consciousness for a New Century* (New York: Crown, 1991); Richard Douthwaite, *The Growth Illusion: How Economic Growth Has Enriched the Few, Impoverished the Many and Endangered the Planet* (Gabriola Island, BC: New Society, 1999); Kevin Phillips, *The Politics of Rich and Poor: Wealth and the American Electorate in the Reagan Aftermath* (New York: Random House, 1990); Ralph Nader, *The Ralph Nader Reader* (New York: Seven Stories Press); Donald L. Barlett and James B. Steele, *America: Who Really Pays the Taxes?* (New York: Simon and Schuster, 1994); and Stanley Aronowitz,

The Knowledge Factory: Dismantling the Corporate University and Creating True Higher Learning (Boston: Beacon Press, 2000).

14. William Greider, *One World, Ready or Not: The Manic Logic of Global Capitalism.* (New York: Simon and Shuster, 1997), 472.

15. Ibid., 468.

16. Fergus Millar, *The Crowd in Rome in the Late Republic* (Ann Arbor: University of Michigan Press, 2002), 208ff.

17. Thucydides, *History of the Peloponnesian War*, trans. Rex Warner (Middlesex, England: Penguin Books, 1970), 20–44.

18. See, for example, G. E. M. de Ste. Croix, *The Class Struggle in the Ancient Greek World* (Ithaca, NY: Cornell University Press, 1981).

19. Drew McCoy, *The Elusive Republic* (New York: W. W. Norton, 1980), 68.

20. Alexis de Tocqueville, *Democracy in America*, trans. Henry Reeve (New York: Oxford University Press, 1947), 433–34.

21. Murray Bookchin, "Municipalization: Community Onwership of the Economy", Green Program Drafts, No. 1 (Burlington, VT: Green Program Project, 1986), 5.

22. See E. F. Schumacher, *Small Is Beautiful: Economics as if People Mattered* (New York: Harper Perennial, 1989 [1973]); Jane Jacobs, *The Death and Life of Great American Cities* (New York: Vintage Books, 1961); Wendell Berry, *The Unsettling of America: Culture and Agriculture* (San Francisco: Sierra Club Books, 1977); Barry Commoner, *The Poverty of Power: Energy and the Economic Crisis* (New York: Alfred A. Knopf, 1976); and Donella H. Meadows, Dennis L. Meadows, Jorgen Randers, and William W. Behrens III, *The Limits to Growth* (New York: Universe Books, 1972).

23. William R. Catton Jr., *Overshoot: The Ecological Basis of Revolutionary Change* (Urbana: University of Illinois Press, 1982).

24. Cf. Richard Douthwaite, *The Growth Illusion: How Economic Growth Has Enriched the Few, Impoverished the Many and Endangered the Planet* (Gabriola Island, BC: New Society, 1992); Herman E. Daly, *Beyond Growth: The Economics of Sustainable Development* (Boston: Beacon Press, 1996); and Donella Meadows, Jorgen Randers, and Dennis Meadows, *Limits to Growth: The 30-Year Update* (White River Junction, VT: Chelsea Green, 2004).

25. In *The Economy of Cities* (New York: Vintage Books, 1969), Jane Jacobs argues that local economic growth is a function of import replacement: "Consider the fact that when cities rapidly replace imports, three direct results follow: 1. The sum total of economic activity expands rapidly. 2. Markets for rural goods increase rapidly because of shifts in the com-

position of city imports. 3. Jobs in cities grow very rapidly" (167). Though Jacobs (more a political economist than an ecologist) still sees a value in economic "growth," her point about import replacement suggests how relocalization might in fact improve local economic conditions, an advantage that might to some degree offset the loss of cheap energy and foreign imports.

Notes to Chapter Two

1. Lewis Henry Morgan, *Ancient Society* (Chicago: Charles H. Kerr, 1910), 6.
2. Kinship mentality is a vast subject addressed by diverse writers; some classic statements include: Numa Denis Fustel DeCoulanges, *The Ancient City*, trans. Willard Swail; Lewis Henry Morgan, *Ancient Society*; Sir James George Frazer, *The Golden Bough: A Study in Magic and Religion* (New York: Macmillan, 1963); Claude Levi-Strauss, *The Savage Mind* (London: Weidenfield and Nicolson, 1962); Henri Frankfort et al., *The Intellectual Adventure of Ancient Man: An Essay on Speculative Thought in the Ancient Near East* (Baltimore: Penguin Books, 1973); Robert Redfield, *The Primitive World and Its Transformations*; (Ithaca, NY: Cornell University Press, 1953); Calvin Luther Martin, *In the Spirit of the Earth: Rethinking History and Time* (Baltimore: Johns Hopkins University Press, 1992).
3. On the kinship roots of ancient Greek and Roman societies, the locus classicus remains Fustel de Coulanges, *The Ancient City*, trans. Willard Swail; (New York: Doubleday, 1956).
4. Harriet Crawford, *Sumer and the Sumerians* (Cambridge: Cambridge University Press, 1991), 20.
5. Writing of the tribes of the seventh and sixth centuries BCE in Italy, Klaus Bringmann in his *A History of the Roman Republic*, trans. W. J. Smyth (Cambridge: Polity Press, 2007) states: "They were all organized in associations of tribes and clans and lived dispersed on the land in hamlets and villages. Clans descended from a common ancestor were linked by personal associations founded on marriage and mutual exchange of goods (*conubium* and *commercium*). Tribal religious sanctuaries afforded a rudimentary basis for the deliberation of common affairs and for common undertakings" (3–4).
6. Cf. Richard Rudgley, *The Lost Civilizations of the Stone Age* (New York: Free Press, 1999), and Alexander Marshack, *The Roots of Civilization: The Cognitive Beginnings of Man's First Art, Symbol and Notation* (New York: McGraw-Hill, 1972).

7. See Arthur C. Parker, *The Constitution of the Five Nations*, and Doug George-Kanentiio, Iroquois Culture and Commentary (Sante Fe, NM: Clear Light, 2000).

8. Cf. Catton, *Overshoot*.

9. The classic statement of population pressures leading to competition over resources remains Thomas Malthus, *An Essay on the Principal of Population* (Teddington, UK: Echo Library, 2006 [1798]).

10. Cf. Maria Gimbutas, *The Civilization of the Goddess* (San Francisco: HarperSanFrancisco, 1991) and *The Slavs* (New York: Praeger, 1971); James Mellaart, *Catal Huyuk: A Neolithic Town in Anatolia* (New York: McGraw-Hill, 1967); Walter A. Fairservis Jr., *The Threshold of Civilization: An Experiment in Prehistory* (New York: Charles Scribner's Sons, 1975); Robert J. Braidwood, *Prehistoric Men*, 2nd ed. (Glenview, IL: Scott, Foresman, 1964); and E. E. Evans-Pritchard, *The Nuer: A Description of the Modes of Livelihood and Political Institutions of a Nilotic People* (New York: Oxford University Press, 1969).

11. Cf. Maria Gimbutas, *The Civilization of the Goddess* and *The Gods and Goddesses of Old Europe 7000 to 3500 BC: Myths, Legends and Cult Images* (Berkeley: University of California Press, 1974); Gerda Lerner, *The Creation of Patriarchy* (New York: Oxford University Press, 1986); Anne Baring and Jules Cashford, *The Myth of the Goddess: Evolution of an Image* (London: Viking Arkana, 1991); cf. also Robert Graves, *The White Goddess: A Historical Grammar of Poetic Myth*, amended and enlarged ed. (New York: Farrar, Straus and Giroux, 1948).

12. William Irwin Thompson, *The Time Falling Bodies Take to Light: Mythology, Sexuality, and the Origins of Culture* (New York: St. Martin's Press, 1981), 133.

13. Alexancer Heidel, trans. and ed., *The Gilgamesh Epic and Old Testament Parallels* (Chicago: University of Chicago Press, 1949), 32.

14. Crawford, *Sumer and the Sumerians*, 23.

15. Ibid., 71.

16. Daniel K. Richter, *The Ordeal of the Longhouse: The Peoples of the Iroquois League in the Era of European Colonization* (Chapel Hill: University of North Carolina Press, 1994), 21–22.

17. Thomas Jefferson, *Writings: Autobiography, A Summary View of the Rights of British America, Notes on the State of Virginia, Public Papers, Addresses, Messages, and Replies, Miscellany, Letters* (New York: Library of America, 1984), 1263.

18. Ibid., 220.

19. Richard K. Matthers, *The Radical Politics of Thomas Jefferson: A Revisionist View* (Lawrence: University of Kansas Press, 1984), 89.

20. Thomas Paine, *Collected Writings*, ed. Eric Foner (New York: Library of America, 1995), 397.

21. Jefferson, *Writings*, 959.

Notes to Chapter Three

1. Aristotle, *Politics*, bk. 2, sec. 2, 111.

2. Ibid., 117–18.

3. Ibid., 119.

4. Ibid., 113.

5. Ibid., 119.

6. Aristotle does not, it is true, give Phaleas the credit he seems to deserve. But the text of *Politics*, we should remember, like most of Aristotle's other surviving texts, is based on somewhat rough notes, probably compiled by students and others, and likely incomplete in various details.

7. Aristotle, *Politics*, bk. 4, sec. 2, p. 327.

8. Ibid., 327–28.

9. Ibid., 329–30.

10. Ibid., 331.

11. Ibid., 333.

12. Cf. I. F. Stone, *The Trial of Socrates* (New York: Anchor Books, 1989), 44, 221–24.

13. Aristotle, *Politics*, bk. 2, sec. 4, p. 119.

14. Ibid., 511.

15. A tentative list in progress of Greek democracies, compiled by Eric W. Robinson, Harvard University, personal communication, 2003.

16. C. Douglas Lummis, *Radical Democracy* (Ithaca, NY: Cornell University Press, 1996), 117.

17. Victor Davis Hanson, "Countryside Character," in *The Times Literary Supplement* (review of Nicholas F. Jones, *Rural Athens under the Democracy*) June 25, 2004, p. 4.

18. Mogens Herman Hansen, *The Athenian Democracy in the Age of Demosthenes: Structure, Principles, and Ideology,* trans. J. A. Crook (Oxford: Blackwell, 1991), 90–94.

19. Josiah Ober, *Mass and Elite in Democratic Athens: Rhetoric, Ideology, and the Power of the People* (Princeton, NJ: Princeton University Press, 1989), 32.

20. Details of Athenian democracy can be found in a number of works, including W. G. Forrest, *The Emergence of Greek Democracy 800–400 BC* (New York: McGraw-Hill, 1966); M. I. Finley, *Democracy Ancient and Modern*, rev. ed. (New Brunswick, NJ: Rutgers University Press, 1985); Hansen, *The Athenian Democracy in the Age of Demosthenes*; Ober, *Mass and Elite in Democratic Athens*; and R. K. Sinclair, *Democracy and Participation in Athens* (Cambridge: Cambridge University Press, 1988).

21. Barry S. Strauss, "The Melting Pot, the Mosaic, and the Agora," in *Athenian Political Thought and the Reconstruction of American Democracy*, ed. J. Peter Euben, John Wallach, and Josiah Ober, 252–64 (Ithaca, NY: Cornell University Press, 1994).

22. Christian Habicht, *Athens from Alexander to Antony*, trans. Deborah Lucas Schneider (Cambridge: Cambridge University Press, 1997), 4–5.

23. Plutarch, *The Lives of the Noble Grecians and Romans*, 2 vols., trans. John Dryden, rev. Arthur Hugh Slough (New York: Modern Library, n.d.), 15.

24. On Solon see Forrest, *The Emergence of Greek Democracy 800–400, BC*, 143–74.

25. Edward E. Cohen, *Athenian Economy and Society: A Banking Perspective* (Princeton, NJ: Princeton University Press, 1993), 61.

26. Aristotle, *Constitution of Athens*, in *Aristotle and Xenophon on Democracy and Oligarchy*, trans. J. M. Moore (Berkeley: University of California Press, 1986), 147–207.

27. Stone, *The Trial of Socrates*, 232–35.

28. Cf. Finley, *Democracy Ancient and Modern*, 124–41.

29. From Plato's "Seventh Letter," quoted in Plato, *Republic*, trans. G. M. A. Grube, rev. trans. C. D. C. Reeve (Indianapolis: Hackett, 1992), ix.

30. Stone, *The Trial of Socrates*, 44–45.

31. Thucydides, *The Peloponnesian War*, trans. Rex Warner (Baltimore: Penguin Books, 1954), 211.

32. Polybius, *The Histories of Polybius*, vol. 1, bk. 6, trans. Evelyn S. Shuckburgh (London: Macmillan, 1889), 467–74.

33. James Madison, "Federalist No. 10," in *A Documentary History of the United States*, ed. Richard D. Heffner, 4th ed. (New York: New American Library, 1985), 42.

34. Ibid., 44.

35. Cf. Fergus Millar, *The Crowd in Rome in the Late Republic* (Ann Arbor: University of Michigan Press, 2002), 15ff.

36. Bringmann, *A History of the Roman Republic*, 45.

37. Ibid., 127.

38. On the fall of Rome, see Bryan Ward-Perkins, *The Fall of Rome and the End of Civilization* (Oxford: Oxford University Press, 2005).

39. Quoted by Patrtick J. Geary in *The Myth of Nations: The Medieval Origins of Europe* (Princeton, NJ: Princeton University Press, 2002), 145.

40. J. G. A. Pocock, *The Machiavellian Moment: Florentine Political Thought and the Atlantic RepublicanTradition* (Princeton, NJ: Princeton University Press, 1975), 116ff.

41. Niccolo Machiavelli, *The Prince and the Discourses* (New York: Modern Library, 1950), 208–9. Cf. discussion of Machiavelli's republicanism in Fergus Millar, *The Roman Republic in Political Thought* (Hanover, NH: University Press of New England, 2002), 64–79.

42. James Harrington, *The Commonwealth of Oceana and a System of Politics* (Cambridge: Cambridge University Press, 1999), 106.

43. On Harrington, cf. Paul A. Rahe, *Republics Ancient and Modern* (Chapell Hill: University of North Carolina Press, 1992), 409–27; see also Pocock, *The Machiavellian Moment*, 383–400; and also G. P. Gooch, *English Democratic Ideas in the Seventeenth Century* (New York: Harper and Row, 1959), 241–57.

44. Harrington, *The Commonwealth of Oceana*.

45. Ibid., 33.

46. Ibid., 12.

47. Cf. Thomas G. West, "Foreword", in Algernon Sidney, *Discourses Concerning Government* (Indianapolis: Liberty Classics, 1990), xxxviii–xxxvi.

48. Sidney, *Discourses Concerning Government*, 103.

49. Harrington, *Commonwealth of Oceana*, 23.

50. Ibid., 22.

51. Cf. Larry Neal, *The Rise of Financial Capitalism: International Capital Markets in the Age of Reason* (Cambridge: Cambridge University Press, 1990); see also Niall Ferguson, *The Cash Nexus: Money and Power in the Modern World, 1700–2000* (New York: Basic Books, 2001).

52. John Trenchard and Thomas Gordon, *Cato's Letters: Or, Essays on Liberty, Civil and Religious, and Other Important Subjects*, ed. Ronald Hamowy (Indianapolis: Liberty Fund, 1995), 44.

53. Ibid., 48.

54. Pocock, *The Machiavellian Moment*, 485.

55. Baron de Montesquieu, *The Spirit of the Laws*, trans. Thomas Nugent (New York: Hafner Press, 1975), 44.

56. George Berkeley, *The Querist*, in *The Works of George Berkeley*, vol. 6 (London: Nelson, 1964), 105ff.

57. On the confusion of money and wealth, cf. Frederick Soddy, *Wealth, Virtual Wealth and Debt* (1926; repr., London: George Allen and Unwin, 1983), 69–92.

58. David Hume, "Idea of a Perfect Commonwealth," in *Essays Moral, Political, Literary*, Online Library of Liberty: http://oll.libertyfund..org/Home3/HTML, 4.

59. Montesquieu, *The Spirit of the Laws*, 126.

60. Ibid., lx "Editor's Introduction," by Franz Neumann, x.

61. David Hume, "Idea of a Perfect Commonwealth," 4–5

62. Ibid., 9

63. Brown, *The Web of Debt*, 404.

64. Alexander Del Mar, *The History of Money in America* (1899; repr., Hawthone, CA: Omni, 1979), vii–ix.

65. For an account of English developments in the sixteenth and seventeenth centuries, see Christopher Hollis, *The Two Nations* (New York: Gordon Press, 1975), 1–27.

66. Larry Neal, *The Rise of Financial Capitalism: International Capital Markets in the Age of Reason* (Cambridge: Cambridge University Press, 1990), 90.

67. Brown, *The Web of Debt*, 70; emphasis in original.

68. Hollis, *The Two Nations,* 29–30; on the story of the Bank of England and its significance see Hollis, *The Two Nations*, chapters 2 and 3. Cf. the account given in Zarlenga, *The Lost Science of Money*, chapters 10 and 11.

69. Alexander Hamilton, letter to James Duane, in *Writings*, 83.

70. On the modern background of finance capital see Carroll Quigley, *Tragedy and Hope* (New York: Macmillan, 1966), 42–77; for more general accounts of money and credit systems, see Zarlenga, *The Lost Science of Money* (2002); Hollis, *The Two Nations*; and Brown, *The Web of Debt*; for nonpopulist views, cf. Ferguson, *The Cash Nexus*; Glyn Davies, *A History of Money: From Ancient Times to the Present Day*, 3rd ed., rev. (Cardiff: University of Wales Press, 2002); John Kenneth Galbraith, *Money: Whence It Came, Where It Went* (Boston: Houghton Mifflin, 1975); and Sidney Homer, *A History of Interest Rates* (New Brunswick, NJ: Rutgers University Press, 1963).

71. Frederick Soddy, *Wealth, Virtual Wealth and Debt: The Solution of the Economic Paradox* (London: George Allen & Unwin, 1926; repr., Palmdale, CA: Omni, n.d.), 70; emphasis in original.

72. Ibid., p. 80.

73. Ibid., 70.

74. Ibid., 79.

75. Ibid., 134.
76. Ibid., 137.
77. Ibid., 186.
78. Ibid., 153.
79. Ibid., 196.
80. Ibid., 182.
81. Ibid., 209ff.

Notes to Chapter Four

1. On American colonial monies, see Zarlenga, *The Lost Science of Money*, 361–72; Alexander Del Mar, *The History of Money in America* (1899; repr., Hawthorne, CA: Omni, 1979), 73–92; and Brown, *The Web of Debt*, 35–45.
2. Benjamin Franklin, "A Modest Inquiry into the Nature and Necessity of a Paper-Currency," in *Writings* (New York: Library of America, 1987), 129; cf. his "Essay on Paper Currency: Proposing a New Method for Fixing Its Value," in Writings, 286–90.
3. Franklin, "A Modest Inquiry," 134.
4. Ibid., 129.
5. Zarlenga, *The Lost Science of Money*, 373–77.
6. Del Mar, *The History of Money in America*, 96.
7. Ibid., 377–87.
8. Martin Van Buren, *The Origin and Course of Political Parties in the United States* (1867; repr., New York: Augustus M. Kelley, 1967), 139–40.
9. Ibid., 161.
10. Cf. Forrest McDonald, *Novus Ordo Seclorum: The Intellectual Origins of the Constitution* (Lawrence: University of Kansas Press, 1985), 139–42, and Donald Gibson, *Battling Wall Street: The Kennedy Presidency* (New York: Sheridan Square Press, 1994), 103–5.
11. Ibid., 165–66.
12. Thomas Jefferson, *Writings: Autobiography, A Summary View of the Rights of British America, Notes on the State of Virginia, Public Papers, Addresses, Messages, and Replies, Miscellany, Letters* (New York: Library of America, 1984), 1283–84.
13. Ibid., 1284–85.
14. Quoted in John P. Diggins, *The Lost Soul of American Politics* (Chicago: University of Chicago Press, 1984), 145.

15. John Locke, *Second Treatise of Government* (New York: Liberal Arts Press, 1952), 17.
16. Jefferson, *Writings*, 841–42.
17. Willard Sterne Randall, *Thomas Jefferson: A Life* (New York: Henry Holt, 1993), 204.
18. George McGuire, "The Brooklyn Gren Flat Tax (A Populist Manifesto)," unpublished ms., 1997, 14.
19. Jefferson, *Writings*, 841.
20. Ibid., 1280; emphasis in original.
21. Ibid., 1395.
22. This scheme is hardly known except to Jefferson scholars, and mostly passed over by them, with some exceptions, including Hannah Arendt, Richard K. Matthews, and Garrett Ward Sheldon; see also Gary Hart, *Restoration of the Republic: The Jefferson Ideal in 21st-Century America* (Oxford: Oxford University Press, 2002); Hart puts Jefferson's ward republics at the center of his program to reform American politics.
23. Paine, *Collected Writings*, 566.
24. Pauline Maier, "The Revolutionary Origins of the American Corporations," *William and Mary Quarterly*, 3rd series, l, no. 11 (1993): 60–61.
25. Ibid., 64.
26. Ibid., 67–68.
27. On independent Vermont, see Michael A. Bellesiles, *Revolutionary Outlaws: Ethan Allen and the Struggle for Independence on the Early American Frontier* (Charlottesville: University of Virginia Press, 1993).
28. Ibid., 137–39.
29. Ibid., 252–53.
30. Andrew Jackson, "Andrew Jackson's Bank Veto," online at http://www.nv.cc.va.us/home/nvsageh/Hist121/Part3/JacksonBankVeto.htm (accessed June 2004).
31. Jack Beatty, *Age of Betrayal: The Triumph of Money in America, 1865–1900* (New York: Random House, 2007), 12.
32. Ibid., 11.
33. Quoted by Reeve Huston in *Land and Freedom: Rural Society, Popular Protest, and Party Politics in Antebellum New York* (Oxford: Oxford University Press, 2000), 114.
34. Ibid.
35. Ellen Meiksins Wood, "Demos vs. 'We the People,'" in *Demokratia: A Conversation on Democracies, Ancient and Modern*, ed. Josiah Ober and Charles Hedrick (Princeton, NJ: Princeton University Press, 1996), 124.

36. Madison, "Federalist No. 10," 44.
37. Ibid., 47.
38. Randall, *Thomas Jefferson*, 301.
39. See Anthony Gronowicz, *Race and Class Politics in New York City before the Civil War* (Boston: Northeastern University Press, 1998).
40. Cf. David Quigley, *Second Founding: New York City, Reconstruction, and the Making of American Democracy* (New York: Hill and Wang, 2004).
41. Montesquieu, *The Spirit of the Laws*, 126.
42. Thomas Paine, *The Rights of Man*, in *Collected Writings*, ed. Eric Foner (New York: Library of America, 1995), 566–68.
43. Thomas Jefferson, "Letter to Samuel Kercheval, 12 July 1816," in *Writings*, 1399–1400.
44. Thomas Jefferson, "Letter to I. H. Tiffany, 1816," in *Thomas Jefferson on Democracy*, ed. Saul K. Padover (New York: D. Appleton–Century, 1939), 21–22.
45. Cf. Henry M. Roberts, *Rules of Order Revised for Deliberative Assemblies* (Chicago: Scott, Foresman, 1915).
46. Frank Bryan and John McClaughry, *The Vermont Papers: Recreating Democracy on a Human Scale* (Chelsea, VT: Chelsea Green, 1989), 82–160.
47. Hart, *Restoration of the Republic*, 117.
48. Ibid., 16.
49. Ibid., 164.
50. Ellen Meiksins Wood, "Democracy: An Idea of Ambiguous Ancestry," in *Athenian Political Thought and the Reconstruction of American Democracy* ed. Peter Euben, Josiah Ober, and John Wallach (Ithaca, NY: Cornell University Press, 1994), 62.
51. Ibid., 61.
52. Francis Bowen, *American Political Economy; Including Structures on the Management of the Currency and the Finances since 1861, with a Chart Flowing the Flucturation in the Price of Gold* (1870; repr., New York: Greenwood Press, 1969), 67.
53. Ibid., 329.
54. Ibid., 406.
55. Mark A. Lause, *Young America: Land, Labor, and the Republican Community* (Urbana: University of Illinois Press, 2005), 122.
56. Edward Kellogg, *A New Monetary System: The Only Means of Securing the Respective Rights of Labor and Property and of Protecting the Public from Financial Revulsions* (1861; repr., New York: Burt Franklin, 1970), 252–53.
57. Ibid., 22.

58. Ibid., 29.
59. Ibid., 46.
60. Ibid., 60.
61. Ibid., 61–62.
62. Ibid., 60.
63. Ibid., 181.
64. Ibid., 80.
65. Ibid., 86.
66. Ibid., 108.
67. Ibid., 160.
68. Ibid., 138.
69. Ibid., 164.
70. Ibid., 307.
71. Ibid., 286.
72. Ibid., 289.
73. Ibid., 279.
74. Ibid., 274.
75. Ibid., 276.
76. Ibid., 61–62.
77. Ibid., 138.
78. Ibid., 184–85.
79. Ibid., 192.
80. Ibid., 230.
81. Ibid., 302.
82. Ibid., 306.
83. "1876 Platform, National, Independent or 'Greenback' Party," online at http://www.geocities.com/CollegePark/Quad/6460/doct/876grbk.html (accessed January 2004).
84. "*The Omaha Platform*; the Populists in 1892," online at http://www.nv.cc.va.us/home/nvsageh/Hist122/Part1/PopulistPlat1892.htm (accessed January 2004).
85. On the influence of Kellogg on subsequent greenbackers and populists, cf. Chester McArthur Destler, *American Radicalism: 1865–1901* (Chicago: Quadrangle Books, 1966), 50–77.
86. Lawrence Goodwyn, *Democratic Promise* (New York: Oxford University Press, 1976); see also Robert C. McMath Jr., *American Populism: A Social History 1877–1898* (New York: Hill and Wang, 1993); and Beatty, *Age of Betrayal*, 303–45.
87. Goodwyn, *Democratic Promise*, 152.

88. Ibid., 556–57.
89. Ibid., 567.
90. High, that is, by Kellogg's standards, where even a 2 percent rate is considered usurious.
91. Alfred Lawson, *Direct Credits for Everybody* (Detroit: Humanity, 1931), 16.
92. Ibid., 17.
93. Lawson's summary of his program follows:

> 1. Gold must be abolished as money and everybody prohibited from using it to pay for anything. 2. Paper currency must be made the standard of exchange and issued in sufficient quantities for all purposes. 3. Interest, and all other forms of payment for the use of money must be abolished and prohibited. 4. Control of supervision of money must be by the government, who will operate all banks and other financial institutions. Private banking must be prohibited. 5. All financial loans must be made by the government. Private loans in business transactions must be prohibited. 6. All credits must be issued by the government direct to everybody. 7. Everybody must be entitled to basic equal credits given by the government. 8. Everybody must perform actual service in return for credits. 9. Limited credits must be issued to everybody without security. 10. Credits must be issued for the upkeep and education of children up to 21 years of age, to be voluntarily repaid by them, if possible, at some future and convenient time. 11. Credits must be issued to everybody past 65 years of age for living expenses, if wanted. The size of such credits to be proportionate to the value of the services rendered by the beneficiary prior to that age. 12. Charity must be abolished and justice take its place. Credits must be issued to the sick and lame. Doctors and nurses will be paid by the government both in money and honors. They must treat all patients with equal consideration. 13. All controversies must be settled by Courts appointed by the government, who will also furnish lawyers for both sides of the case. These lawyers will be paid by the government and prohibited from taking private fees of any nature whatsoever. Disbarment, disgrace, imprisonment or worse, will be the punishment for lawyers who misrepresent anything in connection with a case they are handling 14. Everybody must furnish sworn statements periodi-

cally, showing the amount and character of wealth possessed
and the manner in which it was obtained. (Ibid., 30–31)
94. See Thomas H. Greco Jr., *Money: Understanding and Creating Alternatives
to Legal Tender* (White River Junction, VT: Chelsea Green, 2001).
95. Huey P. Long, "'Redistribution of Wealth,' *The Congressional Record*, 14
January 1935," in Huey P. Long, *Kingfish to America: Share Our Wealth:
Selected Senatorial Papers of Huey P. Long*, ed. Henry M. Christman (New
York: Schocken Books, 1985), 50–51.

Notes to Appendix

1. Jefferson, 1381.
2. Ibid., 1073.
3. Ibid., 1226–27.
4. Ibid., 1307–9.
5. Ibid., 1348.
6. Ibid., 1379–81.
7. Ibid., 1392–93.
8. Ibid., 1395.
9. Ibid., 1399–1401.
10. Ibid., 1402–3.
11. Ibid., 1492–93.

Bibliography

Aldrich, Nelson W., Jr., *Old Money: The Mythology of America's Upper Class*. New York: Random House, 1988.

Allen, Ira. *The Natural and Political History of the State of Vermont*. Rutland, VT: Charles E. Tuttle, 1969.

Allen, W. B., Gordon Lloyd, and Margie Lloyd, eds. *The Essential Anti-Federalist*. Lanham, MD: University Press of America, 1985.

Alm, Richard, and Cox, Michael W. *Myths of Rich and Poor: Why We're Better Off than We Think*. New York: Basic Books, 1999.

Andelson, Robert V., ed. *Critics of Henry George: A Centenary Appraisal of Their Strictures on Progress and Poverty*. London: Associated University Presses, 1979.

Anderson, Hugold. *Government without Taxation*. New York: Exposition Press, 1965.

Andreades, A. *History of the Bank of England: 1640–1903*. Translated by Christabel Meredith. 4th ed. New York: Augustus M. Kelley, 1966.

Appleby, Joyce. *Capitalism and a New Social Order: The Republican Vision of the 1790s*. New York: New York University Press, 1984.

———. *Liberalism and Republicanism in the Historical Imagination*. Cambridge, MA: Harvard University Press, 1992.

Arendt, Hannah. *On Revolution*. New York: Viking Press, 1963.

Aristotle. *The Ethics of Aristotle: The Nichmachean Ethics*. Translated by J. A. K. Thomson. Revised by Hugh Tredennick. New York: Penguin, 1978.

———. *Politics*. Translated by H. Rackham. Loeb Classical Library. Cambridge, MA: Harvard University Press, 1990.

Aristotle, and Xenophon. *Aristotle and Xenophon on Democracy and Oligarchy: Aristotle's The Constitution of Athens, The Constitution of the Athenians ascribed to Xenophon the Orator, Xenophon's The Politeia of the Spartans, The Boeotian Constitution from the Oxyrhynchus Historian.* Translated with commentary by J. M. Moore. Berkeley and Los Angeles: University of California Press, 1986.

Atlas of Otsego County, New York, from Actual Surveys by and under the Direction of F. W. Beers. New York: F. W. Beers, A. D. Ellis, and G. G. Soule, 1868.

Ayer, A. J. *Thomas Paine.* New York: Atheneum, 1988.

Banning, Lance. *The Jeffersonian Persuasion: Evolution of a Party Ideology.* Ithaca, NY: Cornell University Press, 1978.

Barber, Benjamin. *Strong Democracy: Participatory Politics for a New Age.* Berkeley and Los Angeles: University of California Press, 1984.

Beard, Mary, and Crawford, Michael. *Rome in the Late Republic.* Ithaca, NY: Cornell University Press, 1985.

Beatty, Jack. *Age of Betrayal: The Triumph of Money in America, 1865–1900.* New York: Alfred A. Knopf, 2007.

———. *Colossus: How the Corporation Changed America.* New York: Broadway Books, 2001.

Bellesiles, Michael A. *Revolutionary Outlaws: Ethan Allen and the Struggle for Independence on the Early American Frontier.* Charlottesville: University of Virginia Press, 1993.

Berry, Wendell. *Home Economics.* San Francisco: North Point Press, 1987.

———. *The Unsettling of America: Culture and Agriculture.* San Francisco: Sierra Club Books, 1977.

———. *What Are People For?* San Francisco: North Point Press, 1990.

Biehl, Janet. *The Politics of Social Ecology: Libertarian Municipalism.* Montreal: Black Rose Books, 1998.

Bledsoe, Wayne H., ed. *The Advent of Civilization.* Lexington, MA: D. C. Heath, 1975.

Bookchin, Murray. "Municipalization: Community Ownership of the Economy." Green Program Project, Burlington, VT: 1986,

———. *Post-Scarcity Anarchism.* Berkeley, CA: Ramparts Press, 1971.

———. *Remaking Society: Pathways to a Green Future.* Boston: South End Press, 1990.

———. *The Rise of Urbanization and the Decline of Citizenship.* San Francisco: Sierra Club Books, 1987.

Bookchin, Murray, and Dave Foreman. *Defending the Earth: A Dialogue between Murray Bookchin and Dave Foreman.* Boston: South End Press, 1991.

Boorstein, Daniel J. *The Lost World of Thomas Jefferson: With a New Preface.* Chicago: University of Chicago Press, 1981.

Borsodi, Ralph. *Inflation and the Coming Keynesian Catastrophe: The Story of the Exeter Experiments with Constants.* Great Barrington, MA: E. F. Schumacher Society, 1989.

Botsford, George Willis. *The Roman Assemblies from Their Origin to the End of the Republic.* New York: Cooper Square, 1968.

Bowen, Francis. *American Political Economy.* 1870. Reprint, New York: Greenwood Press, 1969.

Bradford, M. E. *A Better Guide than Reason: Studies in the American Revolution.* La Salle, IL: Sherwood, Sugden, 1979.

Bringmann, Klaus. *A History of the Roman Republic.* Translated by W. J. Smyth. Cambridge: Polity Press, 2007.

Brinkley, Alan. *Voices of Protest: Huey Long, Father Coughlin, and the Great Depression.* New York: Alfred A. Knopf, 1982.

Brockway, George P. *The End of Economic Man: Principles of Any Future Economics.* New York: W. W. Norton, 1993.

Brodie, Fawn M. *Thomas Jefferson: An Intimate History.* New York: W. W. Norton, 1974.

Brown, Ellen Jodgson, J. D. *The Web of Debt: The Shocking Truth about Our Money System—The Sleight of Hand that Has Trapped Us in Debt and How We Can Break Free.* Baton Rouge, LA: Third Millennium Press, 2007.

Brunt, P. A. *Social Conflicts in the Roman Republic.* New York: W. W. Norton, 1971.

Bryan, Frank, and McClaughry, John. *The Vermont Papers: Recreating Democracy on a Human Scale.* Chelsea, VT: Chelsea Green, 1989.

Budyko, M. I. *Global Ecology.* Moscow: Progress, 1980.

Burkert, Walter, Rene Girard, and Jonathan Z. Smith. *Violent Origins: Ritual Killing and Cultural Formation.* Edited by Robert G. Hamerton-Kelley. Stanford, CA: Stanford University Press, 1987.

Catton, William R., Jr. *Overshoot: The Ecological Basis of Revolutionary Change.* Urbana: University of Illinois Press, 1982.

Chandler, Alfred D., Jr. *The Visible Hand: The Managerial Revolution in American Business.* Cambridge, MA: Belknap Press of Harvard University Press, 1977.

Chomsky, Noam. *The Prosperous Few and the Restless Many.* Berkeley, CA: Odonian Press, 1993.

Cipolla, Carlo M. *Before the Industrial Revolution: European Society and Economy, 1000–1700.* New York: W. W. Norton, 1976.

Cohen, Edward E. *Athenian Economy and Soceity: A Banking Perspective.* Princeton, NJ: Princeton University Press, 1993.

Commoner, Barry. *The Closing Circle: Nature, Man, and Technology.* New York: Alfred A. Knopf, 1977.

———. *The Poverty of Power: Energy and the Economic Crisis.* New York: Alfred A. Knopf, 1976.

Parker, Arthur C. *The Constitution of the Five Nations, or the Iroquois Book of the Great Law.* Ohsweken: Iroqrafts, 1967.

The Constitution of the United States: With Index and The Declaration of Independence. Washington, DC: The Commission on the Bicentennial of the United States Constitution, 1991.

Cooper, James Fenimore. *The American Democrat.* Indianapolis: Liberty Classics, 1959.

"Corporation." In *Encyclopaedia Britannica.* 13th ed. London: Encyclopaedia Britannica, 1926.

"Corporation." In *The New Columbia Encyclopedia.* New York: Columbia University Press, 1975.

Crawford, Harriet. *Sumer and the Sumerians.* Cambridge: Cambridge University Press, 1991.

Culver, John C., and Hyde, John. *American Dreamer: A Life of Henry A. Wallace.* New York: W. W. Norton, 2000.

Cunningham, Jr., Noble E. *The Jeffersonian Republicans: The Formation of Party Organization, 1789–1801.* Chapel Hill: University of North Carolina Press, 1957.

Davies, Glyn. *A History of Money: From Ancient Times to the Present Day.* 3rd ed., rev. Cardiff: University of Wales Press, 2002.

Davis, John P. *Corporations: A Study of the Origin and Development of Great Business Combination and of the Relation to the Authority of the State.* 2 vols. New York: Capricorn Books, 1961.

Demming, W. Edwards. *The New Economics for Industry, Government, Education.* Cambridge, MA: MIT Press, 1993.

Destler, Chester McArthur. *American Radicalism: 1865–1901.* Chicago: Quandrangle Books, 1966.

Diggins, John P. *The Lost Soul of American Politics: Virtue, Self-Interest, and the Foundations of Liberalism.* Chicago: University of Chicago Press, 1984.

Dobson, Andrew, ed. *The Green Reader: Essays towards a Sustainable Society*. San Francisco: Mercury House, 1991.

Douthwaite, Richard. *The Ecology of Money*. Totnes, Devon, England: Green Books, 1999.

———. *The Growth Illusion: How Economic Growth Has Enriched the Few, Impoverished the Many and Endangered the Planet*. Gabriola Island BC: New Society, 1999.

———. *Short Circuit: Strengthening Local Economies for Security in an Unstable World*. Dublin: Lilliput Press, 1996.

Eccles, Marriner S. *Beckoning Frontiers: Public and Personal Recollections*. New York: Alfred A. Knopf, 1951.

Ellis, Joseph J. *American Sphinx: The Character of Thomas Jefferson*. New York: Alfred A. Knopf, 1997.

Engelbrecht, William. "New York Iroquois Political Development." In *Cultures in Contact: The Impact of European Contacts on Native American Cultural Institutions: A. D. 1000–1800*. Edited by W. Fitzhugh. Washington, DC: Smithsonian Institution Press, 1985.

Engels, Frederick. *The Origin of the Family, Private Property, and the State*. New York: International, 1973.

Engler, Allan. *Apostles of Greed: Capitalism and the Myth of the Individual in the Market*. London: Pluto Press, 1995.

Evans-Pritchard, E. E. *The Nuer: A Description of the Modes of Livelihood and Political Institutions of a Nilotic People*. Oxford: Oxford University Press, 1940.

Fairservis, Walter A., Jr. *The Threshold of Civilization: An Experiment in Prehistory*. New York: Charles Scribner's Sons, 1975.

Farrar, Cynthia. *The Origins of Democratic Thinking: The Invention of Politics in Classical Athens*. Cambridge: Cambridge University Press, 1988.

"FC" [Theodore Kaczynski]. *The Unabomber Manifesto: Industrial Society and Its Future*. Berkeley, CA: Jolly Roger Press, 1995.

The Federal Reserve System: Purposes and Functions. 8th ed. Washington, DC: Board of Governors of the Federal Reserve, 1994.

Ferguson, Niall. *The Cash Nexus: Money and Power in the Modern World, 1700–2000*. New York: Basic Books, 2001.

Finley, M. I. *The Ancient Economy*. 2nd ed. Berkeley and Los Angeles: University of California Press, 1973.

———. *Democracy Ancient and Modern*. Rev. ed. New Brunswick, NJ: Rutgers University Press, 1985.

————. *Politics in the Ancient World*. Cambridge: Cambridge University Press, 1983.

Follett, M. P. *The New State: Group Organization the Solution of Popular Government*. New York: Longmans, Green, 1918.

Forrest, W. G. *The Emergence of Greek Democracy: 800–400 BC*. New York: McGraw-Hill, 1966.

Fossedal, Gregory A. *Direct Democracy in Switzerland*. New Brunswick, NJ: Transaction, 2002.

Freeman, Kathleen. *Greek City-States*. New York: Norton and Norton, 1950.

Fried, Morton H. *The Evolution of Political Society: An Essay in Political Anthropology*. New York: Random House, 1967.

Frost, James Arthur. *Life on the Upper Susquehanna 1783–1860*. New York: Columbia University King's Crown Press, 1951.

Fustel de Coulanges, Numa Denis. *The Ancient City: A Study of the Religion, Laws, and Institutions of Ancient Greece and Rome Translated by Willard Small*. New York: Doubleday, 1956.

Galbraith, John Kenneth. *Money: Whence It Came, Where It Went*. Boston: Houghton Mifflin, 1975.

————. *The New Industrial State*. 2nd ed. Boston: Houghton Mifflin, 1972.

Garrett, Garet. *A Bubble that Broke the World*. Boston: Little, Brown, 1932.

Garrett, Garet, and Murray N. Rothbard. *The Great Depression and New Deal Monetary Policy*. Cato Paper No. 13. San Francisco: Cato Institute, 1980.

Gates, Jeff. *The Ownership Solution: Towards a Shared Capitalism for the 21st Century*. New York: Addison-Wesley, 1998.

Gause, Andrew. *The Secret World of Money*. Hilton Head, NC: SDL Press, 1996.

Geary, Patrick J. *The Myth of Nations: The Medieval Origins of Europe*. Princeton, NJ: Princeton University Press, 2002.

George, Henry. *Progress and Poverty: An Inquiry into the Cause of Industrial Depressions and of Increase of Want with Increase of Wealth*. New York: Robert Schalkenback Foundtion, 1960.

George-Kanentiio, Doug. *Iroquois Culture and Commentary*. Sante Fe, NM: Clear Light Publishers, 2000.

Gibbon, Edward. *The Decline and Fall of the Roman Empire*. 7 vols. New York: AMS Press, 1974.

Gibson, Donald. *Battling Wall Street: The Kennedy Presidency.* New York: Sheridan Square Press, 1994.

Gilreath, James, ed. *Thomas Jefferson and the Education of a Citizen.* Washington, DC: Library of Congress. 1999.

Gitlin, Todd. *The Sixties: Years of Hope, Days of Rage.* New York: Bantam Books, 1987.

Gooch, G. P. *English Democratic Ideas in the 17th Century.* 2nd ed. New York: Harper and Row, 1959.

Goodin, Robert E. *Green Political Theory.* Cambridge: Polity Press, 1992.

Goodwin, Jason. *Greenback: The Almighty Dollar and the Invention of America.* New York: Henry Holt, 2003.

Goodwyn, Lawrence. *Democratic Promise: The Populist Moment in America.* New York: Oxford University Press, 1976.

Gorz, Andre. *Critique of Economic Reason.* Translated by Gillian Handyside and Chris Turner. London: Verso, 1989.

Grant, James. *Money of the Mind: Borrowing and Lending in America from the Civil War to Michael Milken.* New York: Farrar, and Straus Giroux, 1992.

Grant, Michael. *History of Rome.* New York: Charles Scribner's Sons, 1978.

Greco, Thomas H., Jr. *Money: Understanding and Creating Alternatives to Legal Tender.* White River Junction, VT: Chelsea Green Publishing, 2001.

Green Party Platform 2000. Association of State Green Parties Nominating Convention, Denver, CO, June 2000.

Greene, William B. *Mutual Banking: Showing the Radical Deficiency of the Present Circulating Medium and the Advantages of a Free Currency.* Boston: New England Labor Reform League, 1870.

Greider, William. *One World, Ready or Not: The Manic Logic of Global Capitalism.* New York: Touchstone Books, 1997.

———. *Secrets of the Temple: How the Federal Reserve Runs the Country.* New York: Simon and Schuster, 1987.

———. *The Trouble with Money.* Knoxville, TN: Whittle Direct Books, 1989.

———. *Who Will Tell the People: The Betrayal of American Democracy.* New York: Simon and Schuster, 1992.

Gronowicz, Anthony. *Race and Class Politics in New York City before the Civil War.* Boston: Northeastern University Press, 1998.

Gross, Bertram. *Friendly Fascism: The New Face of Power in America.* Boston: South End Press, 1980.

Habicht, Christian. *Athens from Alexander to Antony.* Translated by Deborah Lucas Schneider. Cambridge, MA: Harvard University Press, 1997.

Hacker, Andrew. *Money: Who Has How Much and Why.* New York: Simon and Schuster, 1997.

Halloway, Mark. *Utopian Communities in America 1680–1880.* Mineola, NY: Dover, 1966.

Hamilton, Alexander. *Writings.* New York: Library of America, 2001.

Hansen, Mogens Herman. *The Athenian Democracy in the Age of Demosthenes: Structure, Principles, and Ideology.* Translated by J. A. Crook. Oxford: Blackwell, 1991.

Hansmann, Henry. *The Ownership of Enterprise.* Cambridge, MA: Belknap Press of Harvard University Press, 1996.

Hanson, Victor Davis. "Countryside Character.", Review of Nicholas F. Jones, *Rural Athens under the Democracy. The Times Literary Supplement,* June 25, 2004.

———. *The Other Greeks: The Family Farm and the Agrarian Roots of Western Civilization.* New York: Free Press, 1995.

Hardin, Garrett. *Filters against Folly: How to Survive Despite Economists, Ecologists, and the Merely Eloquent.* New York: Viking Penguin, 1985.

Harrington, James. *The Commonwealth of Oceana and a System of Politics.* Edited by J. G. A. Pocock. Cambridge, UK: Cambridge University Press, 1992.

Harris, C. C. *Kinship.* Minneapolis: University of Minnesota Press, 1990.

Harris, Marvin. *Cannibals and Kings: The Origins of Cultures.* New York: Random House, 1979.

Harrod, R. F. *The Life of John Maynard Keynes.* Harmondsworth, England: Penguin, 1972.

Hart, Gary. *Restoration of the Republic: The Jeffersonian Ideal in 21st-Century America.* Oxford: Oxford University Press, 2002.

Harvey, William H. *Coin's Financial School.* Edited by Richard Hofstadter. Cambridge, MA: Belknap Press of Harvard University Press, 1963.

Hawken, Paul. *The Ecology of Commerce: A Declaration of Sustainability.* New York: Harper Business, 1993.

Hawken, Paul, Amory Lovins, and L. Hunter Lovins. *Natural Capitalism: Creating the Next Industrial Revolution.* Boston: Little, Brown, 1999.

Hawley, Ellis. *The New Deal and the Problem of Monopoly: A Study in Economic Ambivalence.* Princeton, NJ: Princeton University Press, 1966.

Hayak, Friedrich A. *The Road to Serfdom.* Chicago: University of Chicago Press, 1972.

Heffner, Richard D., ed. *A Documentary History of the United States.* 4th ed. New York: New American Library, 1985.

Heilbroner, Robert L. *The Worldly Philosophers: The Lives, Times and Ideas of the Great Economic Thinkers.* 4th ed. New York: Simon and Schuster, 1972.

Heilbroner, Robert L., and Lester C. Thurow. *The Economic Problem.* 4th ed. Englewood Cliffs, NJ: Prentice-Hall, 1975.

Heinberg, Richard. *Powerdown: Options and Actions for a Post-Carbon World.* Gabriola Island, BC: New Society, 2004.

Herman, Edward S. *Corporate Control, Corporate Power.* Cambridge: Cambridge University Press, 1981.

Herodotus. *The History.* Translated by David Grene. Chicago: University of Chicago Press, 1987.

Hobsbawn, E. J. *The Age of Capital 1848–1875.* New York: Charles Scribner's Sons, 1975.

Hollis, Christopher. *The Breakdown of Money: An Historical Explanation.* New York: Sheed and Ward, 1934.

———. *The Two Nations: A Financial Study of English History.* New York: Gordon Press, 1975.

Homer, Sidney. *A History of Interest Rates.* New Brunswick, NJ: Rutgers University Press, 1963.

Hooper, Finley. *Roman Realities.* Detroit: Wayne State University Press, 1979.

Hounshell, David A. *From the American System to Mass Production: 1800–1932.* Baltimore: Johns Hopkins University Press, 1984.

Huntington, Samuel P. *The Clash of Civilizations: Remaking of World Order.* New York: Touchstone, 1997.

Huston, Reeve. *Land and Freedom: Rural Society, Popular Protest, and Party Politics in Antebellum New York.* Oxford: Oxford University Press, 2000.

Inhaber, Herbert, and Sidney Carroll. *How Rich Is Too Rich? Income and Wealth in America.* New York: Praeger, 1992.

Issac, James Paton. *Factors in the Ruin of Antiquity: A Criticism of Ancient Civilization.* Privately published, 1971.

Jackson, Andrew. "Andrew Jackson's Bank Veto." Online at http://www.nv.cc.va.us/home/nvsageh/Hist121/Part3/JacksonBankVeto.htm. Accessed June 2004.

Jacobs, Jane. *Cities and the Wealth of Nations: Principles of Economic Life.* New York: Random House, 1984.

———. *The Death and Life of Great American Cities.* New York: Vintage Books, 1961.

———. *The Economy of Cities.* New York: Vintage Books, 1970.

———. "The Economy of Regions." In *People, Land, and Community: Collected E. F. Schumacker Society Lectures.* Edited by Hildegarde Hannum. New Haven, CT: Yale University Press, 1997.

Jefferson, Thomas. *Jefferson: Magnificent Populist.* Edited by Martin A. Larson. Washington, DC: Robert B. Luce, 1981.

———. *Thomas Jefferson on Democracy.* Edited by Saul K. Padover. New York: D. Appleton–Century, 1939.

———. *Writings: Autobiography, A Summary View of the Rights of British America, Notes on the State of Virginia, Public Papers, Addresses, Messages, and Replies, Miscellany, Letters.* New York: Library of America, 1984.

Jennings, Francis. *The Ambiguous Iroquois Empire: The Covenant Chain Confederaton of Indian Tribes with English Colonies from Its Beginnings to the Lancaster Treaty of 1744.* New York: W. W. Norton, 1984.

———. *The Invasion of America: Indians, Colonialism, and the Cant of Conquest.* New York: W. W. Norton, 1975.

Jensen, Merrill. *The Articles of Confederation: An Interpretation of the Social-Constitutional History of the American Revolution 1774–1781.* Madison: University of Wisconsin Press, 1959.

Johansen, Bruce E. *Forgotten Founders: How the American Indian Helped Shape Democracy.* Boston: Harvard Common Press, 1982.

Johnston, Robert D. *The Radical Middle Class: Populist Democracy and the Question of Capitalism in Progressive Era Portland, Oregon.* Princeton, NJ: Princeton University Press, 2003.

Jones, A. H. M. *The Decline of the Ancient World.* London: Longman, 1966.

Kagan, Donald. *Pericles of Athens and the Birth of Democracy.* New York: Free Press, 1991.

Kaplan, Robert D. "The Coming Anarchy." *The Atlantic Monthly,* 273, no. 4 (1994): pp. no.

Kaufman, Henry. *Interest Rates, the Markets, and the New Financial World*. New York: Times Books, 1986.

Kazin, Michael. *The Populist Persuasion: An American History*. New York: Basic Books, 1995.

Keane, John. *Tom Paine: A Political Life*. Boston: Little, Brown, 1995.

Keesing, Roger M. *Kin Groups and Social Structure*. New York: Holt, Rinehart and Winston, 1975.

Kellogg, Edward. *Labor and Other Capital: The Rights of Each Secured and the Wrongs of Both Eradicated*. 1849. Reprint, New York: Augustus M. Kelley, 1971.

————. *A New Monetary System: The Only Means of Securing the Respective Rights of Labor and Property and of Protecting the Public from Financial Revulsions*. Edited by Mary Kellogg Putnam. 1861. Reprint, New York: Burt Franklin, 1970.

Kennedy, Margrit. *Interest and Inflation Free Money: Creating an Exchange Medium that Works for Everybody and Protects the Earth*. Philadelphia: New Society Publishers 1995.

Kennedy, Paul. *Preparing for the Twenty-First Century*. New York: Random House, 1993.

————. *The Rise and Fall of the Great Powers: Economic Change and Military Conflict from 1500 to 2000*. New York: Random House, 1987.

Kennedy, Susan Estabrook. *The Banking Crisis of 1933*. Lexington: University of Kentucky Press, 1973.

Cecelia M. Kenyon, ed. *The Antifederalists*. Indianapolis: Bobbs-Merrill, 1966.

Keynes, John Maynard. *The General Theory of Employment, Interest, and Money*. New York: Harcourt Brace, 1964.

Kirk, Russell. *The Conservative Mind: From Burke to Eliot*. Chicago: Regnery Books, 1986.

Klebaner, Benjamin J. *Commercial Banking in the United States: A History*. Hinsdale, IL: Dryden Press, 1974.

Korten, David C. *The Post-Corporate World: Life after Capitalism*. San Francisco: Berrett-Koehler, 1998.

————. *When Corporations Rule the World*. San Francisco: Berrett-Koehler, 1995.

Kotlarz, Richard. "An Open Letter: Middle East War and the Rest of the American Revolution." Pamphlet. 2004.

Kotz, David M. *Bank Control of Large Corporations in the United States*. Berkeley and Los Angeles: University of California Press, 1978.

Kramer, Samuel Noah. *History Begins at Sumer*. New York: Doubleday Anchor, 1959.

Krivit, Lawrence R. *The Ruling Minority*. Monroe, NY: Library Research Associates, 1974.

Kunstler, James Howard. *The Geography of Nowhere: The Rise and Decline of America's Man-Made Landscape*. New York: Simon and Schuster, 1993.

———. *Home from Nowhere: Remaking Our Everyday World for the Twenty-First Century*. New York: Simon and Schuster, 1996.

———. *The Long Emergency: Surviving the Converging Catastrophes of the Twenty-First Century*. New York: Atlantic Monthly Press, 2005.

Kurtzman, Joel. *The Death of Money*. Boston: Little, Brown, 1993.

Landis, David S. *The Unbound Prometheus: Technological Change and Industrial Development in Western Europe from 1750 to the Present*. Cambridge: Cambridge University Press, 1972.

Lappe, Frances Moore. *Rediscovering America's Values*. New York: Ballantine, 1989.

Larsen, J. A. O. *Greek Federal States: Their Institutions and History*. Oxford: Clarendon Press, 1968.

———. *Representative Government in Greek and Roman History*. Berkeley and Los Angeles: University of California Press, 1966

Lasch, Christopher. *The Revolt of the Elites and the Betrayal of Democracy*. New York: W. W. Norton, 1995.

Lawson, Alfred. *Direct Credits for Everybody: Showing How Capitalism Will Work*. Detroit: Humanity, 1931.

Leavitt, Samuel. *Our Money Wars: The Example and Warning of American Finance*. Boston: Arena, 1894.

Lemon, James T. *The Best Poor Man's Country: A Geographical Study of Early Southeastern Pennsylvania*. Baltimore: Johns Hopkins University Press, 1972.

Lerner, Gerda. *The Creation of Patriarchy*. New York: Oxford University Press, 1986.

Leveque, Pierre, and Pierre Vidal-Naquet. *Cleisthenes the Athenian: An Essay on the Representation of Space and Time in Greek Political Thought from the End of the Sixth Century to the Death of Plato*. Translated by David Ames Curtis: Atlantic Highlands, NJ: Humanities Press, 1997.

Levy, Leonard W. *Jefferson and Civil Liberties: The Darker Side*. Chicago: Ivan R. Dee, 1989.

Lewis, Martin W. *Green Delusions: An Environmental Critique of Radical Environmentalism.* Durham, NC: Duke University Press, 1992.

Lindbeck, Assar. *The Political Economy of the New Left: An Outsider's View.* New York: Harper and Row, 1971.

Lintott, A. W. *The Constitution of the Roman Republic.* Oxford: Oxford University Press, 1999.

———. *Violence in Republican Rome.* Oxford: Clarendon Press, 1968.

Livingston, James. *Origins of the Federal Reserve System: Money, Class, and Corporate Capitalism, 1890–1913.* Ithaca, NY: Cornell University Press, 1986.

Locke, John. *The Second Treatise on Government.* New York: Liberal Arts Press, 1952.

Long, Huey P. *Kingfish to America: Share Our Wealth; Selected Senatorial Papers of Huey P. Long.* Edited by Henry M. Christman. New York: Schocken Books, 1985.

Lukacs, John. *Outgrowing Democracy: A History of the United States in the Twentieth Century.* New York: Doubleday, 1984.

Lummis, C. Douglas. *Radical Democracy.* Ithaca, NY: Cornell University Press, 1996.

Lundberg, Ferdinand. *The Rich and the Super-Rich.* New York: Lyle Stuart, 1968.

Macesich, George. *Money and Democracy.* New York: Praeger, 1990.

Machiavelli, Niccolo. *The Prince and the Discourses.* Translated by Luigi Ricci and Christian E. Detmold. New York: Modern Library, 1950.

Macmullen, Ramsay. *Corruption and the Decline of Rome.* New Haven, CT: Yale University Press, 1988.

Madison, James. "Federalist No. 10." In *A Documentary History of the United States.* Edited by Richard D. Heffner. 4th ed. New York: New American Library, 1985.

Maier, Pauline. "The Revolutionary Origins of the American Corporations." *William and Mary Quarterly,* 3rd ser., 50, no. 1 (1993): pp nos.

Main, Jackson Turner. *The Anti-Federalists: Critics of the Constitution 1781–1788.* New York: W. W. Norton, 1974.

Malthus, Thomas. *An Essay on the Principle of Population.* 1798. Reprint, Teddington, England: Echo Library, 2006.

Manes, Christopher. *Green Rage: Radical Environmentalism and the Unmaking of Civilization.* Boston: Little, Brown, 1990.

Mannheim, Karl. *Ideology and Utopia.* New York: Harcourt, Brace and World, 1956.

Mansbridge, Jane J. *Beyond Adversary Democracy*. New York: Basic Books, 1980.

Mapp, Alf J., Jr. *Thomas Jefferson: A Strange Case of Mistaken Identity*. New York: Madison Books, 1987.

Marcuse, Herbert. *One Dimensional Man: Studies in the Ideology of Advanced Industrial Society*. Boston: Beacon Press, 1964.

Martin, Calvin Luther. *In the Spirit of the Earth: Rethinking History and Time*. Baltimore: Johns Hopkins University Press, 1992.

Martin, Justin. *Nader: Crusader, Spoiler, Icon*. Cambridge, MA: Perseus, 2002.

Marx, Karl. *Capital: A Critique of Political Economy*. Vol. 1. Translated by Samuel Moore and Edward Aveling. New York: International, 1967.

———. *The Economic and Philosophic Manuscripts of 1844*. Translated by Martin Milligan. New York: International, 1964.

———. *The German Ideology*. Part 1. Edited by C. J. Arthur. New York: International, 1974.

———. *Grundrisse: Foundations of the Critique of Political Economy*. Translated with foreword by Martin Nicolaus. New York: Vintage Books, 1973.

———. "Wage Labour and Capital." In *The Marx-Engels Reader*. Edited by Robert C. Tucker. New York: W. W. Norton, 1972.

Marx, Leo. *The Machine in the Garden: Technology and the Pastoral Ideal in America*. New York: Oxford University Press, 1964.

Mattera, Philip. *Prosperity Lost*. Reading, MA: Addison-Wesley, 1990.

Matthews, Richard K. *The Radical Politics of Thomas Jefferson: A Revisionist View*. Lawrence: University Press of Kansas, 1984.

Mayer, David N. *The Constitutional Thought of Thomas Jefferson*. Charlottesville: University Press of Virginia, 1994.

McCoy, Drew. *The Elusive Republic: Political Economy in Jeffersonian America*. New York: W. W. Norton, 1980.

McDermott, John. *Corporate Society: Class, Property, and Contemporary Capitalism*. Boulder, CO: Westview Press, 1991.

McDonald, Forrest. *Novus Ordo Seclorum: The Intellectual Origins of the Constitution*. Lawrence: University Press of Kansas, 1985.

McGuire, George. "The Brooklyn Green Flat Tax (A Populist Manifesto)." Pamphlet, 1997.

McKibben, Bill. *The End of Nature*. New York: Random House, 1989.

————. *Hope, Human and Wild: True Stories of Living Lightly on the Earth.* St. Paul, MN: Hungry Mind Press, 1997.

McMath, Robert C. *American Populism: A Social History, 1877–1898.* New York: Hill and Wang, 1993.

McQuaig, Linda. *Shooting the Hippo: Death by Deficit and Other Canadian Myths.* Toronto: Viking, 1995.

Meadows, Donella H, Dennis L. Meadows, Jorge Randers, and William W. Behrens III. *The Limits to Growth.* New York: Universe Books, 1972.

Meadows, Donella, Jorgen Randers, and Dennis Meadows. *Limits to Growth: The 30-Year Update.* White River Junction, VT: Chelsea Green, 2004.

Mellaart, James. *Catal Huyuk: A Neolithic Town in Anatolia.* New York: McGraw-Hill, 1967.

Mencken, H. L. *Notes on Democracy.* New York: Octagon Books, 1977.

Merchant, Carolyn. *Ecological Revolutions: Nature, Gender, and Science in New England.* Chapel Hill: University of North Carolina Press, 1989.

Milbrath, Lester W. *Envisioning a Sustainable Society: Learning Our Way Out.* Albany: SUNY Press, 1989.

Millar, Fergus. *The Crowd in Rome in the Late Republic.* Ann Arbor: University of Michigan Press, 2002.

————. *The Roman Republic in Political Thought.* Hanover, NH: University Press of New England, 2002.

Mills, C. Wright. *The Power Elite.* New York: Oxford University Press, 1959.

Mises, Ludwig. von *The Theory of Money and Credit.* Translated by H. E. Batson. Indianapolis: Liberty Classics, 1980.

Montesquieu, Baron de. *The Spirit of the Laws.* Translated by Thomas Nugent. New York: Hafner Press, 1949.

Morgan, Lewis Henry. *Ancient Society.* Chicago: Charles H. Kerr and Co., 1910.

————. *League of the Ho-De-No-Sau-Nee or Iroquois.* New York: Dodd, Mead, 1902.

Morgan, Ted. *FDR: A Biography.* New York: Simon and Schuster, 1985.

Morrissey, Charles T. *Vermont: A Bicentennial History.* New York: W. W. Norton, 1981.

Mueller, John. *Capitalism, Democracy, and Ralph's Pretty Good Grocery.* Princeton, NJ: Princeton University Press, 1999.

Murphy, Liam, and Thomas Nagel. *The Myth of Ownership: Taxes and Justice.* Oxford: Oxford University Press, 2002.

Myers, Gustavus. *History of the Great American Fortunes.* New York: Modern Library, 1937.

Neal, Larry. *The Rise of Financial Capitalism: International Capital Markets in the Age of Reason.* Cambridge: Cambridge University Press, 1990.

Nedelsky, Jennifer. *Private Property and the Limits of American Constitutionalism: The Madisonian Framework and Its Legacy.* Chicago: The University of Chicago Press, 1990.

Nicolet, C. *The World of the Citizen in Republican Rome.* Translated by P. F. Falls. Berkeley and Los Angeles: University of California Press, 1980.

Noble, David F. *America by Design: Science, Techology, and the Rise of Corporate Capitalism.* New York: Alfred A. Knopf, 1977.

———. *Progress without People: In Defense of Luddism.* Chicago: Charles H. Kerr, 1993.

Ober, Josiah. *The Athenian Revolution: Essays on Ancient Greek Democracy and Political Theory.* Princeton, NJ: Princeton University Press, 1996.

———. *Mass and Elite in Democratic Athens: Rhetoric, Ideology, and the Power of the People.* Princeton, NJ: Princeton University Press, 1989.

Ober, Josiah, and Charles Hedrick, eds. *Demokratia: A Conversation on Democracies, Ancient and Modern.* Princeton, NJ: Princeton University Press, 1996.

O'Connor, James. *The Fiscal Crisis of the State.* New York: St. Martin's Press, 1973.

Olson, Mancur. *The Rise and Decline of Nations: Economic Growth, Stagflation, and Social Rigidities.* New Haven, CT: Yale University Press, 1982.

Onuf, Peter F. *The Origins of the Federal Republic: Jurisdictional Controversies in the United States 1775–1787.* Philadelphia: University of Pennsylvania Press, 1983.

———. *Statehood and Union: A History of the Northwest Ordinance.* Bloomington: Indiana University Press, 1987.

Oppenheim, A. Leo. *Ancient Mesopotamia: Portrait of a Dead Civilization.* Rev. ed. Chicago: University of Chicago Press, 1977.

Orr, David W. *Earth in Mind: On Education, Environment, and the Human Prospect.* Washington, DC: Island Press, 1994.

Orwell, George. *The Orwell Reader: Fiction, Essays, and Reportage by George Orwell.* Edited by Richard H. Rovere. New York: Harcourt Brace Jovanovich, 1956.

Paine, Thomas. *Collected Writings.* Edited by Eric Foner. New York: Library of America, 1995.

———. *The Complete Writings of Thomas Paine.* 2 vols. Edited by Philip S. Foner. New York: Citadel Press, 1945.

Painter, Nell Irvin. *Standing at Armageddon: The United States 1877–1919.* New York: W. W. Norton, 1987.

Palmer, Bruce. *"Man over Money": The Southern Populist Critique of American Capitalism.* Chapel Hill: University of North Carolina Press, 1980.

Papworth, John. *Small Is Powerful: The Future as if People Really Mattered.* Westport, CT: Praeger, 1995.

Parker, Arthur C. *The Constitution of the Five Nations, or the Iroquois Book of the Great Law.* Albany: University of the State of New York, 1916. Reprint, Ohsweken, Ontario, Canada: Iroqrafts Ltd., 1991.

Phillips, Kevin. *Boiling Point: Democrats, Republicans, and the Decline of Middle-Class Prosperity.* New York: Random House, 1993.

———. *The Politics of Rich and Poor: Wealth and the American Electorate in the Reagan Aftermath.* New York: Random House, 1990.

———. *Wealth and Democracy: A Political History of the American Rich.* New York: Broadway Books, 2002.

Pirenne, Henri. *Early Democracies in the Low Countries.* Translated by J. V. Saunders. New York: Harper Torchbooks, 1963.

———. *Economic and Social History of Medieval Europe.* Translated by I. E. Clegg. London: Routledge and Kegan Paul, 1953.

Plato. *The Collected Dialogues of Plato, Including the Letters.* Edited by Edith Hamilton and Huntington Cairns. New York: Bollingen Foundation, 1961.

———. *Republic.* Translated by G. M. A. Grube. Revised by C. D. C. Reeve. Indianapolis: Hackett, 1992.

Plutarch. *Essays.* Translated by Robin Waterfield. London: Penguin Books, 1992.

———. *The Lives of the Noble Grecians and Romans.* Translated by John Dryden. Revised by Arthur High Slough. New York: Modern Library, 1992.

———. *Selected Essays and Dialogues.* Translated by Donald Russell. Oxford: Oxford University Press, 1993.

Pocock, J. G. A. *The Machiavellian Moment: Florentine Political Thought and the Atlantic Republican Tradition.* Princeton, NJ: Princeton University Press, 1975.

Polanyi, Karl. *The Great Transformation: The Political and Economic Origins of Our Time.* Boston: Beacon Press, 1957.

Pollock, Norman. *The Just Polity: Populism, Law, and Human Welfare.* Urbana: University of Illinois Press, 1987.

————, ed. *The Populist Mind.* Indianapolis: Bobbs-Merrill, 1967.

Polybius. *The Histories of Polybius.* 2 vols. Translated by Evelyn S. Shuckburgh. London: Macmillan, 1889.

Ponting, Clive. *A Green History of the World: The Environment and the Collapse of Great Civilizations.* London: Penguin Books, 1991.

Proudhon, Pierre-Joseph. *What Is Property?* Edited and translated by Donald R. Kelley and Bonnie G. Smith. Cambridge: Cambridge University Press, 1994.

Quigley, Carroll. *Tragedy and Hope: A History of the World in Our Time.* New York: Macmillan, 1966.

Quigley, David. *Second Founding: New York City, Reconstruction, and the Making of American Democracy.* New York: Hill and Wang, 2004.

Rae, George. *The Country Banker: His Clients, Cares, and Work from an Experience of Forty Years.* New York: Charles Scribner's Sons, 1886.

Rahe, Paul A. *Republics Ancient and Modern: Classical Republicanism and the American Revolution.* Chapel Hill: University of North Carolina Press, 1992.

Randall, Willard Sterne. *Thomas Jefferson: A Life.* New York: Henry Holt and Company, 1993.

Redfield, Robert. *The Primitive World and Its Transformations.* Ithaca, NY: Cornell University Press, 1953.

Resenbrink, John. *Against All Odds: The Green Transformation of American Politics.* Raymond, ME: Leopold Press, 1999.

Ribero, Darcy. *The Civilizational Process.* Translated by Berty J. Meggers. New York: Harper and Row, 1968.

Richard, Carl J. *The Founders and the Classics: Greece, Rome, and the American Enlightenment.* Cambridge, MA: Harvard University Press, 1994.

Richter, Daniel K. *The Ordeal of the Longhouse: The Peoples of the Iroquois League in the Era of European Colonization.* Chapel Hill: University of North Carolina Press, 1994.

Riegel, E. C. *The New Approach to Freedom*. Edited by Spencer Heath MacCallum. San Pedro, CA: Heather Foundation, 1976.

Rifkin, Jeremy. *Biosphere Politics: A New Consciousness for a New Century*. New York: Crown Publishers, 1991.

Roberts, Henry M. *Rules of Order Revised for Deliberative Assemblies*. Chicago: Scott, Foresman, 1915.

Roberts, Jennifer Tolbert. *Athens on Trial: The Antidemocratic Tradition in Western Thought*. Princeton, NJ: Princeton University Press, 1994.

Robertson, Pat. *The New World Order*. Dallas: Word, 1991.

Robinson, William A. *Jeffersonian Democracy in New England*. New York: AMS Press, 1969.

Ronda, James P., ed. *Thomas Jefferson and the Changing West: From Conquest to Conservation*. Albuquerque: University of New Mexico Press, 1997.

Rosenberg, Nathan, and L. E. Birdzell Jr. *How the West Grew Rich: The Economic Transformation of the Industrial World*. New York: Basic Books, 1986.

Rostovtzeff, M. *Rome*. Translated by J. D. Duff. London: Oxford University Press, 1960.

Rothbard, Murray N. *The Case against the Fed*. Auburn, AL: Ludwig von Mises Institute, 1994.

———. *For a New Liberty: The Libertarian Manifesto*. Rev. ed. New York: Collier Books, 1978.

———. *A History of Money and Banking in the United States: The Colonial Era to World War II*. Auburn, AL: Ludwig von Mises Institute, 2002.

Roy, William G. *Socializing Capital: The Rise of the Large Industrial Corporation in America*. Princeton, NJ: Princeton University Press, 1997.

Rudgley, Richard. *The Lost Civilizations of the Stone Age*. New York: Free Press, 1999.

Sagan, Eli. *At the Dawn of Tyranny: The Origins of Individualism, Political Oppression and the State*. New York: Alfred A. Knopf, 1985.

———. *The Honey and the Hemlock: Democracy and Paranoia in Ancient Athens and Modern America*. New York: Basic Books, 1991.

Sagoff, Mark. *The Economy of the Earth: Philosophy, Law, and the Environement*. Cambridge: Cambridge University Press, 1988.

Sale, Kirkpatrick. *The Luddites and Their War on the Industrial Revolution: Lessons for the Computer Age*. New York: Addison-Wesley, 1995.

———. *SDS*. New York: Random House, 1973.

Sampson, Anthony. *The Money Lenders: The People and Politics of the World Banking Crisis*. New York: Penguin, 1983.

Samuelson, Paul. *Economics: An Introductory Analysis*. New York: McGraw-Hill, 1964.

Saul, John Ralston. *The Unconscious Civilization*. Concord, ON: House of Anansi Press, 1995.

Saxonhouse, Arelene W. *Athenian Democracy: Modern Mythmakers and Ancient Theorists*. Notre Dame, IN: University of Notre Dame Press, 1996.

Schumacher, E. F. *Small Is Beautiful: Economics as if People Mattered*. New York: Harper Perennial, 1989.

Seavoy, Ronald E. *The Origins of the American Business Corporation, 1784–1855: Broadening the Concept of Public Service during Industrialization*. Westport, CT: Greenwood Press, 1982.

Shade, William Gerald. *Banks or No Banks: The Money Issue in Western Politics, 1832–1865*. Detroit: Wayne State University Press, 1972.

Shafarman, Steven. *We the People: Healing Our Democracy and Saving Our World*. Van Nuys, CA: Gain, 2001.

Sharkey, Robert P. *Money, Class, and Party: An Economic Study of Civil War and Reconstruction*. Baltimore: Johns Hopkins University Press, 1959.

Sheldon, Garrett Ward. *The Political Philosophy of Thomas Jefferson*. Baltimore: Johns Hopkins University Press, 1993.

Shuman, Michael H. *Going Local: Creating Self-Reliant Communities in a Global Age*. New York: Free Press, 1998.

Sidney, Algernon. *Discourses Concerning Government*. Edited by Thomas G. West. Indianapolis: Liberty Classics, 1990.

Silk, Leonard, and Mark Silk. *The American Establishment*. New York: Basic Books, 1980.

Simmel, Georg. *The Philosophy of Money*. London: Routledge and Kegan Paul, 1978.

Sinclair, R. K. *Democracy and Participation in Athens*. Cambridge: Cambridge University Press, 1988.

Slater, Philip. *A Dream Deferred: America's Discontent and the Search for a New Democratic Ideal*. Boston: Beacon Press, 1991.

Smith, Adam. *The Theory of Moral Sentiments.* Amherst, MA: Prometheus Books, 2000.

———. *The Wealth of Nations.* Edited by Edward Cannan. New York: Modern Library, 1937.

Soddy, Frederick. *The Role of Money: What It Should Be, Contrasted with What It Has Become.* New York: Harcourt, Brace, 1935.

Starr, Chester G. *The Economic and Social Growth of Early Greece 800–500 BC.* New York: Oxford University Press, 1977.

Statistical Abstract of the United States: The National Data Book. Washington, DC: U.S. Census Bureau, 2000.

Ste. Croix, G. E. M. de. *The Class Struggle in the Ancient Greek World from the Archaic Age to the Arab Conquests.* Ithaca, NY: Cornell University Press, 1981.

Stockman, David A. *The Triumph of Politics: The Inside Story of the Reagan Revolution.* New York: Avon Books, 1987.

Stone, I. F. *The Trial of Socrates.* New York: Anchor Books, 1980.

Herbert J. Storing. ed. *The Anti-Federalist: Writings by the Opponents of the Constitution.* by Chicago: University of Chicago Press, 1985.

———. *What the Anti-Federalilsts Were For.* Chicago: University of Chicago Press, 1981.

Strauss, Barry S. "The Melting Pot, the Mosaic, and the Agora." In *Athenian Political Thought and the Reconstruction of American Democracy.* Edited by J. Peter Euben, John Wallach, and Josiah Ober. Ithaca, NY: Cornell University Press, 1994.

Strouse, Jean. *Morgan: American Financier.* New York: HarperCollins, 1999.

Syme, Ronald. *The Roman Revolution.* Oxford: Oxford University Press, 1987.

Szatmary, David P. *Shay's Rebellion: The Making of an Agrarian Insurrection.* Amherst: University of Massachusetts Press, 1980.

Talmon, J. L. *The Origins of Totalitarian Democracy.* New York: Praeger, 1960.

Tawney, R. H. *The Acquisitive Society.* New York: Harcourt, Brace, 1920.

———. *Religion and the Rise of Capitalism: A Historical Study.* New York: New American Library, 1954.

Taylor, Alan. *The Divided Ground: Indians, Settlers, and the Northern Borderland of the American Revolution.* New York: Alfred A. Knopf, 2006.

————. *William Cooper's Town: Power and Persuasion on the Frontier of the Early American Republic.* New York: Alfred A. Knopf, 1995.

Taylor, John. *An Inquiry into the Principles and Policy of the Government of the United States.* Indianapolis: Bobbs-Merrill, 1969.

Taylor, Lily Ross. *Roman Voting Assemblies from the Hannibalic War to the Dictatorship of Caesar.* Ann Arbor: University of Michigan Press, 1966.

Temin, Peter. *The Jacksonian Economy.* New York: W. W. Norton, 1969.

Thomas, John L. *Alternative America: Henry George, Edward Bellamy, Henry Demarest Lloyd and the Adversary Tradition.* Cambridge, Press MA: Belknap Press of Harvard University Press, 1983.

Thompson, E. P. *The Making of the English Working Class.* New York: Vintage, 1966.

Thompson, William Irwin. *The Time Falling Bodies Take to Light: Mythology, Sexuality, and the Origins of Culture.* New York: St. Martin's Press, 1981.

Thucydides. *The Peloponnesian War.* Translated by Rex Warner. Baltimore: Penguin, 1954.

Timberlake, Richard H., Jr., *The Origins of Central Banking in the United States.* Cambridge, MA: Harvard University Press, 1978.

Tindall, George Brown, ed. *A Populist Reader: Selections from the Works of American Populist Leaders.* New York: Harper and Row, 1966.

Toqueville, Alexis de. *Democracy in America.* Translated by Henry Reeve. New York: Oxford University Press, 1947.

Tokar, Brian. *The Green Alternative: Creating an Ecological Future.* San Pedro, CA: R. & E. Miles, 1987.

Toynbee, Arnold J. *A Study of History.* 2 vols. Abridged by D. C. Somervell. New York: Oxford University Press, 1958.

Trautmann, Thomas R. *Lewis Henry Morgan and the Invention of Kinship.* Berkeley and Los Angeles: University of California Press, 1987.

Trumpbour, John, ed. *How Harvard Rules: Reason in the Service of Empire.* Boston: South End Press, 1989.

Turnbull, Shann. *Democratising the Wealth of Nations from New Money Sources and Profit Motives.* Sydney: Company Directors Association of Australia, 1975.

Turner, Frederick Jackson. *The Frontier in American History.* New York: Holt, Rinehart and Winston, 1962.

Ungar, Irwin. *The Greenback Era: A Social and Political History of American Finance, 1865–1879.* Princeton, NJ: Princeton University Press, 1964.

Van Buren, Martin. *Inquiry into the Origin and Course of Political Parties in the United States.* 1867. Reprint, New York: Augustus M. Kelley, 1967.

Veblen, Thorstein. *The Theory of the Leisure Class.* New York: Dover, 1994.

Vico, Giambattista. *The New Science of Giambattista Vico.* Translated by Thomas Goddard Bergin and Max Harold Fisch. Ithaca, NY: Cornell University Press, 1970.

Wallace, Anthony F. C. *Jefferson and the Indians: The Tragic Fate of the First Americans.* Cambridge, MA: Belknap Press of Harvard University Press, 1999.

Walzer, Michael. *The Revolution of the Saints: A Study in the Origins of Radical Politics.* New York: Atheneum, 1972.

Ward-Perkins, Bryan. *The Fall of Rome and the End of Civilization.* Oxford: Oxford University Press, 2005.

Watson, David. *Beyond Bookchin: Preface for a Future Social Ecology.* Brooklyn, NY: Autonomedia, 1996.

Weinstein, James. *The Corporate Ideal in the Liberal State: 1900–1918.* Boston: Beacon Press, 1968.

Williams, T. Harry. *Huey Long.* New York: Random House, 1981.

Wills, Gary. *Inventing America: Jefferson's Declaration of Independence.* New York: Random House, 1978.

Wilson, Thomas. *The Power "To Coin" Money: The Exercise of Monetary Powers by the Congress.* Armonk, NY: M. E. Sharpe, 1992.

Wiltse, Charles Maurice. *The Jeffersonian Tradition in American Democracy.* New York: Hill and Wang, 1960.

Wolf, Peter. *Land in America: Its Value, Use, and Control.* New York: Pantheon Books, 1981.

Wolfe, Tom. *The Bonfire of the Vanities.* New York: Bantam Books, 1988.

Wood, Ellen Meiksins. *Democracy against Capitalism: Renewing Historical Materialism.* Cambridge: Cambridge University Press, 1995.

———. "Democracy: An Idea of Ambiguous Ancestry." In *Athenian Political Thought and the Reconstruction of American Democracy.* Edited by J. Peter Euben, John Wallach, and Josiah Ober. Ithaca, NY: Cornell University Press, 1994.

————. "Demos vs. 'We the People:' Freedom and Democracy Ancient and Modern." In *Demokratia: A Conversation on Democracies, Ancient and Modern*. Edited by Josiah Ober and Charles Hedrick. Princeton, NJ: Princeton University Press, 1996.

————. *The Origin of Capitalism: A Longer View*. London: Verso, 2002.

————. *Peasant-Citizen and Slave: The Foundations of Athenian Democracy*. London: Verso, 1988.

Wood, Ellen Meiksins, and Neal Wood. *Class Ideology and Ancient Political Theory: Socrates, Plato, and Aristotle in Social Context*. New York: Oxford University Press, 1978.

Wood, Gordon S. *The Radicalism of the American Revolution*. New York: Alfred A. Knopf, 1992.

Wood, John H. "Money: Its Origins, Development, Debasement, and Prospects." *Economic Education Bulletin*. 39, no. 8 (1999): pp. nos.

Woods, Thomas A. *Knights of the Plow: Oliver H. Kelley and the Origins of the Grange in Republican Ideology*. Ames: Iowa State University Press, 1991.

Woolley, C. Leonard. *The Sumerians*. New York: W. W. Norton, 1965.

Zarlenga, Stephen A. *The Lost Science of Money: The Mythology of Money—The Story of Power*. Valatie, NY: American Monetary Institute, 2002.

Zerzan, John. *Future Primitive and Other Essays*. Brooklyn, NY: Autonomedia, 1994.

Zimmerman, Joseph F. *The Massachusetts Town Meeting: A Tenacious Institution*. Albany: SUNY Graduate School of Public Affairs, 1967.

Zinn, Howard. *A People's History of the United States*. New York: Harper and Row, 1980.

Zuckerman, Michael. *Peaceable Kingdoms: New England Towns in the Eighteenth Century*. New York: Alfred A. Knopf, 1970.

Zunz, Olivier. *Making America Corporate: 1870–1920*. Chicago: University of Chicago Press, 1990.

Index

Accountability
    in corporate finance capitalism, 7–8, 10
    in kinship societies, 46–47
    of representation, 2–3, 168–70
Adams, John, 50, 157–58
"Agrarian Justice," 51
Allen, Ethan, 114
Alternative monetary systems
    debt-based system v., 5–6, 9–10
    democracy and, 145–46
    implications of, 145
    of Kellogg, 6, 10, 138–48, 152–53
    of Lawson, 151–52
    low-interest loans in, 5–6, 138–48
    money in, 139, 144–48, 152–53
    in *A New Monetary System*, 6, 132
    practicality of, 146–47
American Political Economy, 131
American populism, 100–153. *See also*
        Jefferson, Thomas; United States;
        Ward republics
    Jacksonian era of, 117–18
    public credit and, 100–107
    slavery and, 121–22
    socialism v., 20–22, 108
    in Vermont, 18, 113–17
    wealth circulation in, 106–12
Ancient Society, 29–30
Antipater, 67
Anti-Rent Wars, 119
Appropriation
    by conquest, 55–56
    failure of, 47
    wealth circulation v., 5
Arginusae, battle of, 71
Aristotle
    The Constitution of Athens by, 57–63
    on democracy, 57–63
    Harrington on, 80
    on inequality, 62

middle classes preferred by, 60, 63
    on Phaleas, 3, 57–63
    Politics by, 3, 57–63, 80
    Rhetoric by, 70
    slavery and, 62
    on virtue and politics, 58–59, 63
    on wealth circulation, 4, 63
Assembly. *See* Democratic assembly
Athenian Economy and Society, 68
Athens
    The Constitution of Athens and, 57–63
    assembly of, 65–66, 69, 72–74, 125–26
    citizenship in, 64–65
    criticisms of, 69–74
    democracy of, 64–74
    inequality in, 71–72
    jury trials in, 66
    kinship traditions in, 62, 67–68
    leadership in, 66
    legislation in, 65
    middle classes in, 65
    oligarchs in, 72, 74
    origin of, 67
    prehistory of, 67–68
    property in, 65
    slavery in, 64
    U.S. compared with, 66
    women in, 64

Bank of England, 91–94, 132
Bank of the United States, 118
Battle of Arginusae, 71
Beatty, Jack, 118–19
Bellesiles, Michael A., 115–16
Berkeley, George
    The Querist by, 85–87
    on wealth circulation, 84–87
Big business
    as antidemocratic, 9
    big government v., 8–9